Charles Minor Blackford

LETTERS FROM LEE'S ARMY

OR

**Memoirs of Life In and Out of
The Army in Virginia
During the War Between the States**

Compiled by
SUSAN LEIGH BLACKFORD

*From original and contemporaneous memoirs,
correspondence and diaries*

Annotated by her husband
CHARLES MINOR BLACKFORD

Edited and abridged for publication by
CHARLES MINOR BLACKFORD III

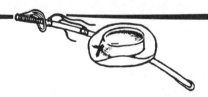

INTRODUCTION TO THE BISON BOOKS EDITION BY
GORDON C. RHEA

University of Nebraska Press
Lincoln and London

⊗

First Bison Books printing: 1998

Library of Congress Cataloging-in-Publication Data
Blackford, Susan Leigh, b. 1835.
Letters from Lee's army, or, Memoirs of life in and out of the army in
Virginia during the War Between the States / compiled by Susan Leigh
Blackford from original and contemporaneous correspondence and
diaries; annotated and edited by Charles Minor Blackford; edited and
abridged for publication by Charles Minor Blackford III; introduction
to the Bison Books edition by Gordon C. Rhea.
p. cm.
Originally published: New York: Scribner, 1947.
An abridged version of Memoirs of life in and out of the army in
Virginia during the War Between the States (1894) compiled by Susan
Leigh Blackford.
Includes index.
ISBN 0-8032-6149-7 (pbk.: alk. paper)
1. United States—History—Civil War, 1861–1865—Personal narratives,
Confederate. 2. Virginia—History—Civil War, 1861–1865.
3. Blackford, Susan Leigh, b. 1835—Correspondence. 4. Blackford,
Charles Minor, 1833–1903—Correspondence. 5. Lynchburg (Va.)—
Biography. I. Blackford, Charles Minor, 1833–1903. II. Blackford,
Charles Minor, 1898 or 9- III. Blackford, Susan Leigh, b. 1835.
Memoirs of life in and out of the army in Virginia during the War
Between the States. IV. Title.
E605.B63   1998
973.7′82—dc21
98-29020   CIP

INTRODUCTION

Gordon C. Rhea

On a pleasant Sunday evening in June 1861, twenty-seven-year-old Charles Minor Blackford tearfully embraced his wife and children, glanced longingly at his Lynchburg, Virginia, home, then mounted his "noble old roan" and rode off to war. The letters that passed between Charles and his wife, Susan Leigh Blackford, during the tumultuous years that followed comprise the core of this delightful volume. Husband and wife wrote with the intention of preserving a record of their experiences for posterity. Their missives described life at the battlefront and at home with candor and immediacy rare in Civil War literature. "I fear all these stories bore you, but they illustrate the spirit of the war, and of the camp," Charles reminded Susan. "They are lost to history usually, and hence I take this mode of preserving them for my children."[1]

Charles and Susan Blackford's letters weave a spellbinding tale bursting with unforgettable characters and events. Charles bore witness to many of the American Civil War's momentous battles and hobnobbed with the Army of Northern Virginia's foremost personages. He penned riveting accounts of the excitement of combat and the drudgery of camp life. Susan remained home in Lynchburg with the couple's three young children. Her written legacy provides a somber glimpse into the hardships of life in wartime Virginia, where the task of caring for a family assumed daunting proportions and deprivation and anxiety became routine. The letters open a revealing window into the thoughts and concerns of an intensely engaging young couple swept up in the maelstrom of war. They stand in the foremost rank of primary material generated during those eventful years.

Charles and Susan Blackford came from distinguished Virginia families. The second of five brothers, Charles was born on October 17, 1833, in Fredericksburg. His father, William Matthews

Blackford, was a man of relative prosperity and impeccable social stature with a pronounced gift for speaking and writing. He served as President Tyler's chargé d'affairs in New Granada (later Colombia), edited the *Fredericksburg Herald*, and while Charles was still young, moved to Lynchburg to edit the *Lynchburg Virginian*. He lived until April 1864 and kept a detailed diary, which Susan later praised as the "reflections of a thoughtful and scholarly man." Charles's mother, Mary Berkely Minor, also claimed exalted Old Dominion lineage. Her father, John Minor of Fredericksurg, had fought under Lighthorse Harry Lee in the Revolutionary War and served for many years in Virginia's General Assembly.

Charles became interested in literary endeavors at an early age. While a teenager, he published a set of pamphlets mocking life in Lynchburg. He attended law school in Charlottesville, took his degree in June 1855, and returned to Lynchburg to practice. The following February he married Susan Leigh Colston, two years his junior and a member of one of Albemarle County's leading families. By 1861 the young couple presided over a thriving household of three children in Lynchburg.

At the outbreak of the Civil War, the Blackford brothers took up arms and fought with distinction for the Confederacy. The eldest brother, William Willis Blackford, served on the staff of General Robert E. Lee's flamboyant cavalry commander, James Ewell Brown "Jeb" Stuart, and rose to the rank of lieutenant colonel of the First Engineers. His wartime memoir—first published in part as an appendix in Susan Blackford's *Memoirs of Life In and Out of the Army in Virginia during the War between the States* and later as *War Years with Jeb Stuart*—is a classic account of the Confederate mounted arm. The family's third brother, Benjamin Lewis Blackford, fought in the Eleventh Virginia Infantry and attained the rank of lieutenant of engineers. Launcelot Minor Blackford, the next youngest brother, started with the Rockbridge Artillery and advanced to become adjutant of the Twenty-fourth Virginia Infantry. And the youngest Blackford boy, Eugene, served bravely with the Fifth Alabama Infantry despite painful bouts of phlebitis. He became major of the regiment, and it was to him that Thomas J. "Stonewall" Jackson issued the orders to launch the famous Confederate flank attack at Chancellorsville on May 2, 1863.[2]

Charles believed fervently in Virginia's cause. He answered the call for volunteers in May 1861 and was commissioned lieutenant in the Wise Troop, named for Henry A. Wise, a former governor of Virginia. The outfit was to become Company B of the Second Virginia Cavalry.

Charles's service put him in the thick of combat, and he faithfully wrote home about the pageantry and vagaries of war. His pen recorded his exuberance during the war's early years, his depression over Gettysburg, his frustration after Chickamauga, his consternation over Grant's relentless grinding, and his resignation when defeat came at Appomattox. He participated in the opening battle at Manassas and spent the winter of 1861–62 in camp at Leesburg. In May 1862 he was elected captain of Company B of his regiment. Sickness kept him from the Shenandoah Valley Campaign and the campaigns around Richmond during June and early July. He recovered in time, however, to join the campaign against John Pope in central Virginia. There he witnessed the normally stoic Stonewall Jackson dash into the heat of battle brandishing a sword in one hand and a flag in the other. Sickness kept him from the fights at Second Manassas and Antietam, but he returned in the fall to command a detachment of pickets in the Shenandoah Valley. That winter at Fredericksburg, he gazed upon the corpse-strewn field below Marye's Heights and wrote a haunting account of the carnage. He also visited his childhood home in the devastated town. Federal surgeons had used the dining-room table to perform amputations and had left arms and legs heaped on a small table nearby. "I poured them out into the back yard and managed to get the table out to camp and will send it home in a few days," Charles informed Susan.

On December 16, 1862, Charles was appointed judge advocate of the Confederate First Corps, with the rank of captain of cavalry. He served in this post until the end of the war, which spared him the rigors of line duty, although he still accompanied the army on its campaigns. He left stirring accounts of the summer of 1863. "I crossed 'Mason's and Dixon's Line' today," he wrote as the army marched into Pennsylvania, "and am now some five or six miles within the boundaries of the Keystone State, surrounded by enemies and black looks, Dutchmen and big barns." He watched the disastrous Confederate charge on July 3 at Gettysburg, which he predicted "will be the theme of the poet, painter and historian of all ages." Lee's failure at Gettysburg, in conjunction with the fall of Vicksburg, depressed him deeply. "The outlook is far from bright," he wrote, "and this looks very much to me as the turning point of the war." He railed against Southern newspapers for making a bad situation worse. "Our sky is dark and the worst feature is that our people seem to be letting down," he informed Susan. "We have had only our first reverses, yet many people have gone into a fainting fit. The press seems to take infinite delight in publishing everything to increase the depression and chill the enthusiasm of the army."

September 1863 saw Charles journeying by boxcar to Georgia with the First Corps. He was soon adding his voice to the insistent chorus denouncing Braxton Bragg for failing to exploit his victory at Chickamauga. "The suicidal policy which Bragg has adopted has rendered futile the victory which Longstreet won for him," he complained to Susan. "Our great victory has been turned to ashes." He could not resist comparing Bragg with Lee, whose fortunes he had followed in Virginia. "The difference between this army and Lee's is very striking," he asserted. "[W]hen the men move in the Army of Northern Virginia they think they are doing the proper thing, whether it be backward or forward, and if all the success anticipated is not secured, at all events it is not Lee's fault. Down here the men seem to feel the wrong thing is being done whatever it be and when success is secured they attribute it to anybody else than Bragg."

Ulysses S. Grant's Overland Campaign in the spring of 1864 persuaded Charles that the South's cause was doomed. "Grant has shown no remarkable generalship—only a bull-dog tenacity and determination in a fight, regardless of the consequences or the loss," Captain Blackford wrote home. "Ultimately such bloody policy must win," he concluded. He and Susan contemplated a bleak future. "I am not surprised at your being gloomy at the outlook for we will have a terrible struggle for mere bread and meat, but we will pull through, exactly how I do not know," Charles wrote. "When the war is over, if I am spared," he added in an attempt to lift her spirits, "we will at least be together, and I have no fear but that I can make a living."

From the start of the war through its finish, combat fascinated Charles, and he depicted with contagious enthusiasm the dry business of marshaling troops and equipment. "One not familiar with artillery can little imagine how grand a sight it was," he informed Susan in a typical passage. "Each gun had four horses, with outriders and officers on horseback and several men mounted on the gun; then the caisson of each gun with its four horses and the like equipment of men, making thirty-two in all. Their ammunition wagons, forges and ambulances, all at full speed, making a procession, which, under the circumstances, was very inspiring." Even numbers sprang alive under his pen. "Few people have an idea of the extent of a column of an army," he instructed Susan. "If General Lee had seventy thousand infantry, twelve thousand cavalry, one hundred and seventy-five guns and the usual impedimenta his column would extend over sixty miles."

Charles's most impressive talent was his knack for describing people. "I felt myself in the presence of a great man, for surely there never was a man upon whom greatness is more stamped," he effused of Lee. "He is the handsomest person I ever saw; every motion is instinct with natural grace, and yet there is a dignity which, while awe-inspiring, makes one feel a sense of confidence and trust that is delightful when it is remembered that there are at present so many contingencies dependant upon his single will." As for Longstreet, "I would trust him to manage men on a battlefield as implicitly as any general in the Confederacy, but when not excited his mind works too slow and he is almost too kind hearted to have control of a department."

For Stonewall Jackson, with whom he associated closely, Charles developed admiration but not affection. "There is a magnetism in Jackson, but it is not personal," he related to Susan. "All admire his genius and great deeds; no one could love the man for himself. He seems to be cut off from his fellow men and to commune with his own spirit only, or with spirits of which we know not." A touching incident, however, caused Charles to soften his opinion. Shortly after the battle of Antietam, Charles watched a young mother thrust her infant into the Confederate hero's arms and ask him to bless the child. Jackson clasped the baby to his breast and closed his eyes in prayer. Bystanders removed their hats, and the mother leaned forward. "It was my wish at the moment that I were a poet or a painter, to put the scene in immemorial words or upon an eternal canvas, the picture of him sitting there on his old sorrel at the end of the wrecked and torn up rail line, the grey section house to one side, the breastworks of logs and iron at the other, while behind were the trees, their autumn foliage turning brown," Charles recorded of the occasion. "Around-about the soldiers in their worn and patched clothing, in a circle at a respectful distance, while his staff officers sat a little to one side. Then Jackson, the warrior saint of another era, with the child in his arms, head bowed until his greying beard touched the fresh young hair of the child, pressed close to the shabby coat that had been so well acquainted with death." Conceded Charles: "For the first time it brought to me that this stern, enigmatic man whom I admired, respected but never loved, had another side to him I had never before seen; that of a tender man of family."

The letters are most poignant when they deal with the personal side of life. Charles and Susan adored one another and wrote with unusual candor and sensitivity. "I am today twenty-eight years old," Charles reminded Susan on October 17, 1861, "and, by agreement, we were to spend the day thinking about each other as much as possible, but I have been so much engaged I fear I have not carried out my part of the agreement as I should have done." On Christmas Eve Charles expressed sadness at being "with you only in spirit tonight as you sit with the children's presents around you in our sweet room all alone with tears in your eyes as your memory reverts to the happy hours at the same time last year." Early in 1863 their children Willy and Lucy became sick. "At eleven o'clock Wednesday night," Susan sadly informed Charles, "as I knelt by [Willy's] bedside, he ceased to breathe and his pure spirit took to flight without a struggle." Then Lucy took a turn for the worse and died. "She never smiled after Willy's death," Susan wrote. "Yes, my darling, in that short time I have seen *two* of our precious children laid in the cold, dark grave. Willy and Lucy are now only bright and beautiful dreams." Yet despite her grief, she remained solicitous of Charles. "One of my most grievous thoughts is that you will have to bear this terrible strain alone," she wrote. "I hope you have received letters from Mr. Minor and myself that have prepared you for this last sad news, so it may not come with such over-whelming force."

At the close of hostilities, Charles returned to Lynchburg im-poverished. He devoted his efforts to building a successful law prac-tice, engaged in railroad ventures, and served as city attorney. But he never forgot that his family possessed a priceless literary trea-sure in his and Susan's wartime letters. He persuaded Susan to arrange the family's writings, including those of his father and brother William, into a more permanent format. Laboring for five years, she wove extracts from these writings into a compelling lit-erary tapestry. Charles assisted in editing and annotating the work. He was so pleased with the result that in 1894 he retained J. P. Bell Company in Lynchburg to print thirty-five copies. Produced in two volumes, the book was entitled *Memoirs of Life In and Out of the Army in Virginia during the War between the States.* Charles stipulated that it was for "the private reading of my immediate family and a few intimate friends." No copies were to be sold or given away, "but when advisable, a copy may be lent to a friend who may desire to read it."[3]

Charles continued writing after the war. In 1881 he authored a legal history of the Virginia Midland Railroad Company. He pro-duced a historical sketch of the Book of Common Prayer in 1893, followed in 1900 by a critique of the trial of Jefferson Davis. In 1901 he published *Battle of Lynchburg,* which remains one of the few accounts of that engagement. Charles died on March 10, 1903, and was buried at Spring Hill Cemetery in Lynchburg. Susan died in 1916 and was buried next to her beloved captain.[4]

Shortly after World War II, Charles's grandson, Charles Minor Blackford III, who had served as a lieutenant-commander in the Navy, undertook to edit and abridge the *Memoirs* "in a fashion that gives the book absorbing interest for the general reader." He short-ened the work to one volume that focused primarily on Charles's wartime experiences. This required eliminating most of the writ-ings by Charles's father and by his brother William, as well as trun-cating Susan's contributions dealing with home life in Lynchburg. Charles Scribner's Sons published the abridged version under the title *Letters from Lee's Army* in 1947 to an enthusiastic reception. Henry Steele Commager, writing for the *New York Herald Tribune,* praised the book's "singularly vivid" depiction of the war, and the *American Historical Review* proclaimed it "an important addition to the source literature of the Civil War."[5]

It is interesting to compare Charles's original letters with the versions in Susan's *Memoirs* and in his grandson's *Letters from Lee's Army*. Charles often wrote on a board balanced across his knees in the midst of a bustling camp. The results sometimes lack polish, but they convey the same romantic ardor and expressive turn of phrase that grace the edited versions. In editing the letters for publication, Charles and Susan did make minor stylistic modifications. For example, on August 17, 1862, Charles began a letter from a bivouac near Raccoon Ford on the Rapidan River with the observation, "I wrote you a note on yesterday morning informing you that we were about to move—not knowing wither—nor do I yet know except that we have passed Orange C H and then turned down Rapidan River some five miles and bivouaced for the night." In the *Memoirs*, the passage was altered to state, "In my letter yesterday morning I told you we were about to move, and we did, but I know nothing more now than I did yesterday except that we have come to this point." The final permutation in *Letters from Lee's Army* reads, "In my letter yesterday I said we were going to move and we did, but I know nothing more than I did yesterday, except we have come to this point, near Raccoon Ford." The improved language in the *Memoirs* was likely Susan's, but Charles put his stamp of approval on her work.[6]

Letters from Lee's Army is for serious scholars of the American Civil War and casual readers as well. Its focus is necessarily provincial, as it recounts only the Blackford family experiences and events that its members witnessed. If you seek an exposition on the war's strategies and battles, you should turn elsewhere. But if you are looking to understand the war's impact on literate Southerners, you have come to the right place. Your reward will be an intimate acquaintance with Charles and Susan Blackford and an unforgettable view of their world through their eyes.

NOTES

1. Charles Minor Blackford III, ed., *Letters from Lee's Army, or Memoirs of Life In and Out of the Army in Virginia during the War between the States*, comp. Susan Leigh Blackford (New York, 1947), 258. Subsequent quotes are from this source unless otherwise identified.

2. Material relating to the Blackford brothers, including Launcelot and Eugene, appears in L. Minor Blackford, *Mine Eyes Have Seen the Glory* (Cambridge MA, 1954).

3. Susan Leigh Blackford, comp., *Memoirs of Life In and Out of the Army in Virginia during the War between the States*, 2 vols. (Reprint, Lynchburg VA, 1996), 1, "Notice." The two-volume *Memoirs* was well-neigh impossible to find until it was reprinted by Warwick House Publishing.

4. Authorship of *Annals of the Lynchburg Home Guard* (Lynchburg VA, 1891) is sometimes mistakenly attributed to Charles Blackford. In fact, his son Charles M. Blackford Jr. wrote the piece.

5. *New York Herald Tribune Weekly Book Review*, February 9, 1847, 3; *American Historical Review* 53, no. 1 (October 1947): 195.

6. Charles M. Blackford to Susan L. Blackford, August 17, 1862, copy in Fredericksburg Spotsylvania National Military Park Library, Fredericksburg VA; Blackford, *Memoirs of Life In and Out of the Army in Virginia*, 1, 181; Blackford, *Letters from Lee's Army*, 108.

CONTENTS

PREFACE   xvii

CHAPTER I   The Beginning   1

CHAPTER II   The March   7

CHAPTER III   First Blood   15

CHAPTER IV   Alarms and Excursions   38

CHAPTER V   Leesburg Visit   71

CHAPTER VI   The Front Shifts   78

CHAPTER VII   Jackson Is a Roundhead   84

CHAPTER VIII   Along the Rappahannock   108

CHAPTER IX   The Judge Advocate   154

CHAPTER X   To Gettysburg—And Back   172

CHAPTER XI   Our Sky Is Dark   192

CHAPTER XII   The River of Death   209

CHAPTER XIII   East Tennessee   231

CHAPTER XIV   Grant Comes to Virginia   242

CHAPTER XV   Lynchburg   259

CHAPTER XVI   Petersburg   266

CHAPTER XVII   Richmond   274

CHAPTER XVIII   Charlottesville   278

CHAPTER XIX   The Confederacy Crumbles   288

APPENDIX   297

INDEX   301

PREFACE

MY memory of my grandfather is limited to one little scene. I was four years old when he died. I remember a hurried trip from Washington to Lynchburg with my mother. I remember my surprise, when we reached the old house, at the quiet and hush of everyone. We were let into the little study in the rear where a group of silent people sat around. Awed by the strange welcome I sat in a bentwood chair and stared at the plaster owl atop the opposite bookcase. After a bit someone came in and motioned to us. Mother and I went upstairs, through the dressingroom into the huge bedroom. My grandfather lay in a large brass bed. I remember him saying: "Come to me!" I crawled up on the bed and hugged him. Then someone hustled me off the bed and into the next room; he was dying.

The war left the Blackford family, whose fortunes were mainly in securities and mortgages, penniless. But my grandfather had his home and profession. Some of their former slaves still lingered around, bewildered and helpless, doing housework and yardwork for less than their spending money before the war. My grandmother had to buy their clothes for them and to teach them how to shift for themselves. But even in my time some of the third generation were still coming to my uncle for advice and assistance when in trouble.

The Southern Railroad system was the conception of my grandfather Blackford. He estimated the cost of buying up the string of bankrupt railroads through the Piedmont while my other grandfather, William Goff Sears, estimated the cost of connecting them up and putting them into good condition. They took the proposition to Morgan and the rest is railroad history.

As a progressive citizen he was one of the first to have electricity in his home, a telephone, modern plumbing and, unfortunately, modern furniture. The wiring ran exposed under the ceiling of each room to a droplight in the center of the room, each light with a scalloped shade of white glass.

Grandfather liked to entertain. He had at least two complete services for twenty-four and extended the diningroom almost to the sidewalk to have enough room. My father frequently told me that Claude Swanson's political career started at one of these dinners. As I remember it some congressman died or retired and the question of his successor was being talked over at the table. My grandfather turned to Mr. Swanson and said, "Why don't you run, Claude?" While the latter was protesting modestly a young lady at the table leaned over and said: "Claude, if you run and win I'll marry you!" He ran, and won both the election and the girl.

The present Lady Astor visited there frequently when a girl.

I remember my grandmother as a frail, thin little woman always dressed in black with a little triangular cap rimmed with lace on her head. She was a typical Southern, or rather Virginian woman of her day: proud, but humble before God, lavish at the table but keeping an account of every penny, every pound of flour and an inventory of every object in the house. She entertained her friends and relatives without thought to herself, but they had to be persons that came up to her rigid standards of breeding.

"To be a gentleman," she often told me, "you have to learn your table manners before seven, your social manners before twelve and your moral obligations before twenty-one."

The Blackford family through its history in America has been always a typical middle-class American family: never very famous, never obscure. It is not one of the First Families of Virginia except by marriage. It first settled in New Jersey in 1745. When the Revolution broke out the father remained loyal and moved to Nova Scotia, where he died; but his sons all joined the Revolutionary Army. Our branch settled in Maryland, then in Virginia. Benjamin Blackford fought at Yorktown, was a friend of George Washington, had a hand in building the first steamboat, and was a man of strong personal honesty. It is told that one of his sons-in-law failed in Charlottesville for ten thousand dollars. He heard of it in Winchester, loaded a wagon with ten thousand silver dollars, drove it across the Blue Ridge and paid off his son-in-law's debts over the tail-board of the wagon as it stood in the main street of Charlottesville. He opened up the first iron mines in Virginia, and he and his wife were active in the movement to return the slaves to Africa. His wife wrote and published several tracts on the subject. Of my great-grandfather there is an excellent description in William W. Blackford's *War Years with Jeb Stuart*. The Blackfords have done their share in fighting our wars, making our laws and developing our natural resources, and, with God's help, may they continue to do so.

This book is compiled from the letters of my grandfather and grandmother written to each other during the war and which my grandmother printed privately in 1894. That work consists of two volumes, mostly in fine print, and contains many items not of interest to the general reader or even to members of the family of this generation. The original contains my great-grandfather's diary (extracts), some of W. W. Blackford's memoirs, now published as *War Years with Jeb Stuart,* and other material.

Such a book could not be written about the past two wars as censorship and the prohibition against diaries has made it impossible to write graphic letters or notes from the battle-front. We now look upon the Civil War as a romantic war; the sting of suffering and loss in its wake has passed. My grandmother remained bitter until almost the end of her life. She had reason: she lost three children directly through conditions caused by the war. "Little Nannie" of this book died at the birth of her first child, and my father, born just after the fall of the Confederacy, could never take his rightful place in science and medicine because of his physical condition. The actions of the Federal soldiers given in the latter part of the book are mild to many stories I heard throughout Virginia as a child and cause one to understand why "Damnyankee" was one word in the South for two generations.

Charles Minor Blackford 3rd.

LETTERS FROM LEE'S ARMY

CHAPTER I

THE BEGINNING

DURING the first three weeks after the John Brown Raid, as it was always called, a cavalry company was organized in Lynchburg called "The Wise Troop," a name selected in honor of Henry A. Wise, then Governor of Virginia and very active in encouraging the formation of military companies. The uniform of this troop seems now to me, who saw it many times afterwards so differently costumed, as very singular, even partaking of the absurd. It consisted of bright blue pantaloons with a gold cord down the sides, the brightest scarlet horsehair tufts hanging down behind them. The papers made great fun of them and pretended to think the British had invaded our homes again. The gay attire was, however, only a holiday dress; when the company was really equipped for the field, as it was two years afterwards, the Confederate grey was adopted and the red coats disappeared —either seeking the dye-pot to appear in some more somber hue or being relegated to some colored camp-follower who rejoiced in the startling tint.

The company, later known as Company B of the Second Virginia cavalry, will be mentioned often in these pages for with it my life and love were bound up during three of the four years of war. As soon as it was formed my husband joined it and was sent to Richmond for the purpose of securing arms. Mr. Blackford took active part in the organization of the company and gave much attention to drill, but having no military education he was only a non-commissioned officer at the outset. The day the company received orders to prepare for active service he rose from the position of fourth corporal to first lieutenant by reason of the resignation of all the officers above him but the captain. The order for service developed the past-muster age of most of them or else brought to light some physical trouble never before known.

Captain R. C. W. Radford was the first captain selected and John S. Langhorne was the first lieutenant. When the war broke out Radford was made colonel of the Second Virginia Cavalry and Mr. Langhorne was made captain in his stead. Very soon after the first battle of Manassas Captain Langhorne was made Major of the regiment and Mr. Blackford elected Captain.

No State in the South had been more devoted to the Union than Virginia. It was literally the child of her loins, and she could not stand calmly by and see it destroyed without solemnly protesting against the sacrilege. Her electoral vote was for Bell and Everett, the avowed Union candidates, although for many years her people had been Democratic by a large majority. The sentiment of the Virginian people was strongly against the violent action of South Carolina and the other Southern States in withdrawing from the Union merely because a sectional President had been elected. They thought that the South should wait and take no action until its rights were so violated that forebearance would cease to be a virtue. Despite the example of all the other Southern States, their seductive prayers and their unreasoning taunts, Virginia, although she called a constitutional convention, refused to pass an ordinance of secession until Lincoln called upon her to furnish eight thousand troops to make war upon her Southern sisters and was preparing to march an army over her soil to subjugate the Southern people. Then Virginia, having exhausted every effort as a peace-maker to prevent war, with a full knowledge that she would be the Flanders of the war, calmly bared her bosom to the storm and placed herself and her people in the forefront of the battle.

Yet the winter of 1860 and 1861 was with us one of unprecedented gaiety. The spirit of fun and frolic seemed to take possession of our people both young and old, and for months entertainments were given in generous emulation as to the novelty and elegance of the amusements offered. Party after party succeeded each other in rapid succession. One of the first was a masked fancy party, the most successful entertainment of its kind I ever saw. The lovely Mamie King took the part of Mary, Queen of Scots. She was regal indeed in her velvet robe and long train, her high lace ruff about her graceful neck and a girdle of pearls about her waist. Her sister, Lilly King, was younger, piquant. She appeared as a saucy little vivandiere, with short skirts, a red cap and a canteen. No one ever dreamed that this canteen, bought to make up a saucy costume, would ever have a grimmer destiny and still be kept, over eighty years later, as a cherished heirloom.

The leaders of Lynchburg society at that time were Mr. and Mrs. Samuel Garland, Jr. Suppers at the Garlands' were things to be remembered. The superb saddle of mutton was a piece of resistance and alongside was an old Virginia ham, red as a ruby, and with a melting tenderness that rivaled the best Westphalian; also there were turkeys and salad, raw Lynnhaven oysters, served from bowls cut from blocks of ice, canvasback ducks, partridges and venison—all ending in pyramids of frosted cake, cut glass bowls of jelly, trembling and sparkling in the light as if set with diamonds—everything made under the eye, and often by the hands of the accomplished hostess. The popping of the champagne bottles added to the jollity of the scene, which was closed, as far as the supper-room went, by a short toast of welcome. Dancing the lancers and cotillions was usually kept up until a late hour. None of us then knew that within two years of that time Mrs. Garland, and their little boy would be resting in the cemetery and Mr. Garland stark and cold on the bloody field of Boonsboro.

Of the other parties I can only recall one other; at Dr. Murell's, I think, and represented an Irish wake.

Directly after Lincoln's call for troops the whole course of our ordinary life was changed. All our usual avocations were at an end, and a new life began for women as well as for men. The sound of drum and fife could be heard from morning until night. The men were drilling and equipping themselves for war while the women, with tearful eyes and saddened hearts, spent their time making coats, pantaloons, shirts, haversacks and every kind of work that would make their men more comfortable or healthy in the field. As I look back upon those sad days I wonder how I lived through them and their sorrow. I well remember now those lonely evenings; after my two children were asleep I would sit in nervous anxiety. I would picture him that was dearer to me than life lying stark upon some lonely battlefield or wounded on a stretcher. There can be no sorrow like that—it was the sorrow of death itself. It would seem to me, as I looked upon it then, that my husband would be the common aim of every northern musket and that escape was impossible.

Mr. Blackford's company was in camp with five or six companies of the same regiment just this side of the Fair Grounds, part of which is now a public park. Mr. Blackford was temporarily detailed as adjutant of the companies present. He was offered the adjutancy of the regiment but declined, preferring to stay with his company and in the line. Every evening I drove out with the children in our little one-horse phaeton, carrying every visit something which I thought would make him comfortable. I would sit and watch the drill and dress parade, and when it was nearly dark, would kiss my husband good-night and, weeping with the children, would return to my desolate home.

I shall now quote from his own pen an account of what occurred when orders came for his company to march. My own recollections of that time are so mingled with tears and anguish that I cannot give an accurate account of what happened. He says in a memorial note kept by him:

We remained in camp in mere routine until Sunday June 2d, when, just after breakfast Colonel Radford received a dispatch which I noticed made him look very grave, and he handed it to me without a word of comment. It was an order to send two companies immediately to Manassas which was then the point nearest the enemy. He directed me, as acting adjutant of the regiment, to place two companies, company A, Captain Terry, and B company, Captain Langhorne, my company, in readiness to march by daylight the next morning. He told me at the same time that, having discharged that duty, I might spend the rest of the day with my family provided I came back before sunset. The news was received with various emotions by the men, but as a rule with pleasure. There was a general belief prevailing, that unless we go speedily to the front the war would be over before we had any hand in it. I had no such thought nor had Col. Radford. I thought it would be many a year's struggle at the least and made my arrangements accordingly. Few shared my apprehensions and even my father, whose judgment was so sound in many things, seemed buoyed up by the hope that the danger, though great, would soon pass away.

As soon as I had delivered my orders and seen the preparations commenced, I had my horse saddled and rode home reaching there in time for late breakfast. My face announced my errand to my wife as soon as I entered her chamber where she was dressing and came near fainting in my arms. As soon as she recovered she packed my valise and had me several days rations cooked but it was a sad day for us both.

The day was as fair as the weather could make it, joyous and bright and we sat most of the day out in the arbor with the children, Nannie and Willy. After dinner we went over to father's that I might bid them good-bye. They were much distressed, but bore up with much fortitude; all their sons, when I left, would be in the field. Under the circumstances I fear I should have broken down. Father kept up his cheerful hopefulness, or appeared to do so for the benefit of the others but his worn and haggard face showed how deeply he was suffering. We went back home again and gathered in the arbor for our last talk together. Nanny was then four years old and Willy two, but they seemed to feel that some deep grief hung over us and clung around us as if to shield us from it. Those two hours were so sad that they left a scar on our hearts that has never been erased from either of us.

At seven o'clock that evening I had to leave my loved ones, Willy I never saw but once again. I told my servants good-bye and confided my household to their faithful care, and after a tearful embrace of my wife and children, and one parting, longing look at my cheerful home, I mounted my horse and took the road to my camp. I remember every incident, even the spot where I turned and took one last look at my home and the route I rode on my return. I remember that people, white and black, sitting in their yards or porches enjoying the wonderful evening bade me good-bye as I passed and showed their sympathy by some kind word. I was riding my noble old roan, I called him old as a term of endearment, for then he was only six. He bore me through four long years of war and there was nothing in Lee's army, man or beast, which was more constant in the discharge of duty.

When I reached camp I found every man in place and everything ready for the start in the morning for we were to march all the way. The lights were soon out and all was quiet. What thoughts crowded the brains of the two hundred men about me I could not tell, but I tossed from side to side with a heart full of anxious foreboding for my home and my State.

CHAPTER II

THE MARCH

Continuing Mr. Blackford's record:

THE next morning, Monday June 3d 1861, I was up at day-break to see that the tents were properly struck and packed in the wagons. When I look back at it in the light of subsequent experience it would seem we were going upon a picnic instead of a march to war. We had two wagons for each company, besides private wagons owned by the officers of each making six in all. We learned before the war was over that beside the transportation of the quartermaster and commissary departments, one wagon for a brigade was enough. Every soldier ought to be required to carry what is necessary for his comfort and that no army can be mobile and efficient until this is done. Baggage is well called "impedimenta" and every old soldier knows this even if he has not read Caesar's Commentaries.

We were equipped largely at our own and the community's expense and were armed with double-barrel shotguns, pistols and sabres. It was supposed the shotgun would be an efficient arm but it was too frail and was soon abandoned. After the first battle of Manassas we supplied ourselves with the captured arms of the enemy and had good carbines for the rest of the war. We never did secure the Winchesters whose repeating qualities made the enemy's cavalry so formidable towards the close of the war.

The men were very well mounted. Every horse, like its rider, had a strain of gentle blood, at least blood that could be traced back to some good old Virginia stock which was famous for pluck and endurance. I had two horses, one a substantial hack for my servant and the other a very fine roan, the finest riding horse I ever saw. He was my constant riding horse, and though I owned several others during the war, he was ever fit and ready for use. I never rode him in battle and he was never hurt.

My servant was a free negro named John Scott. He had been servant for Captain Gardener in the Mexican War, and like my old roan, served me most faithfully through the whole war. He was very taciturn but ever in good humor and I do not remember ever calling him once during the whole time that he did not answer. In camp, on the march, even under fire, he never forsook me when he thought he could be of any use.

Father came out at sunrise to see the last of me and walked by my side as I rode at the head of my column through town to the ford just below the Waterworks dam. He seemed depressed but did his best to keep up his spirits to cheer me. I was, of course, much depressed but I did not show it, for I had too many things to do and too many were dependent on me for advice and comfort. I acted as adjutant to the squadron which was under the command of Captain W. R. Terry as well as lieutenant of my company. Captain Langhorne, though a brave officer, knew nothing of details or how to look after the thousand wants which arise and must be met when a hundred men are leaving home under such circumstances and it is a strange thing, but true, that as soon as the average man enlisted as a private he became almost a machine and relied on his officers to do his thinking, and placed upon them the whole responsibility of his daily life. Captain Langhorne's deficiencies in these details devolved much more work upon me and I had to be a sort of a dry nurse to my whole company and I continued so as long as I was with it.

The company marched down Fifth to Main Street, down Main to Ninth, down Ninth* to Jefferson hence up Jefferson to Sixth, and then crossed the canal near the pumphouse to the ford about where the Glamorgan Works now stand. Before we entered the river we halted to see that everything was

*Lynchburg, Va., is situated on a steep hillside with many streets ending on abrupt cliffs above the James River. Ninth Street is the first street allowing passage down to the lower part of town by the river. C.M.B. III

ready. Hundreds of people came down to the river to bid us good-bye. Many wives and mothers committed their sons and husbands to my care. Two of them, that I remember, soon received back their loved ones placed under my care in coffins, shot on the field of battle.

At ten o'clock Captain Terry gave orders to move and we plunged into the river amidst the cheers of men and the tears of the women upon the bank. We were fairly started on our warpath. From the top of the hill on the opposite side I stopped to take a long farewell look at my home. I could see the whole town stretched out before me. Diamond Hill, my own house and even my chamber window, where I knew my wife and little son were sitting and straining their eyes to catch the last sorrowing look at the squadron as it crossed the ridge. I could linger only a moment; then, dashing away the resistless tear, I applied myself to my many duties.

We reached Amherst Courthouse before night, but owing to the negligence of the officer acting as quartermaster and commissary, we found no provisions had been made for men or beasts, and there was no disposition on the part of the inhabitants to show us any hospitality or to relieve our wants except for money. By ten o'clock, however, provisions had been obtained for men and horses and we were quite comfortably quartered in the Courthouse. By virtue of my rank I was assigned a bench inside the bar and though it was very hard I slept soundly. The next morning we started as soon as we fed our horses and got something to eat. We were much surprised by the little attention shown us by the people of Amherst. I cannot understand it unless they had no notice of our coming and were unprepared to meet the needs of so many. During our march of some twenty-six miles through their county not a cup of buttermilk nor a word of cheer was tendered us. When we crossed the Nelson County line all was changed and our reception was enthusiastic; people came from miles in wagons and carriages, with their families, to see us pass. At every crossroad we had an ovation. Enough pies, cakes and buttermilk were tendered us to feed a brigade. At Lovingstone I found it hard to get through the enthusiastic crowd, and their hospitality was so great that it quite overcame several of my men and I had to have them brought away under guard. The squadron was the first armed band they had seen and they treated it right royally. The hats of most the men were crowned with flowers and around my horse's neck some girls twined a beautiful wreath.

Our second night was more uncomfortable than the first, and from the same reason. Our acting-quartermaster was sent forward to select a camp and he placed it in a narrow road just south of the covered bridge over the Rockfish River; a steep hill rose from the road on one side and a high fence closed it on the other. That was no place to put up a tent and no place to picket the horses except in fence corners. A heavy cloud had been muttering in the west all afternoon, and at sundown, just as we got to our camp-ground, the worse to be found in two counties, it burst upon us. Everything but the men, who took cover in the covered bridge, got wet. After the storm was over we fed the horses but went supperless to bed, as even if we could have found a place to make a fire to cook by the wood was too wet to burn. I slept in my wagon, many of the men in the covered bridge. During the night there was a stampede among some of the horses and they dashed through the bridge to the great alarm and danger of the hundred men sleeping on the floor of the bridge. Some of the men who jumped up at the first alarm were knocked down but no one was hurt and order was soon restored.

About daylight the next morning I was awakened by a messenger bringing me a note from Mr. and Mrs. Jesse L. Heiskell who lived a mile or two north of the Rockfish and directly on our road asking me to extend an invitation to the whole command to breakfast with them. It was joyous news as we had no place to cook and nothing to cook if we had a place. The men were soon up and more than usual time was given for washing and dressing for everyone wanted to look as spry as possible. The sun came out very brightly and it was an ideal day. When everybody was washed and brushed and dry again we started out with longing appetites and reached the house about eight o'clock. In the lot adjoining his barn we found ample provender for our horses and the house was one vast dining-room. I was put in command of the entertainment. In the porch there were three or four tubs of mint julep, over which I placed a guard with orders not to allow more than one drink without my permission. While the men were being served the officers went into breakfast, and such a breakfast for hungry men! Everything known to Virginia housekeepers was there, and in such abundance that the last relief that went into breakfast had just as much and just as good as was served to the officers at the first table. I hurried through and divided the men up into reliefs, putting each relief under the charge of a sergeant, and then the reliefs were taken into breakfast successively.

The exploit in housekeeping I have never known equalled. Mrs. Heiskell told me she had heard of our arrival at the river about bedtime and had determined to give us a breakfast. Couriers were sent out to the neighbors and they rapidly assembled, bringing chickens, eggs, butter, ham and every possible delicacy; then with their cooks they set to work and by daylight the bountiful supply for two hundred men, of which we so joyfully partook, was ready.

When all had eaten to repletion the squadron was formed in front of the house, sabres presented, three cheers given, and I returned thanks in the name of the command. We wheeled into column and marched away very gay and happy. En route through the counties of Nelson and Albemarle our receptions continued very much like a triumphal march.

Within a mile or two of Charlottesville we met a messenger with an invitation to lunch at the University, which of course, we accepted, and when we reached the foot of the lawn we found a very handsome spread and a considerable crowd of professors, their wives and daughters, and students all assembled to do us honor and supply us with the viands, among them, of course Mr. Minor and sister Nannie. After a pleasant hour spent there we marched on to town and were quartered for the night in the town hall and were the recipients of much hospitality. I was the guest of Prof. Holcombe of Maiden Lane.

The fifth day of our march brought us to Culpeper Courthouse after a march of thirty-one miles which was much too severe for such hot weather. Here Colonel Philip St. George Cocke was in command and the garrison consisted of the 19th Virginia Regiment. He was engaged in forwarding troops to Manassas and organizing that regiment. He is an excitable person, with an exaggerated opinion of the importance of his position as commander at Culpeper. He had around him a number of young snobs, who, in the capacity of his aids, were rendering him ridiculous and themselves odious. They were generally young sprouts with bobtailed coats and vast importance, from the Military Institute, who obviously thought the war was gotten up that they might dazzle the world by their talents. Here I received my first letter from home which, by the way, was the first one received in the company. The letter was handed me by Ben Blackford who was the surgeon in charge of the hospital and medical stores of the place. He was comfortably fixed and treated me very hospitably.

We were much jaded by our march, both men and horses. A great part of their discomfort and suffering arose from their inexperience in marching and in taking care of both men and horses. Many horses were rendered unfit for use by sore backs caused by awkward and unskilled riding. Some men can ride their horses for days and never injure their backs, while others will be seldom fit for duty on that account. The difference is in the manner they sit upon their horses and the mode of riding. A man who slouches down, rides with a swing, sits sometimes on one side then on another, and never dismounts when the company halts, will always have a sore-backed horse. The proper rules are always to sit straight in the saddle, never sit on one side with uneven pressure, never fret a horse, ride with an even gait, and the instant a halt is called to dismount and loosen the girth. If the halt is a short one the horse is rested, and when the march, or the day is over never take off the saddle until the horse is cooled.

At Culpeper we lightened our wagons by taking most of our luggage out of them and sending it on to Manassas by rail to await our arrival.

Sunday, June 9th, 1861.

We started this morning at daybreak passing through a beautiful country where people received us with open arms although we were not the first troops that had passed. About four P.M. we reached the Fauquier White Sulphur Springs, which was a most beautiful place. We camped in the grove and Mr. Hudgins, the proprietor, gave us the advantage of the baths which we greatly enjoyed. He was also very hospitable in many ways and distributed many buckets of mint julep amongst the men with over-lavish hand, and invited the officers to take their meals at the house with him where we had a very fine spread.

About sunset it was reported that a yankee spy was seen several miles distant and I was sent with two men to catch him. We found that a well-mounted, suspicious looking stranger had been reconnoitering our position around Warrenton. When he saw us at a distance, and before we saw him, he turned and galloped off. We got on his trail, for the road was moist from a recent shower, and his tracks were easily seen, and showed he was riding at full speed. We took a gallop also and rode about seven miles. Within view of Warrenton the tracks suddenly turned into the woods and we lost all trail as it had grown dark.

When we got back to the Springs we found all the neighborhood gathered, and amongst them many pretty girls, and though it was Sunday we had quite a gay party which lasted until midnight.

Monday.

After breakfast the squadron was drawn up in front of the hotel to bid our kind host good-bye. The balcony was filled with ladies and gentlemen, and Mr. Hudgins stood on the steps. I was detailed to tender the thanks of the command for the kindness shown us, and I made quite a little speech, referring to the Rappahannock which flowed at the foot of their lawn, and to the fine associations which it revived as I lay on its banks the night before. This speaking at every point and on all occasions was not a voluntary thing on my part. I was regularly detailed by the commanding officer.

It was determined we should reach Manassas Junction the day we left the Springs, making a distance of twenty-five miles. We were now so near the army that soldiers were by no means so great a rarity as in the country through which we had passed, so our march was not so much of a triumphal procession. Still our reception, if anything, was much more cordial, because every man and woman seemed to hail us as protectors. We had curious ideas of the war then and were expecting to hear the opening guns of a general engagement and feared it would be over before we could take a hand.

We moved through the lovely village of Warrenton down the Alexandria pike. We stuck to the Alexandria pike until we came to the Stone Bridge over Bull Run. There we turned to the right passing Mrs. Henry's house. Our path took us between Manassas Gap Railroad and Bull Run. When we came within sight of Manassas Junction we were halted and Captain Terry rode on to General Beauregard's headquarters. He soon returned with a staff officer who took us to our camp-ground, just outside the infantry camp. As we dismounted we were surrounded by a number of Lynchburg men belonging to the Eleventh Virginia Regiment. Among them Garland, Kean, Kirk, Otey and Wm. M. Blackford. Lewis Blackford, I found, had just received a commission as lieutenant of engineers and had been sent to Norfolk. I laid off the camp and had the tents pitched. The march was over; we were in the war.

CHAPTER III

☆ ☆ ☆ ★ ☆ ☆ ☆

FIRST BLOOD

☆ ☆ ☆ ☆ ☆ ☆

At this point Mr. Blackford's letters commence. The first of interest is from Centreville, June 19th, 1861.

HERE we are again in what we call Home, and you may depend on it I am glad of it. Now for a description of the march of our army and "The Great Battle of Vienna." On Saturday night a detail of twenty-five men was made up from our company of which I was in command, with orders to prepare cooked rations for ten days and be ready to start on Sunday morning. Sunday morning was bright and beautiful, and, at eight o'clock we started out without knowing where we were bound. Forty-three of Captain Terry's men were with us under his command. Four miles from here we were joined by about seven hundred South Carolina infantry. Two cannons from Kemper's Battery went with us from Centreville under Kemper's command. That night we reached Dranesville, a little village in Fairfax about two miles from the Potomac, and directly opposite the camp of the enemy. There I spent the night on the bare ground without tent or shelter in a pouring rain, and strange to say I slept very well. On Monday Col. Maxcy Gregg, the ranking officer of the whole force, went down to make a survey of the place. As soon as he had completed the work we took up the line of march to Vienna, a point about ten miles from Alexandria. We reached the place about four o'clock and spent two hours destroying all the railroad property there which could be of use to the enemy. The job was completed and we had commenced to move off, and had gotten about half a mile from the depot with the head of the column when a distant whistle of a train was heard indicating the approach of a train from towards Alexandria, which we knew must be in the possession of the enemy. We had no rolling

stock on the road. The forces were instantly ordered back, the
cannon placed in battery on the hill at the right of the depot,
looking east and the infantry and cavalry range in line of battle
a little below them. As soon as the line of battle was formed,
and the whole command was awaiting with breathless anxiety
the approach of the train one of Col. Gregg's staff rode up and
asked for Lieutenant Blackford. I answered, "Here," and he
replied, "Take your command rapidly to the foot of the hill
and occupy the road that crosses the railroad." I closed up my
little band and took up a gallop in front of the whole line, the
men following beautifully, and took my position in front of
the enemy just as they hove in sight, my squad being the only
part of our forces they could see. As soon as they saw us they
made ready to fire at us, but at the same time, the fools allowed
the train of flat cars upon which they were travelling to continue moving at the same rate of speed. In an instant however
they were waked up by a shot from the cannon, the effect of
which I could not see, except they at once fired at my detachment a volley from their whole regiment. Strange to say the
balls passed over our heads and no one was hurt. The smoke
had not cleared before another cannon shot from Kemper was
fired. This time he used canister and the effect was terrific. I
saw the shot plow through their crowded ranks on the flat cars
laying them out right and left, and making them jump off the
still moving train. Twelve shots were fired, and the rascals quit
the cars, retreating without order and in great haste. None of
the shots injured the engine or the running gear of the cars,
so after all the men had quit the train it was backed and soon
out of range, picking up the retreating men as it passed them.
I was ordered to follow but the train could go faster than my
horses, especially as owing to the character of the land I had
to go out of the direct line to follow. It was growing dark and
we had to give up pursuit. The exact number of their killed
and wounded is not known. We found only seven dead and
one wounded, but the Washington papers of the next day announced a terrible rebel ambush and they say that two hundred
of their men were cruelly killed or wounded. I do not believe
that the number was so great, but I know that there were many

more killed and wounded than we first supposed, for it was impossible that so many rounds of canister could go through crowded cars, raking them from front to rear without killing a great number.

June 26th, 1861.

I am, as you see, still at Centreville, although I am entirely unable to say how long I will here remain. Although I sent off a letter to you which I commenced last night and finished this morning I feel as if I ought not to allow a single spare moment pass without occupying it in writing to you, my more than better half. We are now doing not more than half the work we did under Colonel Cocke. The commissioned officers have almost nothing to do, so little that I have the dyspepsia for the first time in my life. Merely for exercise I started out today alone on a scout and I have leave to go again tomorrow, when I intend to find out what the enemy are doing around Vienna. John Thomas Smith is going with me. He is a fellow I always like to have near me in time of trouble. He is a true man as ever breathed and one who will go to the cannon's mouth to defend me. We are great friends. I am aware I have said little about the men but I have made no particular mention of any because all, without exception, have shown me nothing but kindness and love.

As I passed the picket line today a neighborhood man told me to look out or Lincoln's men would take me and I heard one of the picket-guard say, "If they take him he will be retaken or Company B will die in the attempt." There was an earnestness in the manner of saying that gratified me much. Even the notorious Charles Green is one of my fast friends. The day I command the scouting party they find out beforehand and come and beg to go with me. I have no better friend in the company than Van Otey, who is a perfect model of a soldier, and as first sergeant has gotten the company into a better state of discipline than ever before. Virginius Dunnington has joined us, and gone to work like a man. Of course Abram Warwick and Chalmers are with me a great deal, but Cross, Massie and Smith are my especial body-guard in time of danger. Jack Christian, Marion Langhorne and Ned Horner of course would be also, but their being sergeants prevents my taking but one of them with me at a time when I have only a small squad. So among my friends I count Tom Smith, Bob Seabury, Henry Hunt and Jack Alexander, so I should mention also Woodroof, who, you know, has always been one of my pets. He is a good man, a gentleman and a brave soldier, never complaining and always willing and anxious to be detailed for the post of toil and danger.

I hear John Scott's wife is sick. I want you to go and see her. John has been a faithful servant and a great comfort. He gives me no trouble, and does more work than any two servants in camp.

Col. Munford passed through Centreville yesterday with four companies of our regiment, and Col. Radford will be here today with four more. Munford went to Fairfax Courthouse. There will now be about twelve hundred cavalry in this neighborhood, so our picket duty is much lightened.

I went out to dine yesterday at a Mr. Cockerille's and enjoyed the dinner very much. I have become so lost to all modesty that I will not hesitate to go to a man's house and tell him I have come for dinner. Most of the people about here are loyal to our side and very kind to us, but occasionally we find a Union man, generally a man of northern birth. At one place we were cheered under the belief that we were yankees. It is reported the enemy has evacuated Falls Church and retired to Alexandria. If so we will move further towards Alexandria, and they will leave it.

Centreville, June 26th, 1861, Wednesday night.

I mentioned in the letter I sent off today that I was going off on a scout to Vienna, and as Vienna is the nearest point to the enemy, I know you will be anxious until I inform you of my safe return. My instructions were to go as far towards Vienna as possible, and to learn all I could about the enemy's movements. To do this I thought it best not to take a party with me, but to go with only one trusty man, and for that man I selected my friend John T. Smith. I dismounted before I reached the station and went a circuitous route among the pines until I obtained a view of the place and discovered no yankees were there. Then we mounted our horses and rode into the village and inspected our battleground. Every person in the place almost had gone over to the yankees, they being yankees generally themselves by birth, and we found therefore, no one at home just at the station. We scouted the neighborhood and took dinner with an ironside Baptist preacher, then returned safely to camp after a ride of about forty miles. We ascertained the enemy were drawing in their lines in that direction.

Centreville, June 28, 1861.

I went yesterday on business to Middleburg taking John T. Smith with me. We had a most delightful day and enjoyed the country through which we rode exceedingly. As soon as we arrived at Middleburg I called on Mr. Burr P. Noland and we were invited to his house to dinner. The luxury of refined society never seemed to me so great. We actually sat in chairs, talked to a lady and ate out of china, and further had everything nice which the country could afford not excluding ice cream which never seemed so good to me.

Both Mr. and Mrs. Noland were as kind as could be, and I never enjoyed a day more. General Rogers also pressed me much to go to his house. Mrs. Noland gave me an account of the things at Martinsburg; they are terrible. The whole place is divided against itself, some for the South, some for the North—Mr. Holmes Conrad for the latter.

That Mr. Conrad should be a unionist is very astonishing. I have no toleration with such. Even some of the women are traitors and two or three walked many miles to inform the enemy of Johnston's approach. A large part of Loudoun, the upper end where the quakers preponderate, is disaffected. There are a great number of yankees in this county who have proved very troublesome, and many of them have been run off. We were treated very kindly between here and Middleburg. At one place the lady of the house came out to the road and made us go in and take some refreshments. We were received everywhere with open arms by the people of Fairfax. They say they can sleep comfortable now we have come.

Centreville, June 30th.

Col. Radford passed through here this evening with the residue of one regiment en route to Fairfax Courthouse. He did not know when we would be sent. I hope not to Fairfax, as I hear the accommodations there for men and horses are bad. I hope we will be sent to join Company A, under Captain Terry, at Fryingpan Church, and I think it not improbable that after we are joined again we will be sent to Leesburg or in that direction. Something is in the wind; of this you may be sure. At least fifteen hundred men have passed our camp to-day on the march to Fairfax, and orders have been issued to all troops at this point to keep their wagons and horses ready to march at a moment's notice. We are, of course, kept in anxious expectation.

I must trouble you to send me as soon as you can the following articles: one small oven, two heavy blankets, dark if possible, some pipes and stems, a bottle of ink, two camp stools and a camp bed, the latter I want made according to the most approved pattern, such as they are now making in Richmond, the principal object being to get them as light as possible, and so made that they will fold up and occupy very little room. Send me also some simple medicines such as laudanum and such others as you may deem best.

Camp Mason, July 5th, 1861.

Well, here I am at another encampment known as Camp Mason, about three and one-half miles from Fairfax, and three miles from Centreville. We commenced moving this morning at nine o'clock and now we are encamped at a much better place though nearer the enemy. After the last wagon was packed this morning I went down to Manassas to see if the spring-wagon had come, and sure enough there was the mess kit in it. It is very well adapted for my purposes but I am sorry father sent me old harness. I wrote for a new one, and this broke on the trip from Manassas up here. The mess chest is elegant, and will add much to my comfort. I am more comfortably supplied with everything than anyone I know in the army, principally owing to your thoughtful love. I am surprised that Captain Langhorne has not more comforts around him. He scarcely has one, and yet he is entitled to more than anyone in the company. I have just unpacked the chest, and at every turn I find new illustrations of your ever thoughtful love. You never sent sugar to a sourer crowd than ours. Our sugar gave out yesterday and when the box arrived my mess had just finished supper, at which they had drunk unsweetened coffee, and this morning we had to use yours entirely. The coffee, tea and all will be of very great service, for though we usually have some sugar and coffee, we sometimes by accident get out, and then a private supply comes in with great effect.

When you send the next box send about ten pounds of coffee-sugar and then I will let you rest, for I can now think of nothing for you to send. Is it possible you have lived on the little money I left you with? I fear you have been suffering for the necessaries of life. Ask father to endorse my name on one of the insurance notes I left with you, and have it discounted and put to your credit at the Exchange Bank, subject to your check, I am very much anxious to commence drawing my pay as I do not know where else I am to get money.

July 6th.

Just as I was writing the last lines yesterday I was startled by the report of firearms at the infantry pickets, and at once we got ready for a march and you would be surprised at how quick the men were ready for the road. It was perfectly dark and raining and I pitied the sentinels on duty. The men in the camp were ready for duty in five minutes. The alarm turned out to be a false one. We are anticipating an attack every day now. A rumor is afloat that an engagement took place near Fairfax station this morning in which forty of the enemy and three of our men were killed, including Col. Ewell, but it is only a rumor and I know nothing of it.

July 7th.

The night passed quietly and this morning everything looks smiling and beautiful. Sunday, strange to say, is the day upon which most military movements commence. I never get up on

Sunday morning without expecting orders to move somewhere before night. You will remember our trip to Vienna was commenced on that date.

We shall soon be deprived of the luxuries of coffee and sugar, both of which have given out at the commissary. Your supply is all we have now. Don't fail to buy me some common brown sugar, and keep it subject to my order. Don't send me what you have at home, for I fear when your supply is gone you will not be able to get any more. You must begin to economise in its use.

A letter from Mrs. Blackford.
Lynchburg, July 8th, 1861.

I did not write you this morning as I usually do, because I have been at father's all day sewing for the soldiers. While I was there I was sent for to see old Mrs. John M. Otey, who was at Mrs. Spence's making arrangements to establish a Ladies' Hospital for the soldiers in opposition to Dr. Owen's. You know perhaps, that he will not allow the ladies to enter his hospital, or do anything for the patients. Mrs. Otey proposes to have a house and matron and a staff of hired nurses, all under the supervision of the ladies, with a change every day of those who are to stay in the hospital and directing the cooking and general service. If the scheme can be carried through it will a good one and the poor men will be more comfortable than they are now. I promised Mrs. Otey I would co-operate with her as far as it was in my power but I did not think I could do any nursing. I think you would not like me to do that. Mrs. Otey said she was very glad to have her son associated with you and that he sounded your praises very loudly.

From Lieut. Blackford, July 9th.

You see this is dated from Camp Blackford so named by the men as a compliment to me. It is the most beautiful situation we have had since we went into service. We are on a hill surrounded by trees enough to give shade and yet not enough to make it damp. Two springs are within fifty yards of us, and, best of all, surrounded by many nice farms which supply the men with provisions and horses with forage. How long we will remain here I cannot say. I take it a very little while, as I think an attack will be made on Fairfax Courthouse by the Federal forces in a few days, when I think we will fall back, first to Centreville, then to Manassas making Bull Run our line of defense, and a strong one it will be. At least that is what I would do, but of course, I know nothing of what will be done.

Fairfax is no place for you now. Wait awhile for developments. Eugene's company passed up on Sunday and joined Rodes' Regiment but he is out of my reach now; Rodes' regiment is the one nearest the enemy and will certainly be in the first engagement. I shall go down to see Eugene as soon as I can get off. Massie came up with him on Friday and reports him well and his company a fine one. I have seen many companies, but none of them compare with Company B. Our men are older than the Home Guard and their characters have improved since coming into camp, and they have a great reputation with the country people around us and get the inside track on all others in consequence.

July 10th.

The ball will open on this line in a few days, if not hours. Of that you can tell more in Lynchburg than I can down here. You will be surprised when I say I really know less of what is going on in other parts of the army than you do. Of course it is right to keep everything as dark as possible, even from our own men; no other way would keep our designs a secret from the enemy. As it is they learn a vast amount.

Just as I wrote the last line a wagon passed by with four women in it belonging to Col. Wheat's "Louisiana Tigers," all dressed up as men. I presume they are vivandieres from New Orleans. They are disgusting looking creatures who have followed the camp. They are being moved back to a safer place in anticipation of an attack.

July 15th—Monday.

I have not written for several days because I have been ill with dysentery. I had a chill and high fever on Saturday night, and just in the midst of it we were ordered back nearer Centreville, and I was carried to Mr. Meachen's where I now am.

Bristow, July 19th, 1861.

Well, I suppose you are delighted to see my handwriting in ink once more, something like myself. Now for my adventures.

On Wednesday evening I was still flat on my back at Mr. Meachen's quite sick. I was summoned in great haste, put into a wagon and rushed off with the troop to Bull Run, at a place called Stone Bridge Ford, the enemy being on the advance from towards Fairfax Courthouse in overwhelming numbers. The whole of Cocke's brigade took the same position, and we were tolerably well established by night but I had to sleep on the ground, which was not good for a sick man. I was sent by the surgeon, the next day, to this place in an ambulance, for I could not sit on my horse. This is a quiet hotel where are boarding some nice people; amongst them was Mrs. Hyde and her pretty, attractive niece, Constance Cary who had come out of Alexandria when the yankees occupied it.

When the troops fell back it was done by preconcerted plan, and done without firing a gun. The enemy advanced, they thought, to certain victory but they were vastly mistaken. You must know that parallel to the Manassas Gap Railroad runs a stream towards the Potomac called Bull Run, along which our army was placed in three positions. The center was at Mitchell's Ford which is the ford where the road to Manassas from Centreville crosses the run; the right wing was down at a ford near where the railroad crosses the same run, and the left wing was under the command of Colonel Cocke, near the stone bridge, which is the bridge over which the pike from Warrington to Washington passes. General Beauregard commands the center in person—who commands the right wing I do not know. From Manassas to Mitchell's Ford is three miles, from Centreville to the ford is four miles. The Federal headquarters are at Centreville. It is about four miles from Manassas to our right wing. I think they call it Blackburn's Ford. From Manassas to the stone bridge is six miles. Most of our troops are on the right and on the center. I have no idea of how many we have. I only know of Cocke's brigade on the left, with which my command is operating under his orders.

About nine o'clock yesterday morning the enemy commenced an attack on Mitchell's Ford and repeated it several times. Our position there is a strong one. All of our men behaved nobly. The Virginians stood with the coolness of veterans, yet fought with the fury of tigers in the charge. Garland's Eleventh regiment of infantry, with our Lynchburg boys, was the first to make a charge. Our loss, however, was very small. I learn that no member of the Home Guard was killed, wounded or missing. Major Carter Harrison, your cousin and mine, I hear was killed. You can imagine my suspense while lying helpless in Manassas and hearing the battle raging within three miles.

The thunder of guns woke me up from a troubled sleep and at first I thought it was a morning thunder shower but as I became more awake, and heard the people in the house calling to each other I realized what had happened; the battle was commencing. I tried to spring out of bed but my first movements showed me I was still in no condition to join my company so all I could do was lay back, trying from the dim sounds to visualize what was going on at the front. Below me in the road I could hear the mustering of forage details that were in the rear, the jangle and rattle of an artillery company going up at a gallop, ammunition wagons creaking as the driver prodded their horses to greater effort. Now and then the hooves of a courier went past while news and rumors were relayed up from the front of the house to the upper floors by excited shouts. I strained my ears to every word. In the next room I could hear a woman praying, between sobs, for her husband. When John Scott came up I scanned his face, it was as stolid and unmoved by the battle as by any routine maneuver. "What is happening, how is the battle going?" I asked anxiously. "Them yankees ain't doin' nuthin," he answered unmoved by the excitement. "Them yankees are just marchin' up and bein' shot to Hell." John Scott was too much of an old warrior not to be able to sort out the facts from the many rumors that were flying about and I felt easier, especially when I discovered the fighting was going on well away from our position in the lines. As the excitement outside and in the house calmed down, the sound of the fighting remained unchanged and soothed by John Scott's unemotional reports I was able to relax and sleep.

Fortunately Cocke's brigade was not engaged yesterday and there is no fighting anywhere on the line today. I expect to join them before my company is engaged.

Evening, July 19th.

Nothing of interest transpired all day. John Scott has come up with my horses, so I can get off as soon as I can sit in my saddle. I shall not try until I am sure the battle is about to begin in earnest, which is thought not to be for several days. We hear that General Patterson and his army of Federals has recrossed the Potomac at Harpers' Ferry and that General Johnston's army is coming down to join us. Many of his troops arrived today and about two thousand passed here today on the railroad from the South, so that by Monday Beauregard may have been reinforced by at least twenty thousand men, well armed and drilled. The spirit at Manassas seems to be that a victory will be won at all hazards. The greatest battle ever fought on the continent will be fought on this line in less than a week, and I must be well enough to be in it. The whole nation awaits the result with breathless anxiety.

The house is filled with ladies whose husbands, brothers and sons will be in the fight and their anxiety to hear from them is painful beyond description. There has been no fighting today. It is rumored that the enemy sent in a white flag for permission to bury their dead. I can hear nothing from Eugene and do not know where he is. I think he was in the fight yesterday.

July 20th.

This day I spent lying down and taking remedies. By night I was so much better I determined to go back to duty. So, with some pain, I mounted my horse and rode back to my company reaching them about nine o'clock much worn down by my ride. The men welcomed me gladly. They had seen no yankees and very little expected the storm that was to break over our heads so soon. A bed of leaves was made for me and I laid down to rest. My own opinion was that a great battle was going to be fought the next day. The thoughts of a thinking man the day before a battle are necessarily solemn, he may be buoyant and hopeful, yet there is a dread uncertainty that comes over his thoughts both as to himself and those dependent on him which makes him grave and almost sad. I was tired and despite the thoughts of the next day's work I soon dropped off to sleep and never moved until roused by my servant, John Scott, early Sunday morning. He told me to get up, something was going on, he did not know what but I'd better get up and make ready. I soon discovered what was about to happen. All the troops around me were up and cooking their breakfast, though it was scarcely light, and every one seemed to think an attack was about to be made upon our lines, but no one knew where. We supposed it would be made down towards the center where it was made on the 18th.

The bivouac of our squadron was on the extreme left near the Henry house as it was called. Mrs. Henry, who lived in it, and was so very old and infirm she refused to move out of it. She was said to have been a Miss Carter, and to have been one of the family who once owned the Sudley farm nearby. Mrs. Henry's house during the day became a strategic point of great importance and was much torn up by shot and shell, by one of which she was killed. In her yard General Bee was killed and near it Colonel Bartow. Near it also it was that General Jackson formed his heroic brigade and received the baptism of fire during which he received the immortal name of "Stonewall." A few days after the battle I got a piece of cedar post from the ruins of the house, and cut some crosses and other things which I sent home as mementoes, and which I still have.

We were thrown into line about sunrise on the brow of a hill which overlooked Bull Run, with quite a wide valley (two hundred yards at least), below us. On the other side the bluff rose quite steeply, but on the top of it there was an open field. We were placed in that position to support a battery of artillery, whose I did not find out for it was moved very soon after the battle began to rage on our extreme left above the stone bridge.

I was still weak and John Scott brought me out to the line of battle another cup of coffee. He also brought some oats for my horse, which had not finished eating when I mounted him. He got an ammunition box to put the oats in and the horse was eating while I drank the coffee. We could distinctly hear the rumble of the yankee artillery on the pike beyond the run, and there was no doubt they were moving in force towards the stone bridge and the Sudley farm and proposed to turn our left wing and sweep down on our side the run and our line. While we stood thus listening to the rumbling artillery and watching the dust as it arose from many hostile feet, we noticed a Federal battery of four guns suddenly dash out of the woods and throw itself into battery in the open space on the other side of the run above the bluff. We were much interested in the beauty of the movement, all of which we could see plainly, as it was not more than five hundred yards distant, but in a moment they opened upon our lines. The first shells went high above us, but the second were better aimed, and one of them struck the box out of which my horse was eating and shattered it to fragments, and then went on amongst the infantry behind us. John Scott did not move, or show any signs of fear. Having fired those two rounds they limbered up and left us as quickly as they came, and before our battery had done them any injury. When I noticed the first fire in some way I never dreamed the creatures were firing at us, so I went on drinking my coffee, but I was very rudely awakened from the dream by the second round when my indifference was changed to indignation, that they should actually have the impudence to fire at us on our own ground, and when we were doing them no harm.

After this there was a lull for a half hour while we remained in line of battle, but with no enemy in sight, then we heard the sound of cannon and musketry on our left, towards the stone bridge. We were moved up nearer the fighting, two other companies having joined us, and the whole thing being under the command of Lieut.-Col. Thomas T. Munford, of our regiment. The sounds indicated that the battle was growing fast and furious on our left, and that our lines were slowly being driven back, at which we were not surprised, as we knew we had but a small force on our left, and it was then obvious that the enemy was hurling upon it their whole force. We waited orders with great impatience and anxiety, for we saw our people were giving way and we could not see why we could not be of use. The battery we were supporting had been moved and there were no other troops very near us. I think Colonel Cocke forgot us, at all events we remained in the same position until near three o'clock in the evening.

About nine o'clock Generals Beauregard and Johnston, with their respective staffs, dashed by us, about fifty persons, handsomely dressed and mounted, and making a very grand show, and one which appealed to our enthusiasm very much, though all of us thought that one of the two generals should have been up with Colonel Cocke much earlier. Doubtless, however, they had good cause for the delay. Immediately behind them, at a sweeping gallop, came the "Washington Artillery," a battalion of sixteen guns. This was the most inspiring sight I ever saw, and fills me with emotion whenever I think of it now. One not familiar with artillery can little imagine how grand a sight it was. Each gun had four horses, with outriders and officers on horseback and several men mounted on the gun; then the caisson of each gun with its four horses and the like equipment of men, making thirty-two in all. Their ammunition wagons, forges and ambulances, all at full speed, making a procession, which under the circumstances, was very inspiring. Following the battalion next came "Hampton's Legion" of infantry under Col. Wade Hampton. Then a long and continuous line of infantry came pouring by as our troops were moved from the center and right wing to meet the attack on the left.

It is very easy, of course to criticise the conduct of the battle, and it is very unfair, as the critic does not know the inside causes, but while we stood there in nervous anxiety we all concluded our generals had been out-generaled, and the enemy had gained a great point upon them in transferring so many troops without their knowledge to the left, and forcing that wing back as they did. Our troops were put to a great disadvantage when run directly into a fight after moving at almost double-quick from six to ten miles on a hot July day, yet many of them were put to the test. We wondered also why, after it was discovered how the attack was made and that the enemy had stretched out his column from Centreville parallel to our front in the march towards Sudley, an attack was not made on his column, or upon the rear of the column, cutting him off from his base. Instead large forces, even after sending troops to the left, were idle all day at Mitchell's and Blackburn's Fords. No use was made of the cavalry until late in the day and then it was scattered about in small detachments, each acting under different orders, its attack was of little avail except to increase the panic of the enemy inducing a greater loss to them of the material of war. If when the enemy commenced to break, a column of cavalry had crossed Bull Run half way between Manassas and the stone bridge, and opened fire upon them as they moved back on the Warrenton Pike the victory would have been far more disastrous to the enemy and our gain in material so much the greater.

As these troops were passing towards the enemy another dismal line was moving back in the opposite direction. I shall never forget them. They were the wounded, some walking, some on stretchers, some in ambulances, all seeking the field hospital, which was near us in the woods, and all giving proof of their persons as well as their tongues of the terrible carnage on the left, and many giving discouraging tidings that our line was slowly giving way. Troops, certainly none but veterans, should never, if possible, be taken into action so as to see a field hospital or to meet the wounded or demoralized men. It has a bad effect and renders them unsteady.

The news given by the wounded men made us very impatient. We felt there was certainly something for us to do but no orders came. About eleven o'clock we were moved again further to the left, but though within range of artillery we had no actual fighting. The enemy continued to advance and at last, about mid-morning we saw signs of demoralization on the part of some of our troops; but about that time we saw a long column of troops in the same direction moving towards us, which, at first, we thought was the enemy, but to our infinite relief we found was General Jackson's brigade which had just been put off a train of cars on the Manassas road. They doubled quick into action and met the enemy's line and were soon heavily engaged. I was not near enough to mark the fighting, or rather my view was too much obstructed to get a view, but we could tell by the constant roar of cannon and musketry that the contest was severe. It was soon after this that Jackson won his "Stonewall," as I have stated before. I got permission to ride a little distance from our command to get a closer view, and while out in an open field viewing the contest the best I could a bright-eyed boy of some sixteen years of age came up to me with a wounded hand and arm and spoke to me by name. I did not remember ever having seen him before, but he said he remembered me when I was a student at the University of Virginia and that his name was Everett B. Early, of Charlottesville. He had run away from home and gone into the fight and been wounded. He had dressed his wound and was on his way back to take a hand again. He gave me a very intelligent account of the battle.

I was kept in a state of great excitement all day and found it hard to set on my horse from weakness induced by my recent sickness. We had nothing to eat. About four it became obvious that the advance of the enemy had been stopped. Then there was a sudden pause in the firing on their side, and then we could hear cheers and shouts on our lines. We were told by a wounded man that Sherman's and Ricketts' battery had been captured and that the enemy were slowly retiring. Still we were kept waiting though the sound of firing showed us the enemy was now in full retreat and the time for the cavalry had come. About five o'clock an officer came up and told Col. Munford the enemy were in full retreat across Bull Run, and ordered him to cross the stream and make for the pike to cut them off if possible and that Col. Radford with the rest of the regiment had already gone. Both parts of the regiment crossed about the same time, and we dashed up the hill, but the order had come too late for much good to be done. We were received by a scattering fire from the routed column, but they had generally thrown away their arms, and those who had not done so did so as soon as they saw us. It was a terrible rout and the face of the earth was covered with blankets, haversacks, overcoats, and every species of arms. We joined Col. Radford and the other six companies of the regiment as we reached the pike and followed the fleeing yankees, capturing many prisoners, until we came to a block in the road made by a great number of abandoned wagons, cannon and caissons, ambulances and other material at a bridge over a creek about two miles of Centreville. Further advance was checked, or at all events we went no further. From the other side of the creek and on top of the hill the enemy had been able to halt a battery long enough to fire one or two shots at our column, one of which killed Captain Winston Radford, of Bedford, a most excellent man and citizen and the brother of our Colonel. Beyond this our loss was very small and my company had only one or two wounded slightly.

Just as we crossed Bull Run I saw Edmund Fontaine, of Hanover, resting on a log by the roadside. I asked him what was the matter, and he said he was wounded and dying. He said it very cheerfully and did not look as if anything was the matter. As we came back we found him dead and some of his comrades about to remove the body. It was a great shock to me, as I had known him from boyhood, and though he was younger than I was we had met during many visits to Hanover when I was younger. We went into bivouac a little after dark, for it had become cloudy and was very dark.

It was a day long to be remembered, and such a Sunday as men seldom spend. To all but a scattered few it was our first battle, and its sights and wonders were things of which we had read but scarcely believed or understood until seen and experienced. The rout of the enemy was complete but our generals showed much want of skill in not making the material advantages greater. The Federal army was equipped with every species of munition and property, while ours was wanting in everything. They were stricken with a panic; wherever the panic was increased by the sight of an armed rebel it discovered itself by the natural impulse to throw away arms and accoutrements and to abandon everything in the shape of cannon, caissons, wagons, ambulances and provisions that might impede their flight, yet they managed, despite their flight, to carry off much. They only lost some thirty-odd cannon for example, while with proper management on our part they would not have reached the Potomac with two whole batteries and so with other properties.

Had there been even a slight demonstration on Centreville that evening the panic would have been so increased that we would have made more captures in cannon, small arms and wagons.

During the evening* as I was riding over part of the field where there were many dead yankees lying who had been killed, I thought by some of Stuart's regiment, I noticed an old doll-baby with only one leg lying by the side of a Federal soldier just as it dropped from his pocket when he fell writhing in the agony of death. It was obviously a memento of some little loved one at home which he had brought so far with him and had worn close to his heart on this day of danger and death. It was strange to see that emblem of childhood, that token of a father's love lying there amidst the dead and dying where the storm of war had so fiercely raged and where death had stalked in the might of its terrible majesty. I dismounted, picked it up and stuffed it back into the poor fellow's cold bosom that it might rest with him in the bloody grave which was to be forever unknown to those who loved and mourned him in his distant home.

The actual loss of the enemy I do not know but their dead extended for miles and their wounded filled every house and shed in the neighborhood. The wounded doubtless suffered much. Their own surgeons abandoned their field hospitals and joined the fleeing cohorts of the living, and our surgeons had all they could do to look after their own wounded, who of

* "Evening" in the South of that time, and still in many parts, means afternoon. C.M.B. III

course were the first served. They received kind treatment however, and as soon as our surgeons were free they rendered all the aid in their power.

The enemy had permitted no doubt of the result to cross their minds, and had not kept it a secret in Washington that the final attack was to be made on Sunday. The day was therefore made a gala day by the people of all classes, and they came in great numbers in every possible conveyance to enjoy the rebel rout and possible share in the rebel spoils. Members of Congress and cabinet ministers, department clerks and idle citizens followed the advancing column in all the confidence of exhorting confidence, and there were not wanting many a hack-load of the *demi-monde* with their admirers to complete the motley crew. Along the road and amidst abandoned cannon and wagons we found many a forsaken carriage and hack with half-eaten lunches and half-used baskets of champagne, and we received most laughable accounts from the citizens on the roadside of the scenes they saw and the sharp contrast between the proud and confident advance and the wild panic of the flight. The men of our company got many a spoil not known to the ordnance department or used by those who filled the ranks.

We bivouacked in the field and without tent or any shelter but the oilcloths, a vast supply of which we had laid in from those upon which our foes had slept the night before. They were of the very best material and we gladly abandoned ours or kept them to throw over our saddles in the rain. A battle is not a sanitarium for the sick or the cold ground a good bed for a feverish and chilly man. I was so worn and weary that I had no doubt whatever that when I awoke in the morning I would be very ill. Before I laid down I fortunately found an opportunity to send a telegram to my wife and owing to a fortunate accident it got off the next morning and relieved the minds of my people at home and the friends of all my men.

Despite my gloomy anticipations as to the effect on my health I slept like a top and awoke the next morning after daylight feeling very much better. I was aroused by a hard rain falling on my face. I got up at once and crawled into my wagon, which fortunately had come up during the night, and then I had my breakfast owing to John Scott's thoughtfulness. I had heard nothing about my brothers, Capt. Eugene Blackford of the Fourth Alabamas and Lieut. W. W. Blackford, of Stuart's regiment of Cavalry. Both, I knew, had been engaged but I could not hear anything of them. Of course I was anxious.

About eight o'clock a staff officer from somewhere rode up and delivered an order calling for details to gather up arms and spoils from the field and to carry prisoners to the rear. I was sent with twenty men to report to Colonel Evans on the latter duty. When I reported I found also a small detail of infantry and the Colonel put me in charge of the whole detachment and turned over to me several hundred prisoners, who looked very uncomfortable in the rain, with orders to take them to Manassas, six miles to the rear. Before we started Colonel Evans took me into a house in the yard of which he had his headquarters and introduced me to Colonel O. B. Willcox and Captain Ricketts of the Federal army, both of whom were wounded and prisoners. Willcox and Evans seemed very good friends and called each other Orlando and Shanks respectively—"Shanks" being Evans' nickname at West Point. Willcox was very courteous but Ricketts was surly and bitter and complained of his accommodations, which were very much better than those of his captor in the yard or than those of the vast proportion of our wounded men and officers. He had a comfortable room and bed and two surgeons to attend his wounds. One would suppose he expected the rebels to have a first-class hotel on the battlefield ready to receive him and that they had violated all the rules of civilized warfare in failing to do so.

We carried the two officers, placed under my care, in an ambulance, and made them as comfortable as possible. We made rapid progress and I soon delivered my charge to some officer at General Beauregard's headquarters. I had some pleasant chats with Colonel Willcox.

The sights of this day were terrible and more heartrending than those of the day before. Our preparations for the battle, so far as the care of the wounded was concerned, were very imperfect and we were called on to provide for those of both sides. The result was that many of both sides suffered much, but no difference was shown them save in the matter of priority of service. The surgeons were busy all day but still many wounds remained undressed for full twenty-four hours. Luckily it was not very hot and the rain was a comfort.

From Lynchburg Mrs. Blackford wrote:

The sound of the cannon were distinctly heard on the hills of Lynchburg, and we well knew that a great battle was being fought from early morn until sunset, and that not only the fate of our country and our homes was at stake, but that each boom which stirred the air might be fraught with the dying sigh of those we loved best. Mrs. Robert C. Saunders, whose husband was in the battle, stood all day on one of the hills near her home in Campbell and listened in agony to every gun. Other ladies whom I knew did the same thing near Pedlar Mills in Amherst County. Mrs. Saunders was all of one hundred and seventy miles from the battlefield. A large number of people came into town Sunday evening from the surrounding country to hear the news of the result, and many stayed long enough to hear sad tidings the next day of those for whom their hearts beat with such nervous strain; amongst the latter was Mrs. Winston Radford, of Bedford, whose husband was killed by a shell from a battery of the enemy commanded by a Captain Arnald.

The next day the rain poured in torrents. Mrs. Robert C. Saunders came up from her home to Father Blackford's to hear tidings of her husband. We could hear nothing Sunday night except that a great battle had been fought. I remained at Father's with Betty Colston and the children waiting and trembling, at one time on my knees praying for my husband's safety and at another trying to prepare myself for the worse news should it come.

This Monday morning was a time of terrible strain on us all. Father and Mother Blackford were very nervous, and he could not go down to his business, but walked about trying to take comfort from every circumstance mentioned. He had prayers in which we all joined. He and Mother had three sons in the battle, and Mrs. Saunders and myself our respective husbands. Old Dr. Thomas Blackford came up and sat with us. He, too, had one or more sons in the fight and was very nervous. My dear little children seemed to understand the trouble which cast its dark shadow over us all and little Nannie clung to me and whispered words of hope in my ear. Father at last went down town to hear what could be heard, while we waited with growing impatience and terror for his return.

At last we heard his footsteps on the front porch, and our hearts stopped beating, but the hurried way in which he opened the front door and the elasticity of his step announced the good news to my eager ear. With one bound we rushed to meet him, and sent out a shout of grateful joy when he caught his breath enough to say, with choking voice, "All safe"! We all gathered around Mother's bed where she was lying, some of us sobbing for joy, while Father offered up thanks to God for having spared our loved ones.

The telegrams which came were from my husband to me, which was the first which had come through, and one from Eugene and William which soon followed. Mr. Blackford's also told that none of his men were hurt, and my first impulse was to rush out and tell the wives and mothers of his men. It was such a happy day! I never shall forget it.

CHAPTER IV

☆ ☆ ☆ ★ ☆ ☆ ☆

ALARMS AND EXCURSIONS

☆ ☆ ☆ ☆ ☆ ☆

From Lieut. Blackford, July 28th.

WE ARE this morning back at what was formerly called "Camp Blackford." Yesterday we received orders to report at this point to Lieut.-Col. Munford, forming a battalion of four companies. I have been appointed acting adjutant of the command, which relieves me of some company details and gives me somewhat more liberty.

Mrs. Langhorne arrived here last night but brought no tidings of you. I fear you are sick again. We are now attached to Longstreet's brigade, Constituted of the Eleventh Virginia, Col. Garland, Seventeenth Virginia, Col. Corse, and First Virginia, Col. Moore, besides a battery of artillery.

July 30th.

I cannot get a furlough, so I have concluded you may come down as soon as I can get board for you, and I think I can get it for you either at Mr. Meachen's or his overseer's, for I know you would rather live in a tent on army rations than not come. Get me a pair of grey pantaloons and bring them down with you. I want enough Confederate grey cloth to make me a dress uniform. Send it to Page to be made according to Confederate State regulations for a first lieutenant of cavalry.

One of the most remarkable incidents of the day of the great battle, to use an Irishism, occurred that night. I tell the tale as it is told but do not vouch for it, though I believe it. After the battle the Federal Army, or rather so much of it as maintained an organization, finding no one following, bivouacked between Centreville and Fairfax Courthouse as a rear guard. A party of Federal officers, firm friends of Colonel

Evans, who seems to have been a great pal with all West Point officers, took a basket of champagne, and under a flag of truce, came to Colonel Evans' headquarters, which were in our front, and had quite a frolic with him. One of them asked if he had seen the White Horse troop which he had commanded a few months before. He said yes, and had directed a battery to fire on them but had shut his eyes so as not to see the effect of the shot. His command was the first engaged in the morning and he fought all day opposed to Colonel Orlando B. Willcox, his most intimate friend in times gone by.

Mrs. Blackford takes up the narrative.

On the first of August I went down, taking Nannie with me. Mr. Blackford met us at Manassas with his wagon, and we went to Mr. Meachen's, which was a beautiful old place, within a quarter-mile of Mr. Blackford's camp. The family sent me an invitation to spend a fortnight with them, and they made my time very pleasant, and I was never more comfortable. They had two sons, Mr. James Meachen and Mr. Arthur Meachen.

The troops were doing nothing, so Mr. Blackford could stay with me a large part of the time. We sat out under the great trees in the yard with Nannie playing around us. Generally some six or eight soldiers were with us, men and officers from our camp and the Eleventh regiment. While I was there Nannie fell from a saddle on a pole in the yard and broke her collarbone. Nannie, of course, was a great favorite, and much petted by the men, both in our yard and in camp. When she was tired she would climb into her father's arms and soon be asleep, much to his delight.

The camp was in full sight. Mr. Blackford had to go to drill, of course, every morning and evening and we always went over to see the dress parade. . . . It was very interesting as there were several hundred cavalry and nearly a thousand infantry. The soldiers got up minstrel shows and private theatricals for our benefit, and we had one or two dinner parties at camp. Major Daniel Warwick was down there with his nephew, Abram, and he gave us a dinner which we thought could not be surpassed. We had the dinner under the trees in the camp. Some ten or twelve persons sat down, three or four ladies besides myself. The dish which was the central figure was a great iron pot full of Brunswick stew which certainly was very good. After dinner we had some music and clog dancing, and it was all so agreeable we accepted an invitation to stay to supper and get some more stew. Just as the supper table was spread the servants moved over towards the pot containing the stew to bring it over to warm at the fire. It was covered up, and they put the hooks into the places made for them and started off with it. Then, to our horror, out jumped a half-grown pig, whose proportions showed how long it had been regaling itself on our anticipated supper. We had a very good supper but omitted the stew.

On the 11th of August orders came to break up camp and move to Fairfax Courthouse so I had to come back home, much to my distress. Mr. Blackford wrote me that after returning from putting us on the cars at Manassas he went by the old camp and looked for Nannie's footprints but the heavy cannon had crushed them all out.

By Father Blackford's diary I note that he mentions the death of Samuel Garland's little boy. It is said he died of a broken heart, as he had never smiled after his mother died, only our host of the gay parties of such a short while before remained, only Mister, now General Garland remained and he was to follow soon, to rejoin his loving family perhaps somewhere else.

About that time two things happened; Mr. Blackford became Captain Blackford and, on September 2nd, at four o'clock in the morning little Susan Colston was born. Dr. Tom Blackford wrote Captain Blackford:

" I am truly pleased at the event, as Mrs. Blackford has suffered very much since her visit to the camp, and I hope she will now be relieved. She dined and spent the day at my house yesterday in better health and spirits than I have seen her for a long time, and I was surprised when sent for at one o'clock to find her in labour. I sent Gabe down with this note in hopes he may find someone by whom to forward it."

From Capt. Blackford. Sept. 3rd, 1861.

The joyous news reached me last night. May God be praised for it. I had been out all day within sight of the enemy's lines as escort for General Beauregard. Who should I find riding with the general but my man, Charles Green. He has the impudence of a town cow and has been detailed at headquarters by the General's express orders. He rode up to me in a very patronizing style and handed me a letter. Noting that it was not in your handwriting I put it in my pocket to read in camp, and therefore have just opened it. My heart bounded with joy of course. In spirit I am by your bedside.

I know you will expect me home this evening but it is impossible. When the paymaster comes I may get a detail to go home a few days to improve the equipment of my company, but if I cannot get that I cannot get off. Having just taken command of my company renders it advisable I should not apply for leave until the Summer campaign is over.

On our scout today with General Beauregard we had a delightful, though tiresome ride. We went down to Munson's Hill and Mason's Hill, from which we had a grand view of Washington, the Capitol, Alexandria and the enemy's outposts, outworks and tents, all of which are in full view.

*Mrs. Blackford explains:**

In several letters of about this time he descants on the curse which whisky was to the army, and he is especially sharp in his criticism of its use by the general officers. He comments, too, very sharply upon the impertinence and presumption of many of the staff officers, many of whom he describes as great fools, puffed up by their little office and looking down with contemptuous pride upon the line officers. He seems especially to have felt the manner in which these little popinjays treated the private soldier. He says that on the battlefield of Manassas John T. Smith was helping a wounded general officer into an ambulance when one of his staff officers cursed

*There are some letters that are left out which would be of great interest now, but at the time the memoirs were written, would have stepped on the toes of too many then still living in Lynchburg. C.M.B. III

him. Smith put the general officer into the ambulance then rode up to the staff officer and told him if he did not apologize he would thrash him. The apology was given. As the war advanced all this ceased. Common hardship and common danger brought them close together, and where there was any merit mutual respect was engendered.

From Capt. Blackford. Sept. 16th. Falls Church.

I returned from Lynchburg to find that my company was detached from the regiment and retained by Longstreet for scout duty. We are all well and in good spirits. It would amuse you to see our mode of living; we live on what the men can get from the country around us—the debatable land between two picket lines—but we live well and eat more than any other men in the world. I cooked my own dinner today, roasting ears of corn in the shuck and frying bacon on the end of a stick. We have no tents and are within sound of the yankee drums. I have never seen men so well and happy. We sleep on our arms and are constantly on duty, but the weather is fine and sleeping on the ground and breathing fresh air is very inspiriting. As I laid down last night I was amused to think of the difference in my lodging last week and this. I laid down in full uniform, with my boots and spurs, sword and pistol with no covering but my overcoat, no pillow but my saddle and no bed but my saddle-cloth, and yet I never had a more delightful and uninterrupted night's rest.

September 19th.

We are further in advance now than any other troops. Stuart's regiment is nearly as far on another part of the line. I have my company here alone, but we are well protected by pickets and outer videttes from surprise. Back at the central picket I have a good time. William was here this evening and looks as handsome as I ever saw him. Stuart sleeps every night on Munson's Hill without even a blanket under or over him. He is very young, only twenty-eight but he seems a most capable soldier, never resting, always vigilant, always active. His wife is at Fairfax Courthouse and comes to see him every day.

September 21st.

We are still on the same duty and there is nothing much to write about but the exploits of Jack Alexander. He has been up to his old tricks again; utterly disregarding all rules of military life, relying on his wit and good fellowship to see him through. Up to now his reliance has not been in vain but at last has reached its limit. He was sent up to Leesburg with two companies for a short time on some special duty, and finding it a very charming place to be stationed, determined to stay there. Col. Radford ordered him to join the regiment near Fairfax Courthouse but he failed to obey the order. It was repeated several times but with the like result. At last Col. Radford reported him to Beauregard and a peremptory order was sent. Even that he did not obey but reported alone in a style which would have made you think the Prince of Wales was on a visit. He was dressed in an elegant suit of black velvet, with ruffled shirt and fancy-topped boots and in a handsome carriage drawn by two handsome black stallions. His arrival created some amusement among his friends, but had no effect on headquarters where General Beauregard declined to see him but sent him word that if he did not report with his company to his regiment within forty-eight hours he would be under arrest.

While I write I hear a very brisk cannonading about five or six miles to our right. I cannot imagine what it is. I never hear such firing without being glad you are not here. Mrs. Stuart now is in a house very near us, and she is always in tears when she hears firing, knowing that, if possible, her husband is in the midst of it. Kiss all the children for me including Betty Colston.

September 26th.

We found out what the firing was about the other day. Two yankee columns approached Falls Church from opposite directions, each thinking the place occupied by the rebels, opened fire, and with considerable loss both retreated leaving the place deserted for several days.

I left camp yesterday before I could get dinner, and con-

sequently at night I had to forage for my supper. I rode up to
a house, where I found an old woman about eighty years of
age, a young woman and two children, one of them not more
than four months old. Their story was pitiful. They had been
driven out of Alexandria several months before. The husband
of the young woman was the son of the old one. He had been
a mechanic, but had died a week before leaving the family in
great want, and then the poor, helpless things were in the very
midst of the field on which it was expected a battle would be
fought, without friends or money. A more heart-rending sight
I never saw. They prepared a plain supper for me but I felt
so much for them my appetite was gone. The old lady sat at
the head of the table, feeding the helpless babe, who could
not understand what the roll of heavy cannon that were just
then passing meant or the embattled hosts so near, but smiled
as unconsciously as if rocking in some cradle where war has
never been known, and as our little Betty will do tonight.

The old lady spoke with gratitude of the mercies the Lord
had shown her, and, turning her almost sightless eyes to heaven,
seemed to place her trust hopefully on the same source of
comfort. The young woman seemed much distressed, and her
tears fell thick and fast as her little boy, about Nannie's age,
told of his father's illness and death. It was a sad meal. I could
do little for them but I did all in my power.

September 30th.

Saturday night, about three o'clock I was startled by the
intelligence that James Chalmers had been shot and badly
wounded upon the outside line of pickets. You may imagine
the news sent a pang to my heart. He had been shot while
riding between pickets near Annandale; he was fired at, without being halted, by two guns but in whose hands we have not
been able to find out—whether those of the enemy or our own
people. Be what it may he was shot in the discharge of his duty
on a dangerous service. The ball crushed both bones of his
arm then entered his stomach. After he was shot he rode two
miles before dismounting at Annandale. Thence he was
brought here in an ambulance, being first moved to a tavern

about four miles off and then to this place where he is comfortably quartered in Mr. Thomas' law office. His arm was amputated on Sunday. He bore the operation as he has borne all his suffering, with manly fortitude, never complaining and expressing gratitude for the slightest attention.

October 2nd.

Your two long, sweet letters of Saturday and Monday reached me this morning enclosing Nannie's sweet letter dictated by my child and written by her mother, my wife; it is a precious memento! I am at loss at to what to advise you to do about breaking up housekeeping. I think you ought not to go to Albemarle under the circumstances mentioned by Mr. Noland, and I am clearly opposed to your boarding in Charlottesville. You have no friends there half as kind as those in Lynchburg or as father's family, and you will be unable to attend to my business, which gives you so much pleasure, and besides a Captain's wife should stay where her husband's and her own fate have been cast, and where she has duties no one else can perform for her. As to your breaking up and boarding in Lynchburg elsewhere I am not prepared to advise you, and we must be governed by developments.

Something must soon happen to change the face of affairs. All the sick have been sent to the rear and every arrangement made as if an attack was anticipated. The river has been blockaded, and that fact alone, I think, will induce some movement on the part of the enemy. The falling back from Mason's, Munson's and Upton's hills was, I think, to draw the enemy from behind their embankments, and, I doubt not, deranged McClellan's plans no little. They expected an attack and are not prepared yet for a general advance, nor am I sure they will this fall.

President Davis is now down here with the army, but he looks painfully frail in health. He keeps constantly engaged. No stone will be left unturned which military skill can suggest. Johnston, Beauregard and Smith are in consultation every day and all day. Smith now commands Johnston's army, Beauregard his own and Johnston (Joseph E.) the whole. If we are to lie quiet here all the winter you of course must come down, as the mountain cannot go to Mohamet. Two weeks may develop much. At present it is not safe for you to come. An immense number of troops are in the line and a great number of cannon. I know at least sixty of the latter, and they may be more. The whole army is concentrated around Fairfax Courthouse and we are in the sound of drums all day.

My brother Launcelot is now down with two guns of his battery near Falls Church, which is occupied by the enemy. Col. J. E. B. Stuart has been made a brigadier of cavalry, and our regiment is in his brigade. Five of my men have been wounded in the past week.

I attended by invitation, as one of General Longstreet's staff pro tempore, a grand review in honor of President Davis, when he reviewed about ten or twelve thousand troops. After it was over General Longstreet invited me to attend a levee at his headquarters where I was introduced to the President, and saw all of the big bugs of the army. You know I am not fond of such bugs, and I was bored.

October 8th.

The most violent storm of wind and rain I have ever seen in camp burst last night. My tent was blown about and the rain was driven in so that everything was wet. But I slept very well despite it. This morning Tommy Ryan—he is Major Langhorne's servant and the most perfect Irishman in every respect I have ever seen—and who hates Col. Radford, because of his disagreement with Major Langhorne, came over to our camp, and I heard him telling, in the most perfect brogue, that last night in the worst of the storm he cut the Colonel's tent ropes and let the tent fall on the Colonel creating a great stir in camp. It was very amusing, but I was in my tent and supposed not to hear it. Of course if I had known of it officially it would have been my duty to put him under arrest and send him back for punishment. I laughed until the tears ran down my cheeks.

October 9th.

William and I went down to see Eugene today, and found

him well and hearty, and wrapped to his ears in blankets to keep warm. We went with him to call on Col. Rodes, his colonel, formerly of Lynchburg. They seemed to be on the very best terms, from which I inferred Eugene had his confidence.

After our visit we returned in time to see the brigade drill, where we met the inimitable Miss Baily and a Miss Skinner of Maryland, daughter of Major Skinner of the First Virginia infantry. I proposed to them that they go to my camp for supper and they accepted. John Scott set up quite a handsome spread. I believe my tent is the nicest in the army and looked very comfortable. The girls brought their escorts, and Kean came along also. I told the ladies that you and Mrs. Kean were picturing Kean and myself in disconsolate woe in their absence and, very likely in tears at the thought.

October 11th.

I have been worried by rumors of war in the past few days, having been in that time either in the saddle or under marching orders, with cooked rations. Some attack with the Fourth brigade was planned, I know not what, but I think of Springfield. We were to have made a silent night attack, but from some cause it was given up. We were, however, aroused again about two hours before day and started on the march. For some reason we were ordered back to await further orders, and here we are still waiting, with our horses saddled and our sabres buckled on. I took the opportunity to run over into the adjoining camp to call on your two cousins, Col. Raleigh T. and Capt. William B. Colston. I found them very manly and intelligent fellows, and they have a reputation as fine soldiers.

I suppose there will be no further need for us today as I have just received an invitation to dine at headquarters! What it means I cannot tell; something remarkable is about to happen I am sure, for never before have I been invited to dine with a general, though I have stood near and seen them eat when I had had nothing all day. Just after the battle of Manassas General Cocke dined with me, but that is reversing the thing.

Evening.

I found the dinner to be a congratulatory affair given General Longstreet by his staff on account of the intelligence having been received of his promotion to a major-generalship. This promotion removes him from his brigade and gives him a division made up of several brigades. The army is now divided into four divisions under Generals Beauregard, G. W. Smith, Van Dorn and Longstreet. I asked the general whether his promotion would separate my company from the brigade. He said not if he could prevent it. He has been very kind to me and has shown me much attention. He sent me a special invitation to go with him to call on the President and to act on his staff at the grand review. I was the only officer of the brigade invited today.

October 15th.

The long roll sounded today at three o'clock in the morning preceded by five rockets sent up from General Johnston's headquarters. The whole army was on its feet in a few minutes, the allegation being that the enemy was advancing. We made ready in five minutes, dressed, armed and the horses saddled. We are awaiting orders and while I wait I drop you this line,— or add to the letter ready to go.

Just as I finished the last sentence an order came to me to report to Longstreet at once with my company. I took them up only to be sent back again—the whole thing turned out to be nothing. It is now one o'clock in the day, and we have been up since three awaiting something to happen.

Centreville, October 17th.

I am today twenty-eight years old, and, by agreement, we were to spend the day thinking about each other as much as possible, but I have been so much engaged I fear I have not carried out my part of the agreement as I should have done.

I am well, and I think this kind of life agrees with me, though I have not taken on any flesh. I weigh the same as I did when I left home—one hundred and twenty-five pounds —but all there is of me is bone and muscle, very tough and very active. I can spring into my saddle without the use of a stirrup and ride all day without fatigue. So I have every reason to be thankful.

I left Fairfax Courthouse last night about eight, after having been up all the preceding night and the whole of yesterday without anything to eat but stray bits of crackers. We reached the place about ten o'clock, when I ate a most delightful supper, I mean delightful to us, and had a charming night's sleep,—on the ground and without cover it is true,—but none the less charming and refreshing. We are now regularly camped, with tents pitched, on the road between Centreville and Union Mills. The elevated points around here are being fortified and everything indicates we shall not retreat any further. The enemy are now at Fairfax Courthouse, where we were yesterday. The view from the high points around Centreville is beautiful, and all around nothing can be seen but tents, tents, tents. The army seems to be in fine spirits and I am confident of victory if we have a fight. It is raining hard but my tent is very comfortable. I have put my tent up to a fireplace and chimney built by an Alabama company which camped here a short while ago. If a battle is to be likely about here I shall invite the Meachens to make our house their home until the turmoil is over.

October 28th.

On last Tuesday, just about dinner time, I received a message from General Longstreet stating that General Beauregard ordered me to go with my company with the reinforcements sent to General Evans at Leesburg; that the enemy had crossed the Potomac, twenty thousand strong, and had to be driven back. We hurried off in a driving rain without provisions or baggage. We went five miles before we caught up with Col. Jenkins, of the 18th South Carolina Regiment, who commanded the detachment of infantry, artillery and cavalry. We went on until twelve o'clock that night, the cold rain piercing to the bone. About twelve the command halted, and I was put in command of a detachment consisting of my company and four guns of the Washington Artillery, of New

Orleans, and sent forward with haste. The report was that the enemy was pressing Evans, and the infantry could go no further in the rain and mud without rest. Col. Jenkins personally rode on to Leesburg to report to General Evans for orders.

Just about daylight, as we came within sight of Leesburg, Col. Jenkins met me on his return and told me that Evans said the enemy was in such force that he must evacuate Leesburg and fall back, and we must fall back to Mrs. George Carter's farm and take position to give battle. This we did and were soon joined by the infantry and all of Evans' command, and then awaited the coming of the enemy. About noon General Evans sent me an order to take my company and picket the Little River turnpike from Aldie, twelve miles down towards Alexandria. I took up my headquarters in the corner of a fence about a mile from Aldie, and spread my company at intervals over the line indicated. In that condition we spent Wednesday night and a bitter cold one it was. Thursday and Thursday night it was also bitter cold. We remained in the same position until Friday when I got an order to rejoin Col. Jenkins at Bull's Mill, about five miles off, with a view of returning to this place as the enemy were all gone. So off we went again, reaching there about nine o'clock in the night. At three that night a courier from Evans came in ordering us back to Leesburg which we reached at sunrise. All this time, bear in mind, my men had no regular meals and had been living on what they could beg at various farmhouses. I lived very badly and what little I got was cooked on a stick, both bread and meat. Meat we fry by putting it on the end of a stick near the fire and bread was cooked by making the dough up in long thin rolls, twisting it around the stick then holding it near the fire until cooked.

As soon as we reached Leesburg we found the enemy had all gone back over on the other side of the river, but there was a rumor they were preparing to cross at a ferry about twelve miles up the river at "Speaks." I was at once ordered to take a small party and go up there and see about it. I took four men, making a hard ride on an empty stomach, through a most beautiful country, using my bay, which had come up from Centreville. When near the ferry, at the infantry picket post, I heard cannon fire and a bomb burst in the woods just ahead. We then dismounted and crept up the hill just over the ferry where we had a good view of the other side, the enemy firing all the time but the bombs bursting behind us. We crept up to the house at which they had been firing and then showed ourselves. Then, strange to say, they ceased firing and moved their battery off without even a salute. I had my field glasses and could see all they did with perfect ease. I found they had four guns and an encampment of about two regiments of infantry. They seemed much amused at us coming out so freely, but only looked at us through their glasses, sitting on a fence seeming to hold a consultation as to what it all meant.

We surveyed each other for about an hour, then both parties retired. We picked up pieces of the shells they had been throwing at the house. In the house we found an old negro man who said he went to bed as soon as they opened fire on the house. He entreated us to go away or they would fire again. I saw nothing to make me think they contemplated crossing so I returned to our bivouac, getting a fine supper in Leesburg and then went to bed on the ground in the rain and slept without moving all night.

The next morning, Sunday, the sun rose on a cloudless sky, it having cleared up during the night. I enjoyed the day much, going to church at Walter Williams' Church in the morning. I rode about with Col. Jenkins in the evening. We struck up a great friendship.

We went to the battlefield of Ball's Bluff, where the battle was fought on Tuesday, October 21st. A word about the battle:

The enemy crossed within two miles of Leesburg at least two thousand strong with three pieces of artillery, and had taken their position before General Evans, who was in Leesburg, was aware of the fact, though it must have taken many hours to make the move.

When they were discovered they were attacked at once and

were most terribly whipped though they fought like tigers. The whole battleground was not more than the size of two squares of a town. The troops engaged were the Eighth Virginia, Col. Eppa Hunton, and the Seventeenth and Eighteenth Mississippi regiments under Cols. Burt and Featherstone—the 13th Mississippi under Col. Barksdale was held in reserve. We had no artillery and only a handful of cavalry who fought on foot.

The gallantry of the troops engaged, and of Hunton, Burt and Featherstone is beyond all praise. Burt was killed. General Baker, of the Federal Army was killed. He was a Senator from Oregon and a man of great ability. Nothing will give a better idea of the sharpness of the engagement than an inspection of the battleground. I saw one thornbush, about five feet high, in which I counted forty-eight balls fired by the Federals, and a small tree in which I counted twenty-six. The enemy had only one battery of four guns, which they lost. All their artillery horses seemed to have been killed. The enemy were driven back into the river. For some reason our troops were ordered back, and the enemy then, during the night, came over with four thousand men and remained in possession for a day or two, then went back.

This (Monday) morning all reinforcements under Col. Jenkins left Leesburg at daybreak, and I am now back in my camp near Centreville.

October 30th.

We had a great display this evening. All the Virginia regiments in striking distance of this place were collected around one of the forts and the State flags were presented to them by Governor Letcher. I suppose we had some ten thousand troops massed and all the generals, colonels and staff officers, making quite an imposing show. The flags are very handsome and all alike, so every Virginia regiment fights under the same flag. Another flag is being prepared for the fighting colors. It is about square, of red ground with a blue cross from corner to corner with stars upon the cross. It is much more beautiful than is the regular flag of the country. The present stars and bars are constantly being taken for the U. S. stars and stripes.

October 31st.

I went this morning to see Eugene and to my sorrow found him sick in bed with what is called camp fever. He is much distressed, because he fears a battle may come on while he is disabled. I think there will be a general engagement during the week, commencing on our right. If it is delayed ten days there will be none until Spring.

Governor Letcher had a grand review of the Virginia troops today, and a grand sight it was. All passed before him in a long column with banners and music. The Governor was surrounded by Generals Johnston, Beauregard, Van Dorn, Longstreet, Jackson, Kirby Smith, G. W. Smith, Stuart, Tombs, Jones, Cocke, Clark and any number of colonels and lesser lights. We have so little of the pomp and circumstance of war that the troops enjoyed it very much.

November 3rd.

I took supper last night with Garland and Kean at the Eleventh regiment. At their tent I met General Kirby Smith, with whom I was much pleased. I like him better than any general in the army I have yet met. He claims all Lynchburgers as his friends and is very popular with us all. You know I always liked his wife and was much inclined to admire him from what I had seen and heard. He does not seem all puffed up by his promotion and his unassuming manner charmed me no little.

From Capt. Blackford's father's diary.
November 7, 1861, Thursday.

I left home on Tuesday morning on the cars for Manassas. Rather a rough set in the cars. We received at Charlottesville a large accession of the same sort—soldiers sent back from the hospitals to camp, scarcely one of whom looked as if he had been an invalid. Various delays occurred and it was not until after dark that we reached Manassas.

I had written Charles to send a horse for me, that I might

go to Union Mills or to his camp, as might be deemed advisable. Knowing the lack of accommodations at Manassas I looked forward with dismay to spending a night there. I was greatly relieved, therefore, by discovering Charles among the crowd, dark as it was. He told me he had made arrangements about Eugene's leave of absence. He sent the order to Eugene by Launcelot, and Eugene was to be brought here that evening in an ambulance, and was perhaps already here. He took me to a tent which he always keeps here with the heavy baggage of his troop, guarded by Sam Sumpter. Charles could not stay long, and of course my plan of visiting his camp was knocked in the head. I awaited impatiently the arrival of Eugene, and just had given him up when the ambulance drove up with him and Lieut. Macon. They had been an hour trying to find the tent.

Eugene was very much exhausted by the drive, but after getting warm by the fire, he seemed refreshed and better. He and I accepted a bunk with Sumpter, three feet wide and only one blanket and a plank between us and the ground. We had an abundance of covering and the tent was comfortable, so in spite of the rain and rough lodging I slept well.

Wednesday morning we got Eugene settled comfortably in the cars, which were much crowded with soldiers going to hospitals, some of whom looked as if they had but little longer in this world. Eugene suffered a good deal during the day, but we reached home safely about six o'clock p.m.

A letter from Capt. Blackford.
November 7th.

General Longstreet ordered the company on some duty a few days since and when the men fell in line I discovered the absence of some six or eight of the best men. I found they had gone hunting without leave, and the sudden call disclosed their absence, which they thought I would never discover. When they returned I put them all on double duty, much to the amusement of the rest of the men. I try and never lose my temper, and hence keep a good control. After I passed sentence one of the hunters sent me a part of the game for supper. William, Kean and Lawrence Meem took supper with me.

I have a plan to visit the battlefield of Manassas tomorrow with Stratton and his father who is here on a visit. I am very ignorant of the positions except those which came under my eye at the time of the fight. I expect to enjoy the trip very much.

General Longstreet sent to me just now to borrow a gun to go hunting, so I presume, no battle is expected for that day at least. Van Otey has gotten hold of a bird-net which we proposed putting to use in a few days, and we intend inviting General Longstreet to go with us. A serenade is going on now at Headquarters by the First Virginia Regiment band.

November 8th.

I was much less interested in the battlefield than I anticipated. Some of its horrors are still fresh. The earth having been washed off, many of the bodies were exposed entirely to view. Strange to say, they seemed to have just dried up without decay. It was the same way with the horses, none of which have either decayed or been devoured by buzzards, but have dried within their skins leaving the bones inside. I send by Mr. Stratton three canes cut from the yard of the Henry house, where the battle was so fierce. The largest one is for Mr. McDaniel. The next size is for Father; it was nearly cut from the tree by a ball, as can be seen now by inspecting the top.

William has made more reputation in the past few days by taking six yankee prisoners. He had only one man with him and went to a house, not knowing any yankees were there. One of them aimed his rifle at him and was about to shoot when William beckoned as if someone was behind the house and the fellow, supposing assistance near at hand, surrendered with his whole squad, presenting William with an elegant fieldglass and pistol.

I tell this as it was told to me at General Stuart's headquarters. I have not seen William since it happened. The affair occurred near Falls Church. He has made much reputation as a soldier, took some eighty prisoners with only ten men near Manassas. He is a dashing officer and stands very high.

The Rockbridge Artillery, with Launcelot in it, has disappeared mysteriously night before last. Where it has gone I have not been able to find out, but Winchester is whispered its destination. It is curious that such movements can be made so quietly and secretly. The Commanding Officer gets an order to be ready to march at some hour, and when the time arrives, told to take such a road and move until told to stop. Thus no one knows its destination and cannot give information in regard to it.

While at breakfast in front of the tent this morning I saw Dennis Sullivan strike a man named John C. Lewis with a great club. Lewis fell like he was dead and Dennis, who was drunk, stood waving his club and daring anyone to arrest him. This was a case for the captain only. I knew he would not strike me and I walked up to him and told him to go to the guardhouse. He hesitated as if doubtful whether he would obey, when I seized him by the throat and gave his cravat a slight twist. To my horror he dropped over apparently dead and there the two men lay, both I thought dead, for I concluded my twist of his cravat had brought on an attack of apoplexy. The men gathered around at once and threw a bucket of water on each. To my joy they both revived. I sent Dennis to the guardtent and put him on bread and water for ten days. I at once instituted a search for whiskey and found that Percival had brought down a keg of it and was retailing it in his tent. I confiscated it and sent it to the nearest hospital and sent Percival to the guardhouse for a few days also, but on regular rations.

Leesburg, November 16th.

We got our marching orders yesterday and have reported here to Col. Jenifer. We are now comfortably camped about a mile from the town in an encampment with four other companies, over which Col. Jenifer has command. Everything here is very quiet. The pickets on the other side of the river are very friendly with our men, exchanging visits, papers and other courtesies. Some of our men went over a mile into Maryland and took dinner with some officers in the yankee camp. A very dangerous and improper thing to do, I think. Tell Father that among the United States officers who have been over here visiting us was John Garland, the son of Dr. John Garland, the dentist of Fredricksburg. He will remember him. He is a returned Californian, who once went to school with me in Fredricksburg. I suppose it is better this way than for the pickets to be firing constantly at each other.

Sunday evening.

Just here I was interrupted by a call from Lieut. Frank Carr, of the Albemarle Troop of our regiment, and afterwards I went to town with him to take tea at Walter Williams, the minister. I spent a delightful evening.

You must not be depressed by the Mason and Slidell affair. It may be the very best thing for our cause. England cannot complain much, as she has always contended she has the right to do what the United States did and what the United States has always denied.

November 25th.

As soon as it becomes apparent there will be no active operations I want you to bring the children and come down for awhile. Mrs. General Evans is now with the General, and Mrs. Jones and Mrs. Stuart are now with their general husbands. Stuart is now near Fairfax Courthouse, yet she is with him. She was with him when his headquarters were within rifle shot of Munson's hill and was barely out of sight when he fought the skirmish at Lewisville which made him a general, but her distressed look shows the constant anxiety she must suffer.

A day or two since some of his cavalry took a yankee captain, whom Stuart asked why the yankee cavalry did not show themselves more. The captain acknowledged that they had no great quality, and what they had was badly trained, but that things would be better now as General Philip St. George Cooke had command over the cavalry, and that he would make Stuart smart. "Yes," Stuart answered, "I know he has command, and I propose to take him prisoner. I married his daughter, and I want to present her with her father; so let him come on."

From the diary of Mr. Blackford's father in Lynchburg. November 24th.

I received a letter from William giving an account of the skirmish of the 18th in which his company was engaged. He was just about to mount his horse when detailed as officer of the day and he did not, therefore, participate in the affair which took place just after dark. William, who is always successful in giving a vivid picture, writes of the scene at headquarters that night. In one room two wounded prisoners, with limbs bare and bloody, suffered operations under surgeons' knives. In another room the corpse of young Chichester, one of Stuart's staff, at the door a wagon with the body of another man killed and in view of all this General Stuart quietly and composedly writing his dispatch.

William was much struck by the appearance of one of the prisoners, a sergeant from Brooklyn who bore the operation with the greatest fortitude. He knew Dr. Minor and the Piereponts. News from the North shows the vastness of their preparations and the bitterness of the spirit in which they are determined to wage the war. A member of congress, from New York City, in a recent speech came out boldly in favor of the policy of placing arms in the hands of the negroes, and Cameron, Secretary of War, indorses the idea.

December 7th.

The Richmond "Dispatch" contains Lincoln's message. Certainly it is unique in style and sentiment. It is his own, beyond doubt. An allusion is made to the defeats they have sustained. The tone is subdued and the doctrines infamous and unconstitutional! Everything indicates a rapid consolidation of the government. The States are prepared to surrender into the hands of the Federal power. There will be unquestionably an exchecquer bank established and the duties will be increased to a prohibitory figure. They are now sighing for the suspension of specie payments by the banks. The liberties of the people are gone, be the issue of the war what it may.

Mrs. Blackford to Capt. Blackford.
November 18th.

There was an indignation meeting last night in town on the subject of salt, which brought the price down to three dollars and a half, so that Messers. Bocock & Parrish will find themselves disappointed in the twenty dollars a sack which they have been charging. I shall write brother about it; he may like me to get some for him.

I hope your stay in Leesburg will be permanent and that I will be able to go and see you. If you cannot get board for me build a log hut or rent two rooms and I can make us all comfortable. The children are healthy and can stand as much as I can and are accustomed to exposure and do not take cold easily. I would be very willing to do my own cooking, and could do everything needful. Aunt Caroline Blackford, your sister Mary and myself are fixing up a box to send Mr. Raymond Fairfax, as he has no home with friends to care for him. I know you will be glad to hear this.

Mr. Launcelot Minor, of Amherst was in town today, and says he has his daughter, Fanny, weaving flannel, and that the sound of the loom is sweeter to him than that of the piano. I do not object to Fanny's doing the weaving, but I think he ought to regret the necessity for her doing so, for it is very hard work.

I wish you could see little Willy; he is so funny. It is sometime after eight and he is not asleep but awake and singing "Dixie." I tell him to hush and go to sleep and he calls, "Diup," in the most impudent way! He is very bad, but so funny in his badness that he amuses me very much.

The prices for everything are incredible. Mr. Garrett told me this evening that Mr. Meem bought a lot of negro clothing for $700 and in two weeks had sold it out for $2,000. Was it not outrageous for him to speculate thus on the necessities of life?

Lynchburg, December 5th.

I went down town this morning to attend to all you wrote me about. Your father promised to see Judge Daniel about hiring Jack, and if he did not want him, to see McDaniel and Irby about sending him to the Salt Works. But I will not allow him to be employed about the caldrons, as he is lame and might fall in and be scalded.

I saw Major Langhorne on the street. He looks pale and thin. I would scarcely have recognized him. He complimented me on my looks, and asked if I was not painted. I answered, "Yes, by God." He admired my dress very much. It is a dark grey poplin gored in princess style, and becoming to me as it makes me look slender.

December 9th.

I have been to call on Mr. and Mrs. Samuel D. Preston. She is, as you know, Texanna Saunders, of Charlottesville. She is very pretty, and much pleased with her new surroundings. He goes back to his battery at Yorktown tomorrow and she to Charlottesville. He is captain. The newspaper is out in an extra today saying the United States Congress had made propositions of peace. I would to Heaven it were true, but I have no belief in it whatever. I fear we have not been sufficiently punished for our national and individual sins.

I stopped awhile to stew some molasses to make some candy for the children. A nice plate of it is by me now which I wish you had. Captain Preston was horrified when I told his wife you wrote long letters every day. He says he fears she will expect him to do the same.

Did you ever feel such weather? Your mother has roses blooming in her arbors now. I never knew that before in December. Have not the moon and the stars been rubbing themselves up lately? I think they are brighter than I ever saw them. Orion and Pleiades are in full view of our chamber window, which opens upon the garden, and I stand there and watch them every night and wonder whether you are looking at them at the same time. It is very pleasant to look at something that your eyes can rest on also. When I feel the warm rays of the sun I thank God for making it so pleasant, and pray that its softest and most soothing beams may rest upon you, my darling.

I went out to take a walk to the Presbyterian Cemetery this evening. As I returned I saw your father coming to meet me. At first I thought he had a telegram saying you were coming home, and then that it announced you were hurt. This thought brought me nearly to a fainting spell, but I soon saw his sweet smile and was reassured before we met. He had come over to pay a visit, and being told where I had gone, followed. We had a pleasant talk and walk together. He brought a message from your mother asking that I bring the children over tomorrow and spend the day, which I will, though I do not like to go from home Sunday.

This time six years ago I was all in the bustle and excitement of getting ready to be married. How grand and important I felt! and when I went to Charlottesville to see our old friends, Lucy Minor especially, I was so proud that I among them all, had won you. I did not then, however, really know what cause I had to be proud.

From Capt. Blackford.
Leesburg, December 6th.

General Evans and our new general, D. H. Hill, rode up this morning and requested me to accompany them on a tour of inspection; so off we went at that breakneck speed over hill and dale, gully and fence, ditch and bog which generals deem essential to their military dignity. We kept up the race without dinner and until late evening, parting with the understanding that I was to join General Hill tomorrow morning and take him up the river. During the day my horse got deeply mired, and in an effort to relieve him, dropped in myself and was covered with mud from head to heels.

I was much pleased with General D. H. Hill. He relieves General Evans of the command of the whole country around here, while General Griffith will take Evans' brigade. I do not know where Evans will go. I think the change is a good one as Evans is too indiscreet for a separate command.

The news from Centreville is that an advance by the enemy is anticipated. I think McClellan's true policy is to keep up a show on his line for the purpose of keeping our army in place and move the main body of his troops to attack elsewhere. He has too much to risk by a battle fought at Centreville.

December 8th.

I am now writing with my new coat on. It is very comfortable and fits admirably. It is much more agreeable than the short jacket which allowed the wind too many liberties. The cap also fits well, and the visor is a great help as it will protect my neck and ears from the biting blast which so often seems so bitter I must be frozen.

I have gotten back my roan horse from Middleburg. He has recovered from his lameness and is very fat and well. I was out again with General Hill and like him better as I know him better. I find him a plain, unpretending Christian gentleman,—a very different man, in the matter of religion, from Evans who is much the reverse.

December 9th.

General Hill took command today, General Evans parting from his command after quite a handsome display of the whole brigade, except the artillery and cavalry. The Confederate battle-flags which have been prepared for all the regiments were presented to the four regiments up here today, and several speeches were made. After the ceremonies I went home with Dr. Clagett to dinner and was most cordially entertained. I enjoyed a glimpse of civilized domestic life very much. The Doctor's family were very kind and made me feel much at home.

Leesburg has as much beauty in it as any place of its size I ever saw, and it affords me much amusement to get introduced occasionally to a girl without letting her know I am married, and then, after saying many gallant things, wind up by some allusion to my wife and children. I went with Col. Munford a few days since to see some young ladies, and we heard them whisper to some other officers present to know whether we were married.

December 10th.

It is now about eleven o'clock at night and I have just left my saddle, on which I took my seat at eight this morning. I have been on a scout with a detachment up river nearly as far as Harper's Ferry. I had the honor today of drawing the enemy's fire, but you see I am unhurt. I was making some observation of the enemy's works in the little town of Berlin, Maryland. I was on a hill on this side of the river. While I was surveying the rascals with my field-glass I saw one of them slip out and take deliberate aim at me, but the ball went over my head. A squad of them followed but their balls also went over my head. On this hint I got behind the wall, where I had an equally good view and they ceased firing. If Col. Radford is ordered up here with the other six companies of the regiment I think it probable Munford and our battalion will be sent up into the beautiful country I was in today to guard it. I should like such a move very much. The country, however, has many disloyal people and a small force among them would suppress that feeling.

A short while ago a Miss Porterfield up in that country showed great heroism in our behalf. She walked five miles at night to warn our pickets that the enemy had crossed and were about to come down and cut them off, which warning saved them. Miss Porterfield and her sister and father have a Confederate flag flying on their house. The yankees have crossed over to their house several times to get the flag but they have preserved it. A squad came over a few nights since and took the old man and held him as a prisoner of war. Communities where public sentiment is divided. as that part of Loudoun County, are much to be pitied, for the strife is bitter and to the death, and one's enemies are either of his household or those who are his neighbors and were his friends.

The glasses of which I spoke are a superb pair, given me by Van Otey when he was compelled to resign and go home. I value them greatly for his sake, and they are of daily use to me and are much better than my own.

Today, while we were crossing an exposed field where the wind blew hard and the yankees were firing at us as we rode over, I made the men take a gallop so as to shorten the exposure. As we crossed I heard a lamb bleating but of course paid little attention to it. After we were safely over I looked back and saw a stalwart fellow from Company A down on the ground wrapping up the lamb in his cape and about to bring it along while the yankee bullets were picking at him with uncomfortable proximity. He says he is a farmer and could not let the animal die from want of some hand to save. The men charged him, however, with an undue love for its tender chops. He proved his motive to be pure by restoring it to its owner whose house was nearby.

I was out again today on reconnaissance to watch a similar party on the other side. They shelled our fortifications with great accuracy, but we did not waste ammunition in responding. I could not tell their motive, but think they were only drilling and practicing. I never saw finer shooting. We were under cover and no one was hurt.

Your brother spent last night with me. A curious incident happened while he was here. We were sitting up very late and I was telling him what a good man I had in John Scott, and remarked that if an alarm was given he would have my horse saddled and at the door of my tent, my wagon horse harnessed, my trunk in the wagon and all my baggage packed before he could think of one of these things. As I finished the sentence, as if in illustration of the truth of what I had said, "Bang! Bang! Bang! Bang!" went the guns of the pickets and the long-roll beat to arms. Before your brother found his saddle-bags my horse was ready for me and my property packed in my Jersey wagon waiting orders to move, down to the carpet on the floor, the table and the camp stools, much to your brother's astonishment and admiration. Then, what astonished him still more, as soon as it was ascertained to be a false alarm, although my tent had been dismantled, before he finished warming at the fire outside everything was snugly replaced, and looked as comfortable as if there had been no excitement.

December 15th.

I spent this Sunday in the saddle. I was Officer of the Day on the picket line and had to inspect every post and have ridden since breakfast. I went alone and had no companions except in the picket posts and I enjoyed the quiet scenery very much. I rode for fifteen miles along the bluffs and I enjoyed the view very greatly. The river was as smooth as a lake, and all nature seemed reposing in a universal Sabbath. Nothing was stirring except occasionally a lazy sentinel on the Federal shore would come out of his tent, take a look at me on the bluff above him and then retire.

For a week or ten days the pickets, who have been relieved every third day, have reported that old John Green, one of the greatest rascals in my company, asked that he may be left at the post nearest the Point of Rocks, sending word that he would rather serve an extra tour of duty than to ride the twelve miles back to camp merely to spend three days. I was perfectly incredulous as to any sense of duty being his motive. At first I permitted it, but on the second request being made I granted it, but determined I would ascertain what it meant. I could see from the mode in which the report was made to me by the returning sergeant that there was something behind. This morning I therefore unexpectedly dropped in on the headquarters of the picket, and on asking for John Green, was informed by the men that he was out on guard. I told them that that was not true and that I must know where he was. Then Emmet Snead burst out laughing, and said he would take me to see him, and we went over to a very comfortable house about two hundred yards from the post. There we found him dressed in a very nice suit of civilian clothes of black cloth and a white cravat. On the road over Snead told me the whole story. Old John had gone to the house to beg something to eat, found it belonged to a nice old Methodist lady of great unction of tone and manner. The old rascal could put a whine in his voice equal to a whole camp-meeting and at once donned that style. He informed the good old soul that he was a Methodist preacher who had enlisted on account of his patriotism, but found the life too hard for him, and his associates so wicked that it vexed his righteous soul to be thrown with them. She at once invited him to stay at her house while he was in that place and he had moved up, bribing each successive picket to make the report brought to me, by inviting them to share his luxurious fare at the good lady's expense. While he was staying at the house he would read the Bible and offer up a prayer every night, and the men would go up to hear him, and he would pray for them by name, describing them as the "most damnable sinners" at which the good woman would groan and the men would laugh, thus making good the story that John had told her of their wickedness. Snead told me that he also had borrowed some money from the old lady.

I came up unexpectedly and even he was abashed. The old woman's face was a study when I told her how he had deceived her, and what a wicked man he was, using no measured words in the description. I made him pay her back the money he borrowed though he denied he borrowed it, and made him return also the suit of clothes which had belonged to her dead husband, then made him walk to camp. I told him that if the sergeant of the guard did not report his arrival before daylight I would send him to the brigade guardhouse and prefer charges. He is a hard man and I have to punish him often.

General Hill is making various strategic moves tonight to deceive the enemy as to our numbers. He has been doing this sort of thing for several nights. Fires are kept burning in secluded woods, and bands play as if in a regiment. Old tents are pitched with no one to occupy, and everything is arranged that a casual observer, or an observer from the balloon the yankees daily send up, would estimate our force at double at what it is. Tonight, at ten o'clock rockets will be sent up at various points from Belmont to Berlin, and tomorrow the yankees will be in a great state of excitement to know what it all means. They think we are concentrating forces here, and will have the effect of lessening the forces on Johnston's front at Centreville.

December 19th.

The weather is the most remarkable I have ever known. It has been perfectly clear for a month and no colder than the average September. I cannot imagine why an advance has not been made, at least upon Leesburg. It is believed that McClellan's intention to have advanced long ago, but that he distrusted the steadiness of his troops. A lady who came across the river a day or two ago says the soldiers everywhere avow they will not advance; that they will resist any advance on our part, but will not attack to be slaughtered. I send this for what it may be worth. Doubtless she heard some such expressions, but if they are ordered they will advance; still the knowledge that there is such a sentiment among the troops is calculated to make a general hesitate. McClellan is very wisely getting his army under proper discipline. It is not of the same materials as ours, but will be very formidable when properly seasoned and well handled. Hill's tricks, that I wrote you about, seem to be causing a stir in Washington from the intelligence that seeps across the river. Pinkerton's men, who are handling the intelligence for McClellan and the Federals, have reported our force as over double what it is.

Col. Munford had gone home. I am in command of the battalion, reporting however, to Col. Jenifer, who has us under his authority along with other troops.

December 21st.

The citizens below here towards Dranesville were in a wild state of excitement and it was reported the enemy was coming up the road towards Leesburg in heavy force. General Hill sent me out to reconnoitre. I took only one man as many of my company were down in that direction on picket already with Lieut. Stratton, with headquarters at Belmont. When I reached Belmont I found Stratton under the impression the enemy were in force at Dranesville, as they had been the day before. I sent him and James T. Smith to reconnoitre the Green Spring road and I went down towards Dranesville. In a short time I met one of my men who had been on outside picket coming back in great haste with the story that the enemy was advancing in two columns, one on the pike, the other on a parallel road; that he had seen them with his own eyes; that one of my men had been captured, but that the outpost at Broad Run would fall back slowly. This was startling news and surely seemed authentic. I made the fellow join me and fairly flew to reinforce the picket at Broad Run which was composed of some of my best men, who I knew would not give up the bridge without some stand. At the rate I was moving I soon reached Broad Run, meeting people fleeing from the approaching enemy in carts, wagons, afoot and on horseback, with women, children, and such household goods as they could pick up and carry off. As I passed them they all, with wild gestures, pointed in the direction I was moving, and signalled me to go back, but I had no time to talk and flew by them. When I reached the picket I found them alert and prepared, with several videttes out a mile towards the enemy. They reported it was E. G. Scott who had been captured and that they thought it was only a scouting party of the enemy who had come back to ascertain whether our troops had occupied it. I went down the road with the whole picket, picking up the videttes as we passed them, but, strange to say, found no enemy. I went on until I reached Dranesville, which to my surprise I found occupied by a scouting party of Stuart's command, with whom Scott was affiliating instead of being captured. The people in the neighborhood knew the yankees had occupied Dranesville the evening before and seeing troops there in large force the next morning supposed them all yankees and hence the false reports which reached us.

Scott had a dispatch for General Hill giving the particulars of the fight of the day before. As soon as I got it I rode back to Leesburg rapidly to relieve the minds of the inhabitants and let the forces which had been sent forward to Goose Creek be returned to camp. The relief in Leesburg when I returned was very great. Many families were preparing to leave town. I have enlarged upon this little incident, but though a trifle, it illustrates camp life and the toils and alarms of war. We have some three or four thousand troops here and every man was moved several miles in consequence of this rumor.

December 24th.

This is Christmas Eve, and I am with you only in spirit tonight as you sit with the children's presents around you in our sweet room all alone with tears in your eyes as your memory reverts to the happy hours at the same time last year. The same memories are constantly before me. I am more uncertain now than ever when I can get off home. I shall take my Christmas dinner at Mr. Hoffman's with Generals Hill and Griffith.

Christmas.

I spent quite an agreeable day. First I had a sweet letter from you, then I went to church and heard a fair sermon from Walter Williams, and then dined at Mr. Hoffman's, with the two generals and the seven misses Hoffman's. I met there also a Mrs. Mason, from near Alexandria, who said she had known your mother when she lived there, and expressed great admiration for her.

December 26th.

While at breakfast a courier came over and said that the order permitting a certain number of furloughs was revoked. I was much down but rode over to see the General. He said the order had been revoked, but he had forwarded mine, as he thought I was especially deserving and that he hoped Beauregard would grant it. We will move our camp as soon as I can get enough men in from picket duty to do it. Our present location, which is just on the edge of town, is very good socially but when the wind blows it is hard to keep the tents standing, or the fires burning. The new place selected is on the South side of a slight hill and with heavy forest to protect us from the wind to the North of us. It will be near the yard of Mr. Thomas Swann's beautiful residence, a place called Mauvin, about a mile from town.

A note by Charles Minor Blackford III.

To close the year nothing is more appropriate than the closing paragraphs in Great-Grandfather's diary. I can imagine the old man sitting in his study in the house which became the residence of the late Senator Carter Glass, upon the ridge of the steep hillside upon which the Lynchburg of that day was built, reviewing 1861 and the vast changes it brought in his life and the lives of those about him. He wrote:

"The year now closing may well be styled *annus mirabilis*. The events of the past year have been well calculated to humble human pride, to shake confidence in what is called human wisdom and to make one tremble for the future of his race.

"A mighty fabric of political greatness shattered at a stroke! Two years ago I deemed the perpetuity of the American Union beyond all preadventure. Now, where is it? Civil liberty is nearly extinct in the United States and is destined to an early and violent death with scarcely a regret expressed by the public. The utter existence of the rights of States will give to those who remain in the Union a strong central government and make them a formidable nation, though with little constitutional or institutional liberty. The last hope for personal liberty is to be found in the Southern Confederacy.

"I have much as usual to be thankful for in a review of the past twelve months. All my sons have joined the army and acquitted themselves like men. Three of them are now captains, one a lieutenant and one a private. Three were in the battle of Manassas and escaped unhurt, and one had the opportunity and did distinguish himself greatly."

CHAPTER V

LEESBURG VISIT

By Susan Leigh Blackford.

THERE is now a gap in our correspondence owing to my going to Leesburg. Captain Blackford had been home most of January on leave and I returned as far as Charlottesville with him. I left Nannie and Willy at the Minors' at the University and started with the baby and her nurse, Frances, on my journey to Leesburg. Mr. Minor's nephew went with me as far as Manassas where I changed cars for the Manassas Gap Road, which then only extended to Strasburg, seventeen miles from Winchester. The train was much crowded with soldiers returning from hospitals and from furloughs. I got on very well until I got to Strasburg about two o'clock in the morning, when we had to leave the cars and go the rest of the way to Winchester in omnibuses. Some of these were quite comfortable and had stoves in them but our soldiers, though gallant enough in battle, were but mortals at last, and manifested this trait by rushing forward and taking possession of all the best vehicles and leaving me only a very dilapidated affair with several of the windows broken out. The roads were beyond description, made so by the many army wagons passing over them. There was no way for Frances and myself even to get into our omnibus except by ploughing through the mud, she with the baby and I with the satchels, lunch basket and other small packages.

After taking our place in the forlorn conveyance, wet, draggled and shivering with the bitter cold, the conductor came around to collect the fare for the trip. I put my hand into my pocket for my purse and to my horror found it gone! It was pitch dark outside and there was no chance of finding it in that crowd, for even had it not been stolen it would be trampled deep into that bottomless mud. My position was distressing, even appalling, for the driver was rough and rude and informed me I would have to get out, as he did not carry passengers for the love of them. I implored him not to put me out on the roadside with the baby that cold night, and informed him I had friends in Winchester who would supply my wants in the morning and that I would pay him double if he would take me there. At last the passengers interceded for me and the man unwillingly consented to take me on. We started, cold and shivering as we were.

Frances and I took it by turns to hold the baby and keep her warm by closely hugging it, while the other would sit on the floor in a vain effort to keep warm. The road to Winchester, after we got out of the mud at Strasburg, was a good turnpike and we were not more than two or three hours making the trip, reaching Winchester just before day.

We were set down at the door of Mrs. Humphrey Powell, the mother of my brother's wife, at that unearthly hour, but had to ring a long time before we roused anyone. At last old "Uncle Simon" the butler let us in. I had written to say that I would be there but found no one there to receive me but Uncle Simon and his wife. They, however, took me to a room and made me comfortable and soon I forgot my troubles in profound sleep in a delightful bed.

The driver, true to his word, was at the house early for his money, and I got the money and paid him. I had dropped a silver cup also in my transit from the cars to the bus, but, strange to say, it was found and brought to me the next day by the driver, who had become quite obsequious after finding I was a person of some consideration in Winchester.

After resting quietly all day I started Thursday in the stage for Leesburg and made the journey of some forty miles very comfortably over a good road. A few miles from Leesburg we were met by Mr. Blackford who had ridden out to meet the stage. He rode by our side into town where we were deposited at the door of Rev. Walter Williams.

I do not remember the particulars of my stay save that it

was very charming. Mr. Blackford and myself rode on horseback all about the beautiful country around Leesburg, visiting every place of interest. We went to the battlefield where the signs of the fierce contest were to be seen everywhere; visited the picket posts and looked over at the yankee guards who would touch their hats and present arms to acknowledge the unusual presence of a lady in such a place. On one evening we rode out to a fort towards Edwards Ferry, and from there we could see the enemy drilling a regiment of infantry and a battery of artillery. We watched them from the parapet of the fort without dismounting, and a number of men came out and stood near us. Suddenly they wheeled and threw their guns in battery and in an instant almost I saw the white puffs of smoke and one shell exploded high above our heads and another between us and the river. Mr. Blackford grabbed my bridle reins and galloped off with me under the cover of a hill while the men got under the embankments.

The enemy continued to fire for half an hour, but we were soon out of possible range and the men were entirely protected so it was only an empty salute but it broke up our enjoyment of their parade and regimental music.

Another evening Mr. Blackford brought his wagon to take Mr. Williams, Mrs. Williams and myself up to a fort on a high hill back of town, the name of which I have forgotten. It was commanded by a company of artillery commanded by Captain Robert Styles, of Richmond. As I jumped from the wagon, after we reached the fort, the lowest hoop of my skirt caught and I fell forward prone on my face in the mud. Fortunately the last three of my hoops were torn off and left hanging on the wagon and thus the drapery of my dress preserved its normal functions, and my modesty suffered no greater shock than that the incident left the unusual display of three pendant hoops. As I was unhurt there was a hearty laugh in which I joined. A number of the men, who had been drilling, had been drawn up close by and had presented arms in honor of our presence. I glanced at them as I arose and they stood like statues, with the most preternaturally solemn faces. I knew they were dying to laugh so I told them to do so, and then, at some sign from the captain, they had three hearty cheers and wound up in a good-natured laugh.

Every woman can appreciate the scarcity of clothes, even that early in the war, and will appreciate my despair when I looked down at my beautiful drab poplin, the one I had worn with so much pride, all covered with mud. Happily for me it all came off when dry and left no stain, but at the time I did not expect it. Captain Styles and his officers said they intended to perpetuate the "impression" I had made by surrounding it with a fence, the hole in the mud my too solid flesh had made.

On Tuesday morning Captain Blackford hurriedly returned from camp with his face pale with anxiety and sorrow and told me to get ready at once and leave Leesburg immediately, as the enemy was crossing the river only a few miles above the town. The despair and misery that came over me I well remember but there was no time for useless wailing. My trunks had to be packed and I had to get away without delay. Mrs. Jno. T. Smith was in town at the same time with her young sister, Miss Laura Dunnington, and they also had to move. As Mr. Blackford's wagon was the only conveyance that could be gotten for love or money there was nothing else to be done but invite them to go with me, so those two ladies, Frances, myself and the baby, with my trunk, all had to be packed into one small wagon. What became of their baggage I do not remember. John Scott, Mr. Blackford's servant, drove and Mr. Blackford detailed Mr. Smith to see us over to the Manassas Gap railroad, a distance of some twenty miles. He had only a few moments to superintend the packing, kiss me and the baby, take the head of his company which was waiting in full sight and ride off. Women who live in times of peace can little imagine the agony of that moment. I will not undertake to describe it.

We toiled and plodded on slowly and sadly over the dreadful roads. Sometimes one wheel would be down in a hole so deep that we would have to get out in the mud that the wagon could be righted. Again it would stick so fast that Mr. Smith and John Scott would prize us out with fence rails.

Once one of the horses laid down, or attempted to, in the mud for which I cannot blame him as he was so tired. Mrs. Smith, Frances and myself walked a great part of the way, while Laura Dunnington sat in the wagon and held little Lucy who was as good as could be.

When we reached Aldie it was so late and the horses so tired, though we had come only ten or twelve miles, we determined to spend the night. The hotel was so crowded we could not get quarters, but we got a good supper and comfortable lodging at a house which was once the home of Hon. Charles Fenton Mercer. Our chambers had splendid wood fires, and we enjoyed them vastly. The house is a quaint old affair. The woodwork inside has never been painted, and in the deep old windows aeolian harps were placed, on which the wind, which was blowing a great gale, played weird and most melancholy tunes. I was miserable anyway and these ghostly sounds filled my heart with sad and gloomy forebodings for the future, and though Laura occupied the room with me, I shed many tears as I thought of the forlorn and hopeless prospect before us.

We left Aldie at eleven in the morning and got to The Plains, a station on the Manassas Gap railroad, in five hours, which we thought was doing well. I had a nice roon with a carpet and a bright fire. I was sorry for Mrs. Smith. Her spirits were low on the thought of parting from her husband.

The next morning we started from The Plains on the train. I waked up with one of my bad headaches brought on by fatigue and exposure to the intense cold; I was at that time, and for many years, a perfect martyr to them. I knew I had a day of terrible suffering before me. The melancholy reflection that I was leaving my husband exposed to so much danger and that each hour was taking me further from him made me suffer more. We went down to Manassas and there changed cars for Charlottesville. At Manassas we saw that activity and movement which even to my unpracticed eye indicated some general military movement. On the train I met Dr. Parker, from Richmond, who did all in his power to relieve my suffering but in vain. When we reached Charlottesville there was much difficulty getting a carriage to take my party up to the University, (Mrs. Smith and her sister continued on to Lynchburg), but at last I reached there and immediately sought my bed and the relief it alone could give, doing little more than kissing my children who were overjoyed to get me back again.

The next morning, though my headache was gone, I was still sick from a deep-seated cold and sore throat and was confined to my room if not my bed. The children seemed well, but I was perhaps too unwell to notice them as I otherwise would have done either that day or the next.

Sunday dear little Willy came to me and in childish talk told me he had a headache. I made him lie down and he soon went to sleep, but when he awoke had a high fever and commenced vomiting, the spells of which lasted all night. Dr. Davis, Mr. Blackford's brother-in-law was at that time much occupied in the hospital and had given up private practice so I sent for Dr. Nelson but as he was the only physician within a wide range he did not get to me until Wednesday when my poor child was unconscious. He died about eleven that night. I wrote my husband:

"It is with a sad and heavy heart I commence this letter to you this evening, knowing the anguish you are enduring from the dreadful tidings contained in the letter Mr. Minor wrote this morning. Yes, my darling, impossible as it seems, our precious little soldier boy has been taken away from us to dwell with God and the angels. I trust you were somewhat prepared by the letters I wrote during his illness. I long to be with you to share this great sorrow and thus help you to bear it, but God has willed otherwise.

"Last Sunday he came to see me and looked prettier than I have ever seen him. He was dressed in his little soldier clothes, his 'bum-bums' as he called them. His hair was parted in the middle and curled around his bright face. He came to my bedside for me to kiss him, and was so sweet and loving I hated him to leave me. As I was unwell I stayed most the day in sister's room, and Miss Lucy Davis says he was sweeter and more gentle than she had ever seen him before. No doubt the disease had made great progress even then. He fell asleep while playing upon the floor and sister covered him up. At dinnertime Mary waked him up and he ate heartily, but after dinner he came to my room and said, 'Mamma, I dot de headache!' From that time he got steadily worse. At eleven o'clock Wednesday night, as I knelt by his bedside, he ceased to breathe and his pure spirit took to flight without a struggle.

"Mr. Minor started this morning with the little coffin to take Willy's body to Lynchburg to be buried but was stopped by Dr. Davis before his carriage reached Charlottesville and told him no trains would go to Lynchburg for several days, as Gen. Johnston was using the cars to move its army or its baggage from Manassas. So he brought the precious little body back and it will be buried in the University graveyard, tomorrow."

CHAPTER VI

THE FRONT SHIFTS

ABOUT this time Mr. Blackford's regiment was very active protecting General Johnston's rear as he withdrew his army to concentrate it below Richmond so as to meet McClellan who was moving his army from around Washington to the peninsula below Richmond by boat. In the middle of March the Federal army thrust into Virginia as far as Bealton on the Orange and Alexandria, (now part of the Southern System). There was only the cavalry to meet them, every regiment was actively engaged and as all their camp equipment was sent to the rear, they experienced much hardship during a long spell of cold, wet weather. Almost every day there were skirmishes with the enemy, only the ground to sleep on and with parched corn for food. I heard Mr. Blackford say that one day when he had nothing to eat, he rode over about dinner time to the camp of the First Virginia Cavalry to dine with his brother William. He found William camped beside a straw rick and was received with great cordiality. Mr. Blackford waited with some impatience for signs of dinner, but none came. Finally, he told William he had had no breakfast and wanted an early dinner, whereupon William put a broken fragment of a stovetop on the fire and when it was hot, covered it with hard corn and told him they had had no other ration for several days. They salted it down and ate heartily without a second course. Then Mr. Blackford returned to his regiment.

Of course during such a time all correspondence practically ceased,—Mr. Blackford had no paper to write upon.

About that time I had to write another saddening letter from Charlottesville where I still was because of the lack of civilian transportation.

University, March 17th, 1862.

I scarcely know how I can write to you when I have such heavy tidings to send you. In less than a fortnight I have been called twice to pass through the fiery furnace of affliction doubly heated. Yes, my darling, in that short time I have seen *two* of our precious children laid in the cold, dark grave. Willy and Lucy are now only bright and beautiful dreams. One of my most grievous thoughts is that you will have to bear this terrible strain alone. I hope you have received letters from Mr. Minor and myself that have prepared you for this last sad news, so it may not come with such overwhelming force.

Little Lucy was seriously ill when little Willy died. On Wednesday her fever abated very much and she became quiet and placid though her countenance was the saddest I ever saw. She never smiled after Willy's death. Thursday she was very sick and never closed her eyes. I shall never forget the eager, seeking eyes that followed me all over the room, and how she would open her poor little dry, hot mouth beseeching me for water, and once, when I held the glass to her lips, she seized it with both hands and drained it to the last drop. Both Dr. Davis and Dr. Nelson came to see her Friday morning and though they thought her extremely ill they were not without hope, as I was. About one o'clock Friday evening she fell asleep never to wake up again in this world.

A long sigh of relief came about four and with it her gentle spirit took flight. I took her in my arms and for the first time in ten days could clasp her to my heart without fear of hurting her. After death a most heavenly smile came over her face and as she lay in her crib robed in a white dress in which she had been christened and covered with white hyacinths and geranium leaves she was very lovely. Her little face must have caught the reflection of the smile her spirit wore when it entered Heaven, perhaps she met Willy at its Portals. While looking at her little Nannie said to me: "Mother, don't you reckon that Willy met Lucy and took her by the hand and led her up to God?"

Mrs. Blackford's narrative.

I go back to my own and my husband's movements. On the 17th of March I went up to my brother's place, Hill and Dale, seven miles from the University. There I remained quietly recuperating my health. Mr. Blackford's regiment came back to the neighborhood of Gordonsville but he was kept constantly out in the terrible weather and in the most active service. The news of the death of our little daughter did not reach him until late March when he got a few days' leave of absence to visit me at my brother's. It was a sad meeting but a great comfort to us both. He stayed only a day then took Nannie and myself back to Lynchburg. The day he was at my brother's was much enjoyed in spite of our sorrow. We heard very distant firing, which, from its regularity, Mr. Blackford pronounced to be a salute of some kind. We afterwards found out it was a salute to President Lincoln fired at Fortress Monroe.

We reached Lynchburg the evening of April first and went directly to the house as his father's house was so filled with refugee relatives he so hospitably entertained, many of whom terribly imposed upon him and made a convenience of his openhanded hospitality.

Mr. Blackford spent three weeks at home. His regiment was camped at Gordonsville and as the enemy had retired it was resting and refitting. Mr. Blackford was recruiting his company and sent back a number of well-mounted men. His stay of course was very grateful to both of us, but he was not well. The physical and mental strain of the preceding month had been too much for him. He suffered much from inflammation of the bowels, a dangerous trouble to a soldier on active service, and to which he succumbed twice during that year, each time after several weeks of laborious and unusual exposure.

Mr. Blackford was very successful during his short stay. The Confederate Cavalry supplied its own horses, and as the supply of horses became less abundant it became harder and harder to keep up a cavalry company, especially one from a city. On this trip he filled the ranks of his company up to its full limit, but after that it was very difficult to keep it up. He could get men enough, but when one of his horses gave out or was killed it was difficult to supply its place.

A whole year had elapsed since Mr. Blackford had left his home and his profession. Our income, therefore, had gradually declined while the prices of necessities had been rising rapidly as they became scarcer and the currency declined in value. Fresh meat was selling at forty cents a pound, coffee one dollar and fifty cents a pound, tea ten dollars, men's boots twenty-five dollars, ladies shoes ten to fifteen dollars and so on. Under these circumstances it was determined I should fill the house with boarders, thus securing me protection and at least enough to eat. Mr. Blackford's pay of one hundred and forty dollars a month did little, at the prices we had to pay for supplies, towards our support. This move was absolutely necessary, but it was the beginning of many troubles and vexations for me and, as I look back upon that period it beclouds even the few rays of happiness which struggled through the gloom naturally incident to such times.

Mr. Blackford's visit did us both good. He left to rejoin his regiment and commence the summer campaign. He still was not well. He went via Charlottesville to pick up his horses at my brother's and John T. Smith with a party of recruits joined him there. He returned to the regiment at the time of elections of officers. This appeared to be one of the weaknesses of the Confederate Army, the officers stood and fell upon their popularity with the remainder of the rank and file of their regiment, brigades or companies, and frequently an able, but strict and unpopular officer would be voted out while some boot-licker would be voted into a position which he was in no way capable of filling. We resume his letters:

In camp near Somerset, April 25th.

This regiment is now in the agony of reorganization and as soon as it is over we will, I suppose, be sent somewhere to the front to keep the enemy in check on their advance. The reorganization is producing great disorganization and I hope it will soon be over. Col. Radford, I understand, is not a candidate for re-election. He is now in Richmond looking, I presume, for a yellow sash. Munford will be made colonel and there will be a scrub race for the other field officers' places in which I have taken no part. I suppose I will be re-elected Captain of my company without opposition. Captains Hale and Flood have been left out and Captains Alexander and Harris will be, and Lieutenants have been scattered to the four winds. I hope mine will be left me, but there is no telling. I send this by Doc Halsey who was not re-elected. I am for Captain J. W. Watts as Lieut. Colonel.

On the 26th, after announcing his unanimous re-election as Captain, he wrote:

When we left Gordonsville I had no doubt we were to join General Jackson and that before this we would have fought a great battle but we were stopped by a courier and have been waiting here for something to turn up. I believe our division under Ewell was to have crossed the Blue Ridge in the rear of Banks and to have attacked him as Jackson advanced on him in front. You gave such a surmise, or rather said you heard such a report in your last letter. I am somewhat curious to know where you heard it, for until the head of the column turned up this way the whole army thought they were to march to Hanover Junction and thence to Richmond. Many brigades ordered their letters to be so addressed. It will give you an idea of the secrecy of military movements. We are ordered to move at daylight, which way I do not know.

Orange County, April 28th.

We are now on the march to join Jackson. We have Elzey's, Trimble's and Taylor's brigades, Flournoy and our regiments and some artillery. I presume a fight is inevitable in a day or so. I do not yet know the meaning of the firing heard yesterday. I am well and in good spirits as usual. Tell Nannie she may look into the "Big Book" whenever you say so.

Madison Courthouse, April 30th.

I was ordered to this place yesterday with about 80 picked men detailed from the regiment and I am in command of the picket line from the Rapidan up to the top of the Blue Ridge running some of the way on the Robertson River. It is an agreeable post and the people are very kind. I am writing now in a doctor's office which he has placed at my command. I have been riding all day and am very tired. The picket is a long one and is covered by several companies but all report to me. The news from New Orleans and North Carolina makes me very unhappy. Our cause is hopeless unless some change takes place. Now it is given out that a place is to be defended to the bitter end and then as soon as the enemy advance we retire without a fight. Such tactics repeated over and over again dishearten the army more than you can imagine.

May 10th.

Col. Flournoy's regiment has come here and I will go back to the regiment with the companies, I suppose. I am very unwell. This constant riding in the rain has made me and a number of my men quite sick. I have fitted up a hospital and the people here are very kind in taking care of my men. I shall be sorry to leave here. I think this is the best post I have had during the war and these are fine people around here.

Mrs. Blackford wrote in conclusion:

When the regiment moved he was sent home, making the trip to Gordonsville in an ambulance. He got home the 17th of May. In addition to his fever he broke out in boils and soon lost twenty pounds of flesh, and that at a time when he was, at best, very thin. But he was so anxious to be with his men who were seeing hard fighting in 'The Valley' as the Shenandoah is known in Virginia that he went off before he was cured. After a month or two of hard riding he brought on a still more serious attack which laid him up and was very dangerous. But again, against the doctor's advice he started out to rejoin his company. He picked up his horses at Charlottesville and reached his company which was camped about three miles from Richmond July 12th.

☆ ☆ ☆ ★ ☆ ☆ ☆

CHAPTER VII

JACKSON IS A ROUNDHEAD

☆ ☆ ☆ ☆ ☆ ☆

From Capt. Blackford. July 13th. Sunday.

I REACHED camp yesterday which I found about three miles from Richmond. My company has been sent up to Jackson's headquarters for some special duty. I was told he sent to the regiment for a Captain who knew something about the country about Fredericksburg and his company. My company was selected as I was a native of that place. I am comfortably camped on the Mechanicsville Pike about a hundred yards from Jackson's headquarters. I am writing from Mr. Peachy R. Grattan's where I came this morning to meet William. This is Mr. Wyndham Robertson's house now occupied by the Grattans.

My men received me with open arms yesterday and seemed to be so glad to see me back that it touched me greatly. I wish I could in some way recruit the ranks somewhat. It is very hard to keep a cavalry company from a town. All the other companies in the regiment have the advantage of mine in the matter of securing horses. I have as many thus far as many other companies but I know that from this time on it will be hard to keep the ranks full.

All I hear are stories about Stonewall Jackson. There are lots of jokes, too, one of which I heard just now:

As he was crossing the Blue Ridge en route to Richmond two Irishmen were sitting by the roadside talking during a rest period. When one said to the other:

"I wish all the yankees was in Hell!"

"And faith," said the other, "and I don't wish anything of the sort."

"The divvel you don't, and why don't you?"

"Because Old Jack would have us standing picket at the gate before night and in there before morning—and it's too hot where we is to suit me!"

I am told by one of the staff that in Monday's fight at Port Republic, in The Valley, Jackson was on the opposite side of the river when the enemy's battery commenced playing on the bridge. He rode up to it and said to the commander. "Fire into those woods over there and not at the bridge." As Jackson was in a blue coat they took him for a Federal officer and obeyed. Upon which he calmly rode over the bridge and at once brought one of his batteries to bear upon the deluded Federal who was still shelling the harmless woods and drove him from his position.

Jackson excites great enthusiasm everywhere, second only to Lee. The regiment is ordered to Gordonsville. I am glad I will not have to march up there with it.

We will move from here tonight or early tomorrow, I think, for I am sure General Jackson got orders or arranged to move tonight when in town. I was invited by Col. A. S. Pendleton, his adjutant, to go with General Jackson and his staff into town this morning. I was proud to be of such a distinguished party although a very small atom of it. We went first to the Governor's mansion and there, I suppose by appointment, we met General Lee. The two generals went into the house, but their respective staffs did not. They were there only a short time; then the two generals and Gov. Letcher came out on the front steps and told the generals good-by. The two then rode around to Jefferson Davis' house where some other generals met them and I suppose they had a council of war—certainly a lunch. While they were lunching and conferring I rode around to Cousin Mary G. Watkins' and got a very nice lunch which she kindly prepared for me in an hour, the period for which we were dismissed at the President's house. Any kind of hospitality is a strain now when bacon is seventy-five and fresh meat fifty cents a pound, potatoes sixteen dollars a bushel and other things in proportion.

When the lunch was over I went back to the President's house where I found the staff officers assembling in front. We still had to wait awhile, but soon the different generals, Longstreet and others, came out, but the particular two were kept to the last and then Lee, Jackson and President Davis came out together, a very distinguished trio, and stood talking on the steps. Lee was elegantly dressed in full uniform, sword and sash, spotless boots, beautiful spurs and by far the most magnificent man I ever saw. The highest type of the Cavalier class to which by blood and rearing he belongs. Jackson, on the other hand was a typical Roundhead. He was poorly dressed, that is, he looked so though his clothes were made of good material. His cap was very indifferent and pulled down over one eye, much stained by weather and without insignia. His coat was closely buttoned up to his chin and had upon the collar the stars and wreath of a general. His shoulders were stooped and one shoulder was lower than the other, and his coat showed signs of much exposure to the weather.

He had a plain swordbelt without sash and a sword in no respect different from that of other infantry officers that I could see. His face, in repose, is not handsome or agreeable and he would be passed by anyone without a second look, though anyone could see determination and will in his face by the most casual glance—much I would say to fear but not to love. I of course speak only from a casual observation and from no acquaintance, but that of a line officer who, in the course of his military duties, has been introduced to his commanding general. A means of observation and acquaintanceship that might be likened to that of a glowworm with the moon.

Davis looks like a statesman. His face is pale and thin but very intellectual and he had graceful manner and easy bearing. He was dressed in a black suit and left a pleasing impression on anyone looking at him.

After the distinguished gentlemen had talked a few minutes on the steps they shook hands very cordially in telling each other good-by, but our observant eyes satisfied us that both Lee and Davis bade Jackson farewell in a manner that indicated they would not see him again for a while,—or in other words that he had been ordered to move. The opinion was confirmed by the manner in which he rejoined his staff. He got on his old sorrel horse, which his courier was holding for him, and without saying a word to anyone, in a deep brown and abstracted study started in a gallop towards the Mechanicsville Pike, which we soon reached. His orders, published to his corps, very strictly enjoined the preservation of the crops along which the army and its trains moved and forbade all officers and men from riding out into the fields on each side of the road. This day Jackson was especially anxious to get back to his quarters. Unfortunately for his speed, the pike was filled with long wagon trains, one set coming in, the other going out. It was impossible to make time under these circumstances and still obey orders. He had not spoken a word since we had gotten underway. He first dodged in and out among the wagons, but his progress was slow, much slower than his needs demanded. He obviously remembered his orders, but determined to violate them.

He told his adjutant to have the cavalcade fall into single file and thereupon dashed into an extensive field of oats, overripe for the harvest, on the left of the pike. Several hundred yards ahead of the place he thusly violated the sacred oat field, there was a very nice brick house sitting back some distance, in a grove of oaks with a lane leading down to the pike. On a porch a round and fat little gentleman was sitting smoking his pipe, with bald head and red face in his shirtsleeves with an eye on his morning "Examiner" and the other on his field of oats. When he saw the cavalcade ride out of the road, he threw down his paper, rushed down the steps and flew down the lane and before we reached the place where the lane and pike united he was standing like a lion in the pathway. He was puffing and blowing, wiping the perspiration off his forehead and so bursting with rage that all power of articulation seemed for a moment suspended.

The General saw him and for the first time in his career seemed inclined to retreat, but our irate friend had regained his speech and made his attack as Jackson drew rein before him.

"What in Hell are you riding over my oats for?" the little

man shouted. "Don't you know it's against orders?"

The General looked confused, fumbled with his bridle rein and was as much abashed as any schoolboy ever caught in a watermelon patch. Before, with his slow speech, he could ever get out a word of explanation, our volcanic friend had another eruption:

"Damnit! Don't you know it's against orders? I intend to have every damned one of you arrested! What's your name anyhow?"

"My name is Jackson," said the General, half as if, for the occasion, he wished it was something else.

"Jackson! Jackson!" in a voice of great contempt. "Jackson, I intend to report every one of you and have you every one arrested. Yes, I'd report you if you were old Stonewall himself instead of a set of damned quartermasters and commissaries riding through my oats! Yes, I'll report you to Stonewall Jackson myself, that's what I'll do!"

"They call me that name sometimes," said the General in the same subdued, half-alarmed tone.

"What name?"

"Stonewall."

"You don't mean to say you are Stonewall Jackson, do you?"

"Yes, sir, I am."

I can give no adequate description of the sudden change. His anger was gone in an instant and in its place came an admiring look that was adoring. His color vanished, his lips parted and tears stood in his eyes. His emotions stilled his tongue an instant, then his speech returned with all the vigor of his vernacular and he shouted as he waved his big bandana around his head:

"Hurrah for Stonewall Jackson! By God, General, please do me the honor to ride all over my damned old oats!"

He would not let the General pass until we had all taken a glass of cold buttermilk with him. He pressed the General to take every variety of strong drink, but buttermilk was all he would accept. So great was our friend's admiration for old Stonewall that even his refusing to take something stronger did not lower him in his estimation as I think it might have done had the refusal come from a lesser light. He made no apology for his oaths, on the contrary emphasized his admiration, as he had his anger, with a choice selection.

The interview over, we hurried on to headquarters and, very soon after, I was informed that we were to go up to Gordonsville tomorrow. I shall watch Jackson closely while I am with him and put down what I see and what I think of him. He is, of course, a great military genius and has made such an impression on the men that "Old Jack" is at once a rallying cry and a term of endearment. The army is full of stories about him and everybody, citizens and soldiers, is trying to get a glimpse of him. Whenever he is recognized by the soldiers, he is cheered. Of course in many brigades which have not served under him he is unknown and he tries to go about unrecognized. I have no chance to learn anything about him socially and will have none. Even if I had, I doubt from what his staff tell me, whether I would be any wiser or know him any better by the opportunities for observation I have otherwise. He seems to have no social life. He divides his time between military duties, prayer, sleep and solitary thought. He holds converse with few.

July 17th.

I write from Mount Airy, Cousin Betty Hill's old home on the banks of the North Anna in Caroline County where I spent many happy hours of my boyhood. But what a change in it, its occupants and me! Time has destroyed many of the homelike surroundings, which Uncle James Minor used to say, there alone never changed. Inattention and want of taste on the part of the present owner have obliterated that air of refinement which once made it so attractive a country residence. Those who lived there when I was a boy are either in the graveyard behind the house or are scattered widely. I am no longer a barefooted boy or a half-grown young man, suffering the agonies of early dandyhood. Instead of being the petted and welcome guest of the house, I am lodged in the barn, and even the dogs bark at me as I ride across the yard.

I left Richmond early yesterday morning with General Jackson and his staff, my company acting as sort of escort for the occasion. We passed by Ashland and hence on by Old Fork Church. Just before we got to Fork Church, we came to a very nice cottage on the right side of the road setting back some forty or fifty feet from it. The house was covered very much by running roses and other flowers, and there were many flowers in the yard, some in boxes, some in beds.

The occupants were obviously more refined than persons of their class usually are. As the cavalcade rode up to the gate a very plainly but neatly dressed matron of forty, with a pleasant face and surrounded by neat looking children, was sitting on the steps watching the soldiers go by. General Jackson who, of course, was in front, asked her for a drink of water. There was nothing in his dress or style, or in that of his staff, to make her suspect that our party was other than "Damned quartermasters and commissaries" but she promptly went inside the house and brought out a stone pitcher of water and handed it to the General without a tumbler or dipper. He was very thirsty and turned it up at once taking a long draught. While his head was so buried she, having noticed the respect and deference with which he was treated, asked me who it was. On being told, her eyes riveted on him with a look of combined curiosity and devotion. When he finished his long pull at the pitcher, he handed it back to her. We watched it with thirsty impatience, longing to slake our parched tongues. Instead, however, of handing it down the line, for we had faced our horses to her yard fence, she poured the water on the ground and carried the pitcher into the house, but came out immediately with another large white one and a dipper, then commenced to water us regularly. When she got to me, I asked her why she carried the other pitcher into the house, and she replied she never intended anyone else should drink out of it, and would hand it down to her children as a memento of Jackson's visit. I have no doubt she will do so, and the story will be told with pride by generations of the family.

We came up the road towards Beaver Dam, passing between

Edgewood and Dewberry. Just before we got to the place where the road turns off towards Dewberry, General Jackson made me ride up beside him and he directed me to go with my company to the neighborhood of Fredericksburg, which is occupied by the Federal General Augur, to send into town and find out all I could about their force, movements, etc., and report to him by couriers, a line of which he would establish at Gordonsville. He left it to my discretion how I was to carry out his orders. After giving me minute directions as to what he wanted, he ceased talking and I rode by his side, once or twice trying to make conversation unsuccessfully. I wanted to drop back with the staff, but did not know whether he was done with me or not. We rode on like a couple of dummies. Fortunately, we soon reached the forks where I had to turn off. I told him so, touched my hat and left him, but I have my doubts as to whether he knew of my presence or absence.

The sun was just setting when I got here and yet old Mr. Dickenson, the proprietor, had gone to bed and was asleep. I was obliged to have to feed my horses and had been supplied with money to buy food. While my men had cooked rations I wanted to get something fresher than that for them. I therefore knocked until I had aroused him and he came to the door in his nightdress. When he peeped out, and saw some seventy or eighty cavalrymen on the lawn he jerked back his head, not being certain to which side we belonged. The colloquy was continued through the door until I convinced him we were Confederates; then he again put the door ajar but was not inclined to show us much hospitality.

I told him that I intended to have forage whether he was willing or not, but would pay him for it before we moved in the morning. With that understood, he was about to go to bed again when he heard me tell one of the officers that my reception was very different from any I had ever had at that house before. That seemed to revive his interest and he asked me my name. When I told him he said, "Yes, yes! I have seen that name cut on the aspens in the yard. Are you any kin to Mr. William Blackford who used to live in Williamsburg?" When I said, "Yes, his son," the old gentleman said: "Hold on there! That's a different thing!" He began calling for different people, family and servants, and soon showed us every possible attention. He had a mighty pot put on and put into it more eggs than I supposed there were on any one farm and served eggs, milk and hoecake to every man in the company. He is having breakfast cooked for us as I write. He wants me to stay in the house, but as we are on neutral territory, which is liable to be raided by yankee cavalry, I thought it best to stay with my men and sleep in the barn— after putting out pickets on all roads of approach, of course.

In the yard I found many aspen trees, high up upon which I found in many places inscribed my name and that of my sister Lucy and the Keans, in letters of varying size and under dates ranging from 1839 to 1853. My earliest inscription was 1844. In one place under the inscription 1837, by Uncle James Minor, is the word "Earthquake." I have often heard he was up the tree carving when an earthquake came which shook the top off the schoolhouse chimney.

I expect to camp for the present at or near Mr. Kean's and send out scouts to the hills near Fredericksburg. The enemy have a cavalry camp at Bowling Green.

July 19, Olney, Caroline County.

I have been scouting towards Fredericksburg for the past two days and I shall lie by today to let my horses rest. Tomorrow, with a competent guide, I shall get almost in sight of Fredericksburg. I have one of my men in town now with his horse hitched to a two-wheeled wagon selling eggs, chickens and tobacco, and picking up all the information possible. I expect him back today and I will send off a courier to Jackson with the information he may get. He was perfectly disguised and had his mother met him she would not have known him. He looked as if he had been raising peanuts and potatoes all his life in Caroline. I gave him a letter to Mr. John M. Marye, who I hear is in town. It is written on a small slip of paper rolled up in a small roll, and then put up in oiled silk so he could put it in his mouth in case of need. Marye is to answer in the same style, but I rely on the sharp wit of the messenger more than anything else. He is a keen trader. I supplied the funds for his wagonload of merchandise and we are to share the profits equally. He is furnishing the wits and risk, and I the money. I told him to invest my share of the profits in shoes and dresses for you— guessing at the numbers of the shoes.

I have enjoyed this day of rest very much. Mr. Kean has lost seven of his negro men; gone over to the enemy. Everybody about here has lost some of their force. The family has been very kind to me. My camp is not far off and we are enjoying our ranger life very much, though there is danger of being captured. We cannot tell when we will run into a body of the enemy. I have been scouting with two parties. I command one party and my lieutenant the other.

Dr. Pendleton's, July 22nd.

I hope you got my short note, or else I fear you shared the anxiety of my army friends that I had been captured near Fredericksburg. I was in danger of it, but owing to my perfect acquaintance with the neighborhood, I was able to elude pursuit although the enemy in large force had thrown their line far in my rear. The people everywhere kept me posted in regards to their movements.

I am going back now, into the same section, but with only one man so as not to attract any attention so there will be no danger. I went within one hundred yards of the yankee camp and looked from the hills into it. I shall continue my huckstering trade, which I found profitable both in a military and a commercial point of view. As I looked down upon old Fredericksburg, surrounded by yankee camps, my thoughts recurred with curious contrasts of my childhood. In this country I have so much to make it revert back to happy childhood hours and to mark such contrasts that I cease to be surprised by such scenes.

I think General Jackson was well pleased with the results of my last trip and I shall endeavor to please him still better on this. Tell mother I had through my spy a very charming letter from cousin Brodie Herndon, in Fredericksburg, in which he sent many kinds of messages to her. I intended to send it to her but when the yankees pressed me so closely I destroyed it, lest if I was captured it might compromise him with them.

On Jackson's staff there is a young man named Henry Kyd Douglas, from Maryland just opposite Shepherdstown whose mother, he tells me, was a Miss Blackford the daughter of a Colonel Blackford. He says he has always heard they are the same family as ours. Do you know them? Ask Father to try and get me some Federal money from the prisoners; it would be of great use to me on such excursions as this. I have hucksters in Fredericksburg now who have some money to buy me things for you. My last man made a few purchases. I told him to get me some writing paper, but he could only find some sheets of note paper with a sutler and that was marked up with vile stars and stripes. The ladies of this neighborhood, like the ladies everywhere else, are ransacking their brains to find modes of comforting the sick and wounded soldiers. How much is it possible for the men of a country to be subjugated when the women show so much spirit? It is said that Greece could not be conquered because its maidens twined their soft tresses into golden bowstrings that their lovers might send winged death hissing to the Persian heart. How much more does the work, the nerve and the sorrowing energy of our women test their unconquered spirit and their cheering faith in our cause? All, of every degree and every age, with praying heart and tearful eye, with one consent are engaged everywhere in unceasing labor, plying the busy needle, handling the constant shuttle, twirling the ceaseless wheel, nursing the sick, watching the dying or binding the wounded limb, all of a common country and from reverent patriotism. Neither history nor romance shows a parallel to the devotion our women are now displaying in every hamlet of our land. This is the age of heroines and I glory in the fact that my wife and mother are among them.

When I started out the last time I was driven back by a brigade of yankee cavalry who did little beside burn Beaver

Dam Depot but I was soon back before Fredericksburg and had the old wagon peddling to the yankees in town. It was in town when the troops began to move out to join Pope towards Culpeper and my man took accurate count of the number of regiments and cannon which he got to me as soon as he could. I at once galloped to the nearest telegraph station which was at Louisa Courthouse, then moved to join my company at headquarters between Gordonsville and Orange. As soon as I got there Col. Pendleton told me that the General was well pleased and wanted to see me at his tent at once. I found the General in a tent with nothing but a roll of blankets strapped up and two camp-stools and a table. He was seated on one stool and motioned me to the other, asking at once for me to tell what I had seen. After I had been talking a few minutes I perceived he was fast asleep. I stopped and waited several minutes. He woke up and said: "Proceed." I did so for a few minutes when I noted he was asleep again so I stopped. He slept longer this time and when he awoke he said without any explanation, apology or further questioning: "You may proceed to your quarters." I did so although I felt somewhat put out that my narrative had proved such a good soporific.

Sunrise, July 29th.

The whole army is moving somewhere and I wait for the order to mount. I snatch a moment to tell you I found your delightful letters awaiting me.

As I write I can see a train of wagons, five miles long, moving towards Gordonsville, yet nobody but General Jackson knows where we are going. It seems strange to see a large body of men moving in one direction and only one man in all the thousands knowing where they are going. I am at headquarters and know nothing nor does the adjutant-general. They will go until ordered to stop.

Mechanicsville, July 30th.

The news this evening indicates some activity on the part of the enemy in our front and many foresee some corresponding move on our part. We are receiving heavy reinforcements. A. P. Hill's division is all here I think. I am very much puzzled by the movements and yet understand them as well as anyone else but General Jackson, who surely keeps his own counsel. I am on very pleasant terms with the staff and sometimes meet the General but he has very little to say to anyone. I fear you will have to give up coffee. It is selling for two dollars and a half a pound and hard to get at that. I would give five hundred dollars a pound for it for your own drinking, but we cannot afford it for so large a family as you have around you now.

Hill and Dale, August 2nd.

You will be astonished to see the date of this letter, and so am I, but here I am and here I spent the night. I was sent to Charlottesville on some business by General Jackson and after that was done came here to spend the night. I find your brother's house full as usual.

Everybody in Albemarle is anticipating the arrival of the yankees but there is no danger while Jackson is in front of them. I go back to camp early this morning. Day before yesterday I was riding with Jackson and his staff investigating some roads which I expect he intends to use. We had not ridden more than five miles and it was not more than two o'clock in the day, when the General suddenly stopped, dismounted at the foot of a tree, unbuckled his sword and stood it by the tree, then laid down with his head on the root of the tree and was asleep in a second, or appeared to be so. I was amazed and glanced at the other gentlemen, who I thought were not so much surprised. The General had not said a word as he went to rest and we were equally quiet while he slept. He laid with his eyes shut for about five or six minutes, got up, buckled on his sword, mounted and rode on without any explanation or comment. He is a curious, wonderful man. No one seems to know much of him, not even those who are with with him hourly. He has no social graces but infinite earnestness. He belongs to the class from which Cromwell's regiment was made except he has no religious hypocrisy about him. He is a zealot and has stern ideas of duty.

August 3rd, (Sunday).

I got back last night very tired and sick but a night's rest has set me up. I find it hard to write intelligibly, as I have no tent or quiet place. I am always surrounded by men and write sitting on the ground with only a plank on my lap as a desk. I made a requisition for at least one tent, which can be used to protect our things from the weather, and as a company office. Of course I will fare as the men do and sleep on the ground, as I have been doing ever since the first of March except when sick. This style of life has made me sick and caused all my troubles with dysentery. I hope I will be gradually hardened to it, but when I wake up in the morning cold and wet I am much depressed by it.

Monday.

I went to church in the Green Springs neighborhood yesterday and heard the Rev. Kelsey Stuart preach a very trashy sermon. I cannot understand how a man with such an audience, and under such circumstances, could preach such a sermon. I dressed up in my new uniform, had my boots blacked, sword and spurs rubbed up very bright, and the black and his housings so polished as to glitter in the sunlight. About ten o'clock and after writing the first part of this letter, I mounted, telling John he need not stay in camp as I would not be back until late in the evening, as I knew I would be invited to some of the swell houses in the neighborhood to dinner, as I knew a number of their inhabitants. I rode off supposing myself to be so irresistible in my resplendent outfit that everybody would want to have me dine with them. I found a very distinguished party gathered at the church. General Jackson was there, and Generals Winder, Pender and A. P. Hill and many colonels, majors and the line officers, all, like myself, dressed in their best, and besides all the beauty and style of the Green Springs country. There was communion service, in which Generals Jackson and Pender joined, and many other officers and men. The clanking swords sounded strangely as each man arranged his so as to enable him to kneel at the chancel rail. We were too near the enemy to lay aside our arms, even in church to worship the God of Peace.

After service I went out and stood by the gate and shook hands most cordially with every acquaintance, and helped many ladies into their carriages but never an invitation did I get from any one. I saw your sister's dear friend, Mrs. Wellington Gordon, whom I had known in better days, and walked up to her with a cordial greeting. She did not remember me, and when I told her who I was seemed shy of my acquaintance and obviously pried enough into my thoughts to divine I had designs on her dinner. She spoke but a word or two and passed hurriedly on, jumped into her carriage and I think did not feel herself safe until it was locked and rolling off. Every acquaintance I had gave me the cold shoulder in the same way, and after all were gone, and I was turning with empty stomach to seek my hungry horse, I heard a plaintive voice ask if that was not Captain Blackford? Turning I found it to be Miss Mary Boyden, the daughter of the rector, who once taught at your brother's. She stopped to ask me to go home with her father and herself to dinner, though of all the crowd they were the only ones to whom hospitality was a burden. They lived too far away for me to try it, so with a very grateful heart, I had to decline. With my feathers drooping I ride back to camp to make my dinner of some roasting-ears of corn I robbed from a field on my way back. Launcelot, my brother, came back with me to share my sumptuous meal. He is looking well and in fine spirits. Amongst that large and wealthy congregation only three or four soldiers, and they either generals or near relations, were invited to dinner. Had it been in Fauquier County every soldier would have been provided with something to eat, whether private or officer.

Headquarters, Valley District, near Gordonsville. Aug. 6th.

I am pressed for time tonight having been in the saddle all day and having received orders to go on a whiskey-spilling expedition tomorrow. I am expecting John and his wagon every hour. His arrival with my camp chest will enhance my comfort very much. All the army is now on the north side of Gordonsville having left the Mechanicsville neighborhood Monday. I was trying to make myself something more comfortable in my bivouac down there when, about two o'clock, John Scott came to me and said I had better send and get some shirts he had taken out somewhere to be washed as we were going to move. Everything was quiet and I asked him with some surprise why he thought so, and he said because General Jackson had sent his servant for his washing. I slipped over to Col. Pendleton's tent and asked him if it were true we were going to move. He said no and asked me why I thought so. I gave him the information John Scott had given me and he jumped up and hurried his servant after his washing and commenced to pack up, saying he was sure to move if Scott were correct but he did not know when. I went back and packed up my few things and made the men do likewise. In less than a half-hour couriers were riding in every direction and in an hour the army was moving.*

I rode awhile with General A. P. Hill who is second in command and whom I know well and pleasantly. We were faced out towards Culpeper Courthouse and I asked him where we were going? He replied that he supposed we would go to the top of the hill in front of us, but that was all he knew. The army consists of Jackson's old Valley army and A. P. Hill's division, amounting to some five thousand more men. John Scott and the wagon just came up as I write. Believe nothing you see in the Lynchburg papers. The heavy cannonading reported by the passengers was thunder or their imagination. I have not heard a cannon since I have been in this neighborhood.

Mr. Garnett's House, in the yard, Culpeper County, Aug. 9th.
I write you in great haste merely to say the whole army is

---

*Robert W. Chambers used this incident in his book, *Secret Service Operator 13*. But he ascribed it as happening to Col. W. W. Blackford instead of C. M. Blackford. C.M.B. III advancing and that we are in a short distance of the enemy, having crossed the Rapidan into Culpeper. I am as well as usual and received your sweet letter yesterday. I will write you a line whenever I can. There will be a fight today or tomorrow. I pray God we may be victoriously spared. If in His great pleasure it is otherwise ordained for me, I pray He may take care of you, my darling and my Nannie.

General Jackson has halted here awhile to let the troops come up and we are trying to get some breakfast. My heart is with you. Kiss Nannie.

Battlefield of Major's Gate, (Slaughter's Mountain), Aug. 11th.

Since the battle I have sent you a short note and a telegram but I do not know whether you got either, or indeed whether they ever reached Gordonsville. I know you suffered intensely from the time you heard of the battle until you heard from me, and there must have been an interval of at least two days.

We attacked the enemy under Banks on the 9th at 4:30 P.M. in a strong position which he chose early in the morning when we were miles away, and drove them three miles on a full run, but night and excessive heat and fatigue prevented our following. We fought the battle really with only part of our forces—I mean only a part were severely engaged. Our loss was small compared with that of the enemy. We captured two cannon, General Prince and some thirty commissioned officers, and four or five hundred men. The victory was decided, but the results, beyond the moral effect on the men of both sides, will not be much. Pope's whole army has come up and vastly outnumbers us, and we must fall back. It is amusing to think Old Jack is standing here in line of battle, defiantly holding the enemy at bay while they are burying their dead under a flag of truce. I was in great danger, my horse having been struck twice by grazing pieces of shells and splinters from trees, and dirt was dashed over me several times from shells. Six or eight men were struck down so close to me as to spatter me with their blood. Launcelot came out all right. His gun was disabled and several men at the same gun were wounded.

I have been trying to write you a detailed account of the battle of Slaughter's Mountain as it is now called. The papers I have seen underrate it very much, yet in every respect it was as great a battle as that of Manassas. For the number of men killed and wounded, the number of men engaged and the length of time it was fought it was one of the most destructive of the war. Our losses in killed and wounded will be a little less than five hundred and that of the enemy, supposing their wounded to be of the same proportion to the killed that ours was, must have been fifteen hundred besides four hundred and fifty prisoners, making their losses near two thousand. On other fields I have seen I could never discover any decidedly great disproportion between their killed and ours but on this one it was so marked that I am sure I do not exaggerate when I say it was three to one. The yankees all admitted the fact when they came on the field and saw both sides, but said we had carried our dead off which was not true. We buried our dead in a few hours with a small detail while they had a large force at work all day. As the enemy ran we had the opportunity of firing into them without receiving any return fire whatsoever.

We were camped on Thursday on the turnpike from Gordonsville to Madison Courthouse, and between the former and Liberty Mills, the head of the column being about seven miles from Gordonsville. About ten o'clock in the morning we got orders from General Jackson to cook three days' rations and be ready to move at twelve which the whole army did, reaching Orange Courthouse that night. The next morning it moved on and rested between Robinson River and Crooked Run. From this position we could see the enemy's line of battle, but no indication of any advance.

As the cannon, caissons and ammunition wagons and the other wagons were crossing Crooked Run there was a delay owing to the mud on the side of the ford where the wagons came out. Major John Harmon was superintending the transit in person, but there was much delay owing to the bad landing place. Harmon has a powerful and sharp-sounding voice and is very profane. It is said he can swear at a mule team and make it jerk a wagon out of a mudhole as nothing else will. He was using his utmost endeavors in this line at the ford that day, but with no great success.

Jackson got impatient, especially for the ordinance wagons, and rode back a little with me as his only companion to hurry them along. Harmon was in full feather and the air was blue with his oaths. As Jackson came up he rather increased his energy. Jackson stood a moment and said very mildly: "Major, don't you think you would accomplish just as much without swearing so hard?"

Harmon turned with a smile that was almost contemptuous and said, "If you think anybody can make a set of damned mules pull without swearing at them you just try it, General! Just try it! I'll stand by and see how damned quick you get tired of it!" With that he stood back and commenced impatiently to walk backwards and forwards and back again while Jackson watched the ford.

The first wagon was light and had a good team and pulled out. Jackson turned with some triumph to Harmon and said, "You see, Major, how easy it is?"

"Just wait," Harmon said, "till one of those damned ordinance wagons comes along! You haven't had anything but a bunch of empties yet; don't holler until you're out of the woods, General!"

As he said it a monster came to the exit of the ford and stalled. The driver jerked the reins and whipped and did everything but swear, having recognized the General on the bank, and after some moments got it out while Harmon stood by obviously enjoying Jackson's impatience.

"Better let me damn 'em, General, nothing else will do!"

Jackson made no reply and another ordinance wagon came along. It was obviously heavily loaded and stuck at the edge of the ford despite every effort of the driver, some suggestions on the part of the General and some pushing by other drivers. Harmon was delighted and laughed a most triumphant laugh.

"What do you say now, General? Try swearing at them yourself, General, since nothing else will suit a mule!"

The General stood impatiently a moment longer, then

gathered up the reins of his horse and moved off saying in a crestfallen tone, "Well, Major, I suppose you will have to have your way!"

Before he had moved fifty yards all the pent up energy of Harmon's nature found vent in a fluent damnation which so startled the mules and their negro driver that the wagon was jerked out of the stream and was alongside the retreating general in half a minute.

I rode on with the General and he turned to the right of the road and took a view of the enemy's lines from a hill on the Crittenden farm. A sharp cannonading had already commenced and several shots were fired at the General before he got back to the Culpeper Road. While we were there he sent me down into a little valley where I found an old lady and four pretty daughters. She was a Mrs. Crittenden and lived in a very nice house which it was obvious would soon be between the two lines, and very unhealthy for that reason. They were preparing food for our soldiers who might come in and getting bandages and lint ready for those who might be wounded, yet at any moment a cannonball might have laid their house in ruins and killed them. I advised them to move, but they said they could not get away before the battle and would prefer staying in their cellar.

When we got to the edge of the woods on the road, just at the place which was called Major's Gate, the General told me to stand there and tell General A. P. Hill, when he came up, to throw his men into line of battle and support Ewell and Early, and then he and his staff rode through the gate and joined Early, whose brigade was out on the hill to the right of the Culpeper Road. It was now about four and a half in the afternoon and very hot. The battle commenced all around me and the smoke was so dense I could see very little, though, in truth, I was in no great humor for accurate observation. Like Casablanca I was obliged to stay where I was and I was in the rear of two batteries firing in different directions and drawing upon themselves a very heavy fire of the enemy. The two lines of fire converged so as to cross about where I was standing. I hope I shall never be in such a place again. The

position was not made more agreeable to me by the reflection
that the shells that were flying close to me had already taken
a chance at my brother Launcelot whose battery was thundering about one hundred yards in my front.

While I stood there several regiments came up the road in
column and deployed into line of battle just before reaching
me. One of these was commanded by Col. W. S. H. Baylor,
of Staunton. He stopped and shook hands with me, and, as
he did so, his regiment, in line of battle, passed us. A shell
exploded in them, killing and wounding six of his men. He
was as calm as if nothing had happened, and merely said,
"Steady men, steady! Close up!" After they had passed Dr.
John A. Smith, of Charleston, Jefferson County, came riding
along on a handsome horse through the fire as if nothing
was going on, and looking as cool as a cucumber. He stopped
and had a chat with me as if it was a nice loafing place.

I noticed a singular thing while waiting here. I was at the
point where troops were thrown into line of battle. I could
see them when in column down the road run out of the
ranks and hide something under the leaves in a fence corner.
I found out later they were playing cards, being superstitious
about taking them into battle. Here, too, I saw what I had
never seen before: men pinning strips of paper with their
names, company and regiment to their coats so they could
be identified if killed.

After what seemed to me a long time the firing on my front
and to the left of the road became very sharp and was nearing
me rapidly, showing that our men were either being driven
or were falling back. I could not see because there were
some low bushes in my front, but in an instant a regiment
or two burst through into the spot where I was standing, all
out of order and mixed up with a great number of yankees.
I could not understand it; I could not tell whether our men
had captured the yankees or the yankees had broken through
our line. In an instant, however, I was put at rest, for Jackson,
with one or two of his staff, came dashing across the road from
our right in great haste and excitement. As he got amongst
the disordered troops he drew his sword, then reached over

and took his battleflag from my man, Bob Isbell, who was carrying it, and dropping his reins, waved it over his head and at the same time cried out in a loud voice, "Rally, men! Remember Winder! Where's my Stonewall Brigade? Forward, men, Forward!"

As he did so he dashed to the front, and our men followed with a yell and drove everything before them. It was a wonderful scene—one which men do not often see. Jackson usually is an indifferent and slouchy looking man but then, with the "Light of Battle" shedding its radiance over him his whole person was changed. His action as graceful as Lee's and his face was lit with the inspiration of heroism. The men would have followed him into the jaws of death itself; nothing could have stopped them and nothing did. Even the old sorrel horse seemed endowed with the style and form of an Arabian.

Just as this scene was being enacted a very handsome and hatless yankee officer, not over twenty-one or two, whose head was covered with clusters of really golden curls and who had in his hand a broken sword, showing he had led the gallant charge which had broken our ranks, laid his hand on my knee as I sat on my horse and said with great emotion, "What officer is that, Captain?" And when I told him, fully appreciating the magnetism of the occasion, he seemed carried away with admiration. With a touch of nature that makes the whole world kin he waved his broken sword around his head and shouted, "Hurrah for General Jackson! Follow your General, Boys!" I leaned over, almost with tears in my eyes and said, "You are too good a fellow for me to make prisoner; take that path to the left and you can escape." He saluted me with his broken sword and disappeared in an instant. I hope he escaped.

Jackson and his men had just gone when, to my infinite relief, General A. P. Hill rode up at the head of Branch's and Pender's brigades, and hearing my account of the orders I was to deliver, put those brigades in support of Jackson's charge and they followed with a shout. My duty being discharged, I rode over to where the Rockbridge Artillery were placed under the command of Capt. Poague, to inquire about Launcelot, and found he was unhurt, and that his gun was disabled by a solid shot and had been sent to the rear, him with it. On my way to the battery I passed the body of General Winder who had been killed near the gate I called "Major's" but which may be that of the Crittenden house. His gallant form was stretched out on the ground with one or two of his staff standing around in great distress. He was still breathing but died quickly afterwards. Col. Snowden Andrews was lying not far off. He, too, was terribly wounded but there was hope enough for him for the surgeons to be at work on him, though with little hope. He had been very kind to some of my men and I found two of them with him. They were doing all they could to help him.

I then rode on to join General Jackson, who had resumed his position in the center. The fight was pretty much over, as the enemy had been driven back some three miles and our men had stopped, owing to coming darkness and the great heat. The General, about night, sent Pendleton and myself along the lines to inquire of brigade commanders whether they were in a condition to advance after a short rest. Without an exception they reported that they were short of ammunition and that their men were too exhausted to go further. They had marched some ten or twelve miles in that intense heat and then fought a great battle. They were so tired that the men were lying about in line of battle dead asleep; they dropped down wherever they were without waiting to get anything to eat. I do not believe anything short of the enemy could have revived them to action.

After riding along our whole front we got back to the General who was standing near a battery which was shelling a woods where we had reason to think the enemy were massed. The General rode up and said something to the officer commanding and turned to go away. As he did so a handsome looking officer dashed up and said, "General, General Banks says—." Then discovering his mistake he whirled around and dashed off regardless of the many demands for his surrender. An infantry officer finding he would not stop fired at him and killed him and brought his horse and dispatches to the General.

I had ridden off some little way, however, and did not see, though I heard, the shot, for which I was glad for it is not agreeable even in war to see individual men killed in your presence by a single shot.

Having reported to the General he went back a short distance and Pendleton and myself laid down on the side of the hill and went to sleep ourselves, supperless. As we got off our horses laid down immediately and seemed utterly worn out.

I have made this letter too long and must close, though I must continue the history of the next two days which are not without interest.

CHAPTER VIII

☆ ☆ ☆ ★ ☆ ☆ ☆

ALONG THE RAPPAHANNOCK

☆ ☆ ☆ ☆ ☆ ☆

August 17th.

IN MY LETTER yesterday I said we were going to move and we did, but I know nothing more than I did yesterday, except we have come to this point, near Raccoon Ford. We started out just as I closed my letter, passed through Orange Courthouse and then turned down the Rapidan River some five miles and bivouacked for the night, and are lying quietly in this beautiful country this morning. My present impression is that we will cross at Raccoon Ford and sweep around to the right in the enemy's rear at Brandy Station, while Longstreet threatens their front, and when Jackson attacks, Longstreet will cross the river and give battle. Thus the enemy will be surrounded and, if we succeed the rout will be complete. The potatoes and onions you sent me arrived just as we were starting this trip, and could not have come at a more acceptable time.

In case of battle do not be uneasy if you do not hear from me at once, for we are so cut off I cannot promptly communicate with you. William spent last night with me. I am uneasy about Eugene, from what William tells me as to his condition. God spare him and our country.

I must finish up while I have the space to write my story. I ended where Pendleton and myself went to sleep on the hillside. Before doing so we divided a small box of sardines between us, some of those you sent me, then we crawled down to the marshy ground below us to get some water. By feeling about in the dark I found a horse track sunk into the mud, which was full, and I drank about half of it, then went back near my horse and laid down close to what I thought was a sleeping man and was dead asleep as was Pendleton in an instant. When I awoke I found my neighbor was a dead yankee soldier, the sun was up and Pendleton was gone. I went down to find my horse track and found the water left in the track was much discolored by the blood which flowed from the dead yankee who was lying some two or three feet above it. The thought that I had slaked my thirst on such water made me very sick, but it soon passed away. I joined my men bivouacked near the General's headquarters. After I got a very poor breakfast of hardtack and stone-cold fried middling I was sent with some twenty men to make a scout on our right towards the Orange and Alexandria Railroad.

At Mitchell's Station we captured a small picket under a very intelligent sergeant. After getting all the information in my reach I came back with our prisoners. The Sergeant was communicative and I took him up to the General's tent, thinking he might give some valuable information. When we got there the staff was standing around the tent, holding their horse and the General's sorrel was just in front, ready for him to mount. My prisoner took his stand at the sorrel's rump to await with the rest of us the General's advent. He at once commenced, I supposed in nervous agitation, to stroke the sorrel's rump with his right hand and to pass his left hand through the tail, pulling out each time a number of hairs. This he did so often that his hand was quite full of them and one of the staff, with some asperity, just as the General came up to the horses's head, ordered him to stop, which he did and at once commenced cramming the hair into his pocket. General Jackson saw what he was doing and, to my infinite relief, said in a mild voice, "My friend, why are you tearing the hair out of my horse's tail?" The prisoner took off his hat most respectfully and with a bright smile said, "Ah, General, each one of these hairs is worth a dollar in New York." Was there ever a more delicate compliment to a man's reputation? The General was both amused and pleased at the tribute, by an enemy, to his fame. He was confused by our presence and actually blushed. He merely directed me to send the prisoner to the rear and did not question him further. I did so, but he carried his trophies with him.

While I was out on the scout Dr. Hunter McGuire went down to Mrs. Crittenden's house to see if it would answer as a hospital. He found them all safe. They had stuck it out, although the bullets had whistled through the trees and bombs had burst in the yard. They begged the doctor to take the house for a hospital, and when he told them it would be very disagreeable to have their house and yard full of wounded men, they replied that they had no higher ambition than to do what they could to give aid and comfort to our men; that they had been subjected to insults by yankee soldiers and would glory in the opportunity of nursing our sick and wounded. Dr. McGuire then referred to the possibility of General Jackson being defeated in the battle which he then thought would take place as soon as the dead were buried. The girls were very indignant at his thinking it possible Jackson could be defeated, exclaiming indignantly, "You, a man, and belonging to Jackson's army, and talk of him being defeated! You ought to be ashamed of yourself and learn courage from a helpless woman." I give the above as Dr. McGuire gave it to me.

When I was at their house the morning of the battle I was the first of our soldiers who had been there. The yankees had left them only an hour or two before. They could not believe it possible that General Jackson was so near and when I assured them he was there in person, near enough to see their house they raised their eyes to Heaven in thankfulness and seemed wonderfully relieved. The sufferings of the people of Culpeper and Fauquier can never be told, but their spirit rises to the occasion and their patriotic devotion is worthy of immortal honor.

Our army stood in line of battle all day on the 10th confronting Pope, for we learned he had come up with heavy reinforcements, and on the morning of the 11th, he sent a flag of truce asking to be allowed to send and bury his dead which was granted. The truce lasted until five in the evening, having been extended because they found much to do.

General J. E. B. Stuart came up on the 10th from Richmond

and on the 11th he went to the front and met many of his classmates and friends of the Federal army. I was with him and he introduced me to Generals Bayard and Crawford, who came over and asked for him, bringing a basket of nice things, which they lunched on and seemed to be very merry. They obviously like Stuart much and were very glad to see him, and it was amusing to hear them talking of their exploits on opposite sides, and how that counter-march had foiled something etc., all being cavalry officers. During the talks something was said about the yankee papers claiming every battle a yankee victory and Stuart bet Crawford a hat in my presence that the yankee papers would claim this battle a victory for the Federals.* Crawford took him up with the remark that even the "New York Herald" would not have the audacity to name this a yankee victory.

Jackson, learning that Pope was in command of so very large an army, withdrew on the night of the 11th without losing a man or a wagon from his front to his old position near Gordonsville. Since then General Lee has come up and the whole, or nearly the whole, of the army around Richmond has been added to ours. Pope should be cashiered for letting Jackson escape him. Had either Lee or Jackson been in his place we would all be either dead or in a yankee prison.

August 19th.

My darling little Nannie,

I wrote a long letter to your mother this morning and will send this to you by the same envelope.

You see this is dated "Stonewall Jackson's headquarters." He is called "Stonewall" because when General Lee saw General Jackson's brigade standing up in the fight at Manassas so nobly he called to his own brigade which was giving way, "Look yonder, boys! Look at Jackson standing like a stone wall!" Thus the title was given both to Jackson and to his brigade, and they are very proud of it as you may imagine.

*This hat was sent over under a flag of truce a few days later and became quite a historical item. See *War Years with Jeb Stuart* by W. W. Blackford C.M.B. III

Since I have been writing you I have heard the sound of muskets being fired and I know it was the death-knell of some of our men who were deserters and were executed on the hill right opposite to my place of bivouac. The poor fellows left our army and went over and joined the enemy, having afterwards been caught. They were tried by Court Martial and sentenced to be shot. Was it not terrible that five men should have died such a shameful death when men are so scarce and when they might have served their country and perhaps lived or, at any rate, have laid down their lives with so much honor! I felt very sad when I heard the guns fire and knew that five living men, perhaps with wives and little children like you, have been launched into eternity with so much dishonor. But this is too sad a subject to write my little girl about.

I am writing from the top of a hill which commands a view of a beautiful valley. On one side of me is General Jackson's headquarters and right in front of me is General Lee's. While I write John Scott and Dick are cooking supper, and in another fence corner my table is spread with the china your mother sent me, ready for our supper, which your Uncle William and Launcelot will take with me. I thought your Uncle William had been taken prisoner, but he turned up this evening much to my relief. We will, I think, move somewhere tonight as the enemy has moved away from our front, and, we think have moved towards Fredricksburg. We have three days' rations cooked ready to start. I had expected to write you a long letter but I have been interrupted and must stop.

August 19th to 26th.

I am doing much work now, as almost all the General's staff are laid up but Pendleton, and I have to serve in that capacity as well as that of captain of my company. I am very tired of this life and wish I was back with the regiment. I am suffering much from dysentery. In the camp at the foot of Clark's mountain we rested two days. We crossed the Rapidan at Raccoon Ford and went to camp. On the evening of the 19th, I was ordered, a little after sundown, to report with twenty men to the General for scout duty. I did so and was kept waiting an hour or so, after which he came out and joined us with Col. Pendleton, and we started off, the General leading the cavalcade. He wandered about all night in by-paths and unused roads in places where neither friend nor foe would ever pass, as far as we could see, without aim or purpose and that it was one of those freaks which sometimes seize him and which make many people think he is somewhat deranged. During the night I was riding at the side of Col. Pendleton in a dark woods, and we had interchanged one or two low-pitched remarks, when I dropped to sleep for a few moments. As I waked up I said in an undertone, but very irreverently and somewhat petulantly, "Sandy, where is the old fool taking us?" From out the darkness my companion responded in an abstracted monotone, raising his head from his saddle-bow over which he was bending: "What?" I recognized Old Jack's voice, my horse went back on its haunches and I disappeared in the gloom of the friendly darkness. I am sure he did not understand what I said. He was either asleep or praying and only knew that some remark had been addressed to him. Hereafter, I shall be more careful in the dark. My horse, which you know is a fine walker, had, while I slept, left Pendleton and ranged up alongside the General.

About daylight the General stopped and laid down on the ground, without a word to anyone, using his canteen as a pillow, and was, or appeared to be asleep in a moment. I stretched out on the top rail of a fence and also slept as soon as I did so while my horse stretched himself on the ground and took a nap. In five minutes there was not a man in the party who was not asleep, but as we were in the rear of our lines it made no difference.

We rested only half an hour, when we started again and rode straight to the top of Clark's mountain which we reached at sunrise and then had a magnificent view, including the whole Federal army under Pope stretched out before us in its various encampments ranging several miles each way

in and around Culpeper Courthouse. It was a glorious
morning and a beautiful sight, but we were all too tired
to enjoy it as we could have done under different circumstances. We were fretted, too, for we could see no reason
or good to be attained by the wearisome journey we had taken
at the expense of a night's rest. Until we reached the top of
the mountain, not a mile from our camp, we learned nothing
of the position of the enemy and our investigation was only
in hog paths and cow tracks which could be of no value to
anyone. We were all, Pendleton as well as the rest of us,
mystified by the expedition, and our conviction was that
Jackson did not know where he was or what he was doing. He
was wandering in another world. After a stay of an hour on
the mountain top we returned to camp badly used up.

The next day we commenced to move forward, the enemy
having fallen back north of the Rappahannock. In the mean-
while General Lee's whole army had come up and joined us
and we had become again a part of the Army of Northern
Virginia, under Lee's immediate command. We pressed forward, following close upon the enemy. I was constantly engaged day and night and my old enemy dysentery set upon
me very badly.

I was often at General Lee's headquarters and spoke to him
the first time. It is impossible for me to describe the impression he made upon me by his bearing and manners. I
felt myself in the presence of a great man, for surely there
never was a man upon whom greatness is more stamped. He
is the handsomest person I ever saw; every motion is instinct
with natural grace, and yet there is a dignity which, while
awe-inspiring, makes one feel a sense of confidence and trust
that is delightful when it is remembered that there are at
present so many contingencies dependent upon his single
will.

I speak of his headquarters but all the interviews I have
had with him were when we were both mounted. I would
ride up to him on the march and make some report from
General Jackson as directed or else deliver a dispatch. He
always had some word to say which cheered me, asked me

questions as to where different brigades or batteries were moving, or something which, if not useful to him, made me feel of some consequence. This was not the case with General Jackson. He is ever monosyllabic and receives and delivers a message as if the bearer was a conduct pipe from one ear to another. There is a magnetism in Jackson, but it is not personal. All admire his genius and great deeds; no one could love the man for himself. He seems to be cut off from his fellow men and to commune with his own spirit only, or with spirits of which we know not. Yet the men are almost as enthusiastic about him as over Lee, and whenever he moves about on his old sorrel, with faded uniform and weather-stained cap slouched down over his left eye, and one shoulder some two inches higher than the other, most men shout with enthusiasm. He rides on rapidly without making any sign of recognition, and no one knows whether he is pleased or not. It is a saying in the army if a shout is heard, "There goes Jackson or a rabbit." The old sorrel is not more martial in appearance than his master, and the men say it takes a half a dozen bomb shells to wake either of them up to their full capacity, but when once roused there is no stopping either of them until the enemy has retreated.

Lee, on the other hand, does not hesitate to avail himself of some of the aids of martial pomp, though perfectly simple in his daily life, walk and conversation. His favorite horse is a handsome grey called "Traveler," and the General is so fine a rider that his horse looks like a picture whenever he is seen. Then Lee wears well-fitted undress grey uniform with the handsomest trimmings, a handsome sword and cavalry boots, making him the grandest figure on any field. The men, in addition to the confidence they have in the genius of Jackson, have for Lee a proud admiration and personal devotion "passing the love of woman." He is called "Marse Robert" and "Uncle Bob" and whenever seen the men shout and rally around him as their darling chief for whom they would willingly die. He receives the adulation of the men with the most graceful courtesy and acknowledges their shouts with uncovered head and a bow which Louis XIV might have envied.

I often think how these two men, so utterly different in their characteristics and style should not only be such friends and have such confidence in each other, but should each seem to be the perfect military leader. Another very remarkable fact is that they are types respectively of the two classes of civilization which have marked and classified the Anglo-Saxon world for more than two centuries. Jackson is as distinct a Roundhead covenanter as Cromwell or Ireton. A Presbyterian by faith, a predestinarian by conviction to the extent of fatalism, and with every practice, habit and style of life which marked the leaders of the Commonwealth. He is not wanting in that forbidding manner and costume which robbed their virtues of so much that was attractive, yet he has all the fiery zeal which makes them successful and formidable.

Lee, on the other hand has all the characteristics of the Cavalier except their vices. Their virtues come to him through a long line of distinguished ancestry from the original Lee who came over with the Conqueror and whose descendants fought under the banner of Charles I and secured to Virginia the legend: "En Vat Virginia Quintam." In appearance, bearing and manner he is a perfect type of all that is admirable in that class, and yet he arouses in others that enthusiasm that is as effective as the zeal of the Puritan as a motive of action. The contrast and parallel might run on still further if I had time.

On the evening of the 21st of August we went into bivouac about a mile from Brandy Station. I was very sick, having been all day and much of the night before in the saddle, suffering so much from dysentery that I could not keep my sword belt buckled without great pain. I asked and obtained leave to be back some half-mile to the residence of Mr. James Barbour, where General Stuart had his headquarters that I might spend the night with William and get the service of a doctor, some medicine and possibly some more nourishing food. I did not get off until after night and when I reached the house I found to my great disgust and discomfort that General Stuart had moved two hours before, and there was no one in the house but an old woman who was taking care of it. She had nothing I could possibly eat. I was too much broken down to go back, so after tying my horse in the yard I laid down on the porch, but I suffered so much I could not sleep. About midnight I discovered my horse, (the black) had broken away and I had to go out to look for him. I found him grazing near the house but as I approached him he moved on and I had to follow him for over a mile before I caught him, and then the exercise made me much worse. The night was one of pain and suffering and if I live a thousand years I shall never forget it, for its agonies, both of body and mind, will ever haunt me; each acting and reacting on the other.

At daybreak I was in the saddle again, without breakfast, and got back to General Jackson's headquarters just as he was about to move and commence the day's operations. My company had finished breakfast but I could eat nothing and only took a hard cracker or two for my day's rations.

As the sun rose we moved on towards the Rappahannock River. Longstreet was to our right and a furious cannonading was going on down at the railroad bridge. When we reached the hills overlooking the river heavy cannonading from side to side was opened up at once along our front, and it continued as we moved up the river. While moving on the crest of the hill a solid shot from the enemy's battery passed through the horse of my sergeant Bob Isbell, who was carrying General Jackson's battle flag, the same he had waved at Slaughter's Mountain. The horse fell over perfectly dead; it was between me and the General, its head lapping on the General's horse and its rump on mine and the ball did not miss the nose of my horse six inches. Isbell was unhurt, jumped up, cut his saddle loose from the dead horse, put it in an ambulance wagon, seized the musket of a man in a passing regiment who had been killed by the same shot and assumed his place in ranks, handing me the battle flag to carry.*

Jackson saw the horse fall at his side but seemed to take no

*Bob Isbell remained in this infantry regiment during the rest of the campaign, when he returned to my company with a horse he had captured and a letter from the Colonel giving high praise for his distinguished gallantry. I recommended him for promotion but no notice was taken of my letter. C.M.B.

notice of it and did not ask any questions about the man who was on the horse. I called his attention to him however and to his having so gallantly and promptly taken his place in the infantry regiment, to which he replied without seeming to appreciate what I said, "Very commendable, very commendable." That was a favorite expression of his. On one occasion when a courier from my company was killed with a message from the General, he asked with some asperity why he did not return, and on being told that he had been killed, made the same remark, "Very commendable."

We moved on parallel to and up the river subject to a continuous cannonade from the other side. The infantry of the corps, out of sight and protected by the hills, were moving in the same direction. As we moved up the river we met William with a message from Stuart to General Jackson. William's orders were, after delivering the message, to go on ahead up the river to Cunningham farm, in the fork between the Hazel and the Rappahannock Rivers, and ascertain as much as possible about the position of the enemy and report to Stuart. General Jackson ordered me to take twenty men and go with him and report the result of the scout to him. I was much pleased with this and we hurried forward, crossed the Hazel near its mouth and then dismounted, leaving the men in ambush and with only two men we walked on until we got into Mr. Cunningham's yard, using his house and outhouses as a screen as we approached. This put us on the bluff almost over-hanging the Rappahannock. Just a little below on the opposite bluff, there was a four-gun battery of the enemy supported by a regiment of infantry. They were apparently not expecting an attack, as most of the artillery were gathered around a party sitting on the ground playing poker. We could distinctly hear the exclamations as the game proceeded, and when there was any gap in the circle around them could see the cards with our glasses. We sent couriers back to tell the Generals the situation and to point out to them a field on our side which could be used by a battery in attack. This hill was below the mouth of Hazel River. After the courier started we waited anxiously to see the result, noting with our glasses, from trees and other high points which we could reach without attracting observation, everything which was going on north of the river in our range.

In about half or three-quarters of an hour we saw Major John B. Brockenborough's battalion of artillery come out on the hill we had indicated and sweep around at a gallop in a battery, and in less time than it takes for me to write it opened fire on the gambling artillerymen of the enemy. The very first shell which reached their side exploded in the midst of the party, killing and wounding several. Until this explosion the enemy either did not see or did not heed the arrival of the battery. So unexpected was the attack that all the infantry and artillerymen ran off, leaving the enemy cannon in battery and the muskets stacked. Brockenborough kept up a most effective fire on the retreating foe. In a few minutes we saw a regiment of our cavalry come out of the woods, dash down the hill towards the river and begin to cross, obviously with the purpose of securing the abandoned guns on the bluff above. William recognized Major Von Borcke of Stuart's and Col. Rosser, and proposed we should join them, so we gathered up our men, crossed the river and came up in their rear. We directed our attention to the abandoned guns while Von Borcke and Rosser followed the fugitives. We got two of the cannon safely over and a number of small arms but soon saw Rosser's men falling back before a brigade or more of yankee infantry. We worked as long as possible and only quit when the regiment got back to us. We made for the ford pell-mell and while we were crossing the enemy had occupied the bluffs above us and fired at us, but with little effect. Most of Rosser's men crossed at the ford lower down. The cannon secured were hauled off by horses sent over from Brockenborough's battery. Had we had ten minutes more we could have gotten all four of them. Brockenborough deserves much credit for his part in the little episode.

After this William and I parted. I joined Jackson and he Stuart. When I reached him Jackson was crossing Hazel River.

Shortly afterwards word was brought that the enemy had crossed the river just ahead of us. He galloped forward, followed by my men and his staff and turned towards the river into the forest. The enemy were shelling the woods heavily. The General became satisfied the enemy were not over in any force and did not propose to attempt to cross. As soon as he came to this conclusion he dismounted in the midst of the severe shelling and seated himself on a stump while he wrote a dispatch to General Lee, which he told me he wanted me to carry. While he wrote we stood around him but he made us scatter so should a shell explode it would not be so disastrous. An infantry brigade was passing at the time, moving up the river just in our front. A shell exploded close by and a boy-soldier in the ranks fell and rolled over almost at the General's feet. At the same time a solid shot or unexploded shell struck just in front of us scattering the dirt all over us and half burying the poor boy and then went on its course without harming any of us. It threw the dust all over the paper on which the General was writing. He shook the dirt off the paper, looked up then in an abstracted manner, got up, walked around the stump, sat down again just as he was and went on writing. Never did I see a man who took so much time to write a short note— at least so it seemed to me, and I doubt not to all the rest who were waiting around him, though others may not so record it. While we waited I am sure a shell exploded near us every quarter of a minute but none of us were hurt. We picked up the poor boy, who, though not over sixteen, seemed a perfect soldier in dress and accoutrements. We could find no wound except a slight incision at the base of his neck in front, from which no blood exuded, but I suppose a small piece of shell entered there and passed into his heart for death was instantaneous. At last the General finished and handed me the dispatch and told me to ride rapidly—which I was very glad to do you may be sure—and in five minutes I was out of the line of fire. Just as I was starting a big shell struck a tree over my head covering me with splinters and leaves.

I hurried back on our line of march some three or four miles and found General Lee resting on the roadside. It was then just noon. I gave him the dispatch and in answer to his questions informed him how things were going on on our part of the line of march. He ordered me to wait awhile, saying he had positive information that the enemy were preparing to cross a reconnoitering party of several brigades just at the point where the shelling was so furious, and that the shelling was preparatory. He had sent one of my men named O'Keefe, with a dispatch about a half-hour before. I knew O'Keefe was a stupid ass and would not be likely to seek Jackson through any heavy shelling, so I offered to return with the dispatch, as General Jackson, I told him, was of the opinion it was only a feint and had gone on up river. He told me no, for he would want to send a more important message as soon as the enemy had actually crossed, news which he was expecting.

I had a fine opportunity of seeing not only Lee but many other distinguished officers while I was waiting. Colonel Charles Marshall, of Baltimore, and Colonel C. S. Venable of his staff were both very polite to me; rather an unusual thing in staff to line officers of subordinate rank. Lee never has any but gentlemen around him.

In a short time a courier rode up bearing a dispatch which said the enemy had crossed the river in some force and had cut Jackson's wagon train in two and was doing much damage, but that General William B. Taliaferro had hurried his brigade forward and had driven them back. General Lee then wrote a dispatch to General Jackson which he directed me to carry him as soon as I could find him, but first to hurry back to Jackson's column and as soon as I struck it to order up in his name any troops I found to the support of General Taliaferro, and to tell that General he must drive the enemy back and remain in that locality to guard until next morning. My horse had had a good feed, thanks to Colonel Venable, and I had had a good lunch, so I started at a rapid rate on the return. Just before I reached Hazel River I came up with General Longstreet and his staff. They were holding a drumhead court-martial over a spy whom they had caught. I stopped to make some enquiries as to what had been heard of the enemy in front. They knew nothing but told me the spy had been condemned and would be shot at once. I was somewhat shocked and rode off rapidly, but I had gone but a short distance when I heard a platoon fire and I knew it was the poor creature's death-knell.

It was about three o'clock in the evening and in the far west an angry bank of dark cloud was forming, from which was to be heard distant thundering. I rode rapidly on and soon came within the sound of the rattle musketry, and I was soon by the side of the regiment commanded by Colonel A. G. Taliaferro, who, you will remember, married your cousin, Agnes Marshall, of Oak Hill. His regiment was in line of battle engaged quite actively and under a heavy fire of small arms and cannon. I rode up to the old Colonel and asked for his brother, the General. He at once recognized me and, as was his habit, was profoundly polite and instead of answering me and letting me go on my way he asked after your health and that of your sister Nannie and opened a general conversation in his peculiar whispering and repeating style. I was on thorns; I wanted to deliver my important message to the General and I did not wish to stand talking, even about you, under such fire. At last he let me know the General was further to our left and I brought the conversation to a close, hurried on and found him. His brigade was in line of battle and was slowly pushing the enemy back towards the river. After giving him General Lee's orders I hurried up the river towards the bridge at the Fauquier White Sulphur Springs, near which I learned General Jackson was stationed. I passed many wagons the enemy disabled in their raid.

It has taken me a short time to write this, but several hours had been occupied in doing what I did, and the storm and night had both set in by the time I had left General Taliaferro and gotten back to my proper road. And such a storm! Many thousand men will remember it as long as they live. It came with a fury unsurpassed. I have never seen such lightning, heard such thunder or felt such a rain. The night was as dark as blackness itself, and I could only find my way by the gleam of the uncertain lightning, the flashes of which were so constant that my eyes were blinded. I could make no progress, and had lost my road and I knew it was impossible to find General Jackson or anyone else. I was in a dense forest, which made the storm more terrible and made it appear more frightful than even the shelling to which we had been subjected early in the day. Men were lying around everywhere, and as I wandered about amidst the vivid lightning, the devastating wind and the falling limbs, I was constantly accused in no very pious nor complimentary terms and warned not to ride over someone if I did not want a bullet through my head. At last a very pleasant voice said from under an oilcloth, "Who is that?"

I answered, "Captain Blackford, of the Second Virginia Cavalry looking for General Jackson."

"How do you do, Charley," said the voice from under the oilcloth, "you'll never find Old Jack in this storm. Get down and get under my oilcloth."

Try as I could, I could not place the voice. I did not answer as I tried to place it.

"You don't know who I am, do you?" the voice asked.

"No, I can't place your voice."

"Don't you remember Davison Penn who went to school with you in Lynchburg ten years ago?" the voice asked.

I remembered Penn. He was the grandson of old Mrs. Bradfute who once lived in old Colonel Maurice Langhorne's house on Diamond Hill and a brother of the beautiful Miss Imogene Penn, who married Mr. James J. Lyons of Richmond. I accepted his invitation, got down, tied my horse to a bush and got under his oilcloth to rest, though as wet as a drowned rat. I was not satisfied I was doing my duty, so I laid down only a few minutes and then, the storm still showing no signs of abatement, bid my host farewell; he was the colonel of a Louisiana regiment. I mounted my horse and again started on my profitless search, cold, wet, and hungry.

It was approaching morning but not a ray of light was visible and the storm and rain were unabated. After awhile

I saw a light down in the valley in the woods and rode to the house whence it shone and dismounted and knocked but no one opened the door or answered my call. I knocked with my sabre hilt louder and more imperiously, and at last someone came to the door who I could see was a soldier. He poked his head out but seeing I was an officer told me I could not come in. I pledged secrecy, told how wet and cold I was, but all in vain; but when I said I was a cavalry officer they seemed to think there was no danger and let me in. There was only one room in the cabin, but in the fireplace there was a big blazing fire and around the room some four or five freshly slaughtered hogs from which the men were cutting pieces of flesh and cooking it on sticks. I never saw such a set of scoundrels as their faces indicated them to be. They were all from Louisiana and were talking in French. I felt a little uneasy and kept my pistol free in case I should need it but they were polite enough and gave me some of their cooked meat which I was glad to get. As soon as I got warm I left them and, to my joy, found the clouds breaking and saw light beginning to streak the East.

With the light of dawn I soon was on the trail of General Jackson and heard he was bivouacked on the hill above the bridge where I heard he was the evening before. I also heard that the General had sent General Early across the bridge the night before with two or three brigades and that the river had risen during the night and washed the bridge away, leaving Early over there without support and exposed to attack from the whole yankee army, for there was no way for him to get back.

At sunrise I found General Jackson on the top of the hill overlooking the river, which was booming; having burst its bounds it was overflowing the whole bottom of the hill with a restless flood, upon which was borne every variety of drift-wood and other debris. Far out we could see the piers and abutments of the bridge in perfect condition, though the bridge itself was gone. Jackson was sitting on his horse entirely alone and very wet, as wet, perhaps, as I was, but whether he had been out all night as I had I could not tell.

I handed him Lee's dispatch, which I think was something of a reprimand for leaving his column so unprotected as to be attacked as it was. At all events the communication did not improve Jackson's temper, which doubtless was somewhat soured by his wet clothes, his long vigil and his anxiety about Early. After reading the dispatch, which he tore up I imagined with some extra vigor, he continued for several minutes to gaze upon the abutments of the bridge, and then, as the rays of the rising sun lit up the landscape, gave his old sorrel a somewhat vicious dig with his spur and started down the hill towards the bridge at a rapid gait, bidding me to follow, which was the only word he addressed to me. When he reached the water, he went straight on, and a few yards our horses were swimming, but as the water at that point somewhat eddied we met no great current until we were very near the southern abutment, but with something of a spurt we conquered the current and landed safely. When we reached the abutment we were the only two persons who were out there, and so remained for near an hour, during which no word passed between us. His staff, or such of them as were fit for duty, had been sent off and did not join him until much later. The first person who swam out was General A. P. Hill, but General Jackson was so abstracted and so rude that he turned around and went back without any commands or instructions.

A number of the soldier and some of the engineer officers soon came out, and as the river was falling rapidly, a volunteer bridge-force was organized and construction of a temporary bridge was commenced, resting on driftwood and trash hung on the piers and abutments; using these hammocks, which nearly touched each other, a passway was completed by four o'clock in the evening which would support a cannon. Before noon the river had subsided so that men could wade out and by four it was within its banks.

I stood all day by General Jackson out on the abutment in the sun, which had become very hot, but I do not think he addressed a single remark to me except the order to follow when he started out. He said little to anyone, nothing by way of conversation. He was obviously suffering from intense anxiety and thought of nothing but securing Early's safety. That Early was not wiped out was wonderful. He could receive no reinforcements, and the whole of Pope's army might have struck him.

I secured hay for my horse from the stacks that had been washed down the river and hung on the abutments, but I got nothing for myself but one army biscuit which a private from the bridge builders gave me. Someone in the neighborhood, about two o'clock, sent the General a very good dinner, with fried chicken, tomatoes, and iced milk which he ate as if in a fit of abstraction, without inviting me to share it with him. He left a considerable amount in the basket in which it was sent and I was strongly tempted to ask him for it, but I was not sure how the request would be received, so I remained silent. I do not think he remembered there was such a person as your husband, whom you value so highly, and I do not blame him, for he had much on his mind and terrible responsibilities pressed on him. I had been subjected to great fatigue, exposure and excitement and the disease had been so increased that by four o'clock I was in a high fever and had a raging headache.

As Lawton's brigade commenced to cross the new bridge late in the evening to reinforce Early and it was obvious the danger was over, Jackson's mind seemed to return to its usual channels, and he turned to me and in a more sympathetic voice said: "I have had nothing to eat all day, have you?" I replied in the negative and he said without a word of thanks or encouragement, "You can retire to your quarters." Where my quarters were I did not know and I was so sick and weak I could hardly get on my horse. However I soon found them and my faithful John Scott fixed me up quite a comfortable place to rest in a fence corner, and I laid down as sick and tired a man as there was in the army and in a few moments was sound asleep. I was much more unwell when I awoke at sunrise than I was when I laid down.

General Early recrossed about daylight after two nights and a day of great danger and hardship. He had held the whole yankee army in check all that time with about two brigades. Soon after I got up, Col. Pendleton, who slept near me, told me that the General was angry with General Talia-ferro for not having come up that night of the rain, and had sent for him. I explained to the Adjutant why Taliaferro had not come up, and that I had given him General Lee's order to stay where he did stay and not to leave until the next day. Pendleton replied that he supposed Taliaferro would explain and that all would be satisfactory. When he came up General Jackson asked him why he had not joined the rest of the corps that night, but was so hasty he did not give Taliaferro a chance to explain, and was very rude and unjust to him. Taliaferro behaved with much dignity and, as he was not allowed to explain, made no explanation, though I was close at the time and could have proved he was not to blame. My opinion is that Jackson, and not Taliaferro, was to blame.

Soon after breakfast the army moved across the river to the Fauquier White Sulphur Springs, where I am now lying stretched out on a cot with a high fever and the doctors at-tending to me. I am very sick and much prostrated. I was in no condition to undergo the terrible fatigue and exposure of the past week. I don't know what will become of me. The army will move forward today towards the mountains for the pur-pose of outflanking Pope. I suppose that Longstreet will probably keep the direct line in Pope's front, but of all this I know nothing.

A note by Mrs. Blackford.

Here Mr. Blackford's letters cease for awhile as he was too ill to write or be moved for several days. Then he was sent home and laid up for several weeks. He left [when recovered] by the cars to Charlottesville where he picked up his horses left at Mr. Colston's "Hill and Dale" then continued via Madison Courthouse and Winchester to Bunker Hill where he found his company again on duty at General Jackson's headquarters.

A letter from Capt. Blackford. Bunker Hill, October 14th.

I am here at headquarters but with nothing to do but lie on the ground and while away the time. Nothing from you as yet, but I know the letters have gone to the regiment and have sent for them. Today we had some excitement arising from Stuart's return from his "grand Rounds" in Pennsylvania. He went as far as Chambersburg, capturing five hundred prisoners and six hundred and fifty horses, destroying two large manufacturing establishments and a quantity of military stores, and clothing his men perfectly. He was supposed to be a yankee brigade as he passed some points in Pennsylvania and was fed by the citizens with everything nice. When the people complained of his pressing their horses and such things they were told that McClellan was to blame for not protecting them better. It was a well planned raid and successfully executed. His loss was only one man slightly wounded and one captured. The captured man was so drunk he could not ride and had to be left behind, but his horse and arms were brought off. General Jackson is in ecstasy. He met General Stuart at forty yards from his tent and exclaimed: "How do you do, Pennsylvania!" I am anxious to see William who was on the trip I suppose. Had I been here I would have gotten leave to go off on the General's staff. It would have been worth a whole campaign for pleasure. Tell Eugene I am on the lookout for a horse for him and have offered four hundred dollars for one which I know to be first rate. Send me a blanket and two quires of paper. We have only poor beef to eat, and that without salt, and flour without lard, salt or soda, with which to cook our biscuits. This country has been laid waste. Even the green corn out in the fields has been used up. What the people are to do I do not know.

In my absence, for want of care, my men have become much infested with vermin, derived largely from camping so often on camp grounds recently used by Federal and Confederate troops alternately. I find it impossible to keep them off me, but I am having a thorough scouring and washing and hope I will get the men in better condition. I heard one of the men, who was inspecting his clothes, say yesterday: "Come out, old fellow; I've raised the black flag now: no more prisoners: I paroled you last week and you're back in the ranks this week fighting me with twenty grand-children at your back." Sumpter asked me whether I knew what was the matter with B— who was very unwell. I said no. He replied, "He's lousy." I was shocked, as he is the neatest man in the company. "Yes," he continued, "that is the matter with him and we are all afraid to tell him." I ordered Sumpter to tell him, and he at once made an investigation and found it was so. He will now be well soon.

Bunker Hill, October 17.

This is my birthday. I am twenty-nine today and I have no birthday gift to send you unless it be a kiss which I may waft you on the breeze. Nannie must catch it and give it to you. Captain Samuel Henry Early, who is now on General Jubal A. Early's staff, came for me today and took me over to dine with him, for which I was grateful, for I had nothing. The whole army was ready to move, I know not where. Generals Lee, Longstreet, Jackson and Stuart have been all day in the front reconnoitering and it looks as if we are about to have a general battle, but we poor line officers know nothing. I would be glad of anything to break the monotony of the life I am leading now.

Martinsville, October 20th.

As I told you in my last letter there has been a forward movement all along the line but it has not brought on an engagement, though it may do so at any time. We are now in the country in which so much of your girlhood was spent. I often imagine you as a girl dashing about on horseback through these beautiful hills and valleys and wonder what you would have thought could you have seen a picture of your future husband as he is now with his surroundings. The country is of course much changed since you were here five years ago. Now it is one vast camp and much devastated, having been in the hands of first one then the other army.

I went to the Presbyterian church yesterday and there I met a Mr. Morrison, to whom I had been accidentally introduced the day before. He took me home with him to dinner, which I enjoyed no little. Who Mr. Morrison is I do not know but he gives exemplary dinners and has two nice looking daughters, even though they ignore the second 'p' in pumpkin —an omission which no wise affected the virtue of their pies made from it.

In the evening I went to Mr. Holmes Conrad's and was heartily welcomed by the whole family and took supper with them. Jackson's corps is now engaged in tearing up the railroad track. Yesterday evening the houses belonging to the Baltimore and Ohio Railroad Company were burned including the handsome depot. This burning I regard as very foolish and only injures private property and alienates good-will. It in no wise advances our cause. Burning bridges and tearing up tracks retard the movements of the enemy, but not burning up a depot, or the houses of the railroad employees. The people here are a majority Union in their sentiments; especially is this so with the laboring classes and the railroad employees. The men, of course, keep quiet, but the women are very open-mouthed in their abuse of us, and swore like troopers when the depot was burned.

Bunker Hill, October 26th.

We are back here and did up the Baltimore and Ohio very thoroughly. It will take the yankees a month to repair damages so as to restore communications thoroughly. Why we were not attacked when stretched out as we were will ever be a mystery to me. It showed great want of skill on the part of the Federal generals.

One of the days we were on the excursion I was placed in charge of a picket-post on the railroad nearest the enemy, in the direction of Harper's Ferry. I had about fifty men under me and I could see the picket of the enemy, of equal force, about three hundred yards down the railroad toward the ferry. My picket was stationed at the house of a section foreman, whose young and pretty wife was a great rebel. Her husband, whatever his sympathies, was in the employ of the railroad company and had thought it best to remain inside the Federal lines. She was quite a refined person for one of her position and more educated than might be expected. She was kind to us and delighted above all things in hearing of Lee, Jackson and Stuart, for whom she had the most romantic fascination.

It happened that on the second day there General Jackson and one or two of his staff rode out to inspect the enemy's position from our post. He stood and gazed from his horse through his glass long at the enemy's position, during which time our pretty hostess found out who it was and seemed almost overcome with the double emotion of awe and admiration. She watched him earnestly, and just as she thought he was through and might go off, she ran into the house and brought out her baby, quite a handsome boy of about eighteen months and handing it up to the General asked him to bless it for her. He seemed no more surprised at this strange request than Queen Elizabeth at being asked to touch for the "King's Evil." He turned to her with great earnestness and, with a pleasant expression on his stern face, took the child in his arms, held it to his breast, closed his eyes and seemed to be, and I doubt not was, occupied for a minute or two with prayer, during which we took off our hats and the young mother leaned her head over the horse's shoulder as if uniting in the prayer. The scene was very solemn and unusual.

It was my wish at the moment that I were a poet or a painter, to put the scene in immemorial words or upon an eternal canvas, the picture of him sitting there on his old sorrel at the end of the wrecked and torn up rail line, the grey section house to one side, the breastworks of logs and iron at the other, while behind were the trees, their autumn foliage turning brown. Around-about the soldiers in their worn and patched clothing, in a circle at a respectful distance, while his staff officers sat a little to one side. Then Jackson, the warrior-saint of another era, with the child in his arms, head bowed until his greying beard touched the fresh young hair of the child, pressed close to the shabby coat that had been so well acquainted with death. And what did he ask the Lord for the child amid the destruction and dislocation of war so strewn about at his feet? What could he ask for but divine protection from bullets and starvation and the dislocation of war which already had cost me two of my little loved ones. For the first time it brought to me that this stern, enigmatic man whom I admired, respected but never loved, had another side to him I had never before seen; that of a tender man of family.

When he finished he handed the child back to its mother without a word, who thanked him with streaming eyes while he rode off back down the roadbed.

I spent the night before with William at General Stuart's headquarters, where I found everything as gay and lively as if there was no such thing as a war going on. They were encamped at Mr. Stephen Dandridge's beautiful place, "The Bower," where there are now staying five or six beautiful girls, and every night there is a gay party in the house, where the General and William lead the dance until one o'clock. I was tired and dirty and did not go into the house, but spent the evening out in the camp in a very agreeable tete-a-tete with the Honorable Charles Lawley, an M. P. and correspondent of the "London Times." He is very intellectual and very agreeable. I was charmed with him. On the death of his father he will be Lord somebody; I do not remember who.

With General Stuart as a guest, there is also the correspondent for the "London Illustrated News," Mr. Vizetelly. He is sketching for his paper. He has a sketch of Stuart and his staff and many other scenes. He is not a statesman like Mr. Lawley, but he has seen the whole world and what is in it and is the best talker I have ever heard, though he seems to look upon the world only with reference to the amount of amusement it will afford him. Many Englishmen are now visiting our army and are acting as aides upon the staffs of different generals.

Berryville, October 31st.

I got back to the regiment, much to my joy, last week as Jackson has no further use for my company. I was very warmly welcomed back by all the officers and men and find it very pleasant.

General Longstreet has recommended me for the new position of Judge Advocate of his corps, which, if I am appointed, will put me on his staff. Owing to the great difficulty in getting horses, I find it hard to keep my company up to its full complement of men that I shall be glad to make the exchange, but I do not know what my chances are or when the appointment will be made—not for some time I suppose. There is some talk of Munford being made a brigadier, in which case Lieutenant Colonel Watts will become Colonel, and he told me yesterday, I would be Major. In which case, of course, I would not accept the staff appointment even if tendered me.

I have been today on a scout near your old home. Edgemont in Loudoun County. From the top of the mountain at Snicker's Gap we saw the enemy below very plainly. Edgemont is in the space between the opposite pickets. I find it hard to write as we have no camp and are only bivouacked. I am sitting on a bundle with a plank on my lap, upon one end of which is a lantern and an inkstand.

November 2nd.

Though this has been Sunday it has had its excitements. I had a very comfortable breakfast at an old Mrs. Washington's where I have arrangements to get breakfasts and suppers better than we can get them at camp where we have about only one skillet to every ten men. Even a Captain has to sop out of the skillet with the others. We are cut off from our wagons and have no conveniences. After breakfast I got a good wash and shave and went up to the Episcopal church to hear Reverend Mr. Suter preach.

The enemy were advancing their lines and had taken possession of Snicker's Gap and I thought it possible the regiment would be called out, so, like all the others who attended church, I went with my sabre and pistol and had John Scott hold my horse in the yard. The service was a nervous one, for we could hear an occasional cannon fire and several of the generals and many of the artillery men and officers were called out. I anticipated that we would be also, but, as our regiment had been on heavy duty we were allowed to rest and sat through the whole service. I saw a lady sitting by a colonel, her husband I suppose, who was called out of church from her side. As he left her, her head sunk over the back of the pew in front and I saw her shiver in agony of prayers and tears. War was brought very close to her and she felt all its horrors.

Mr. Logan Osborne's, November 6th.

I am in command of a picket line on the Shenandoah now, with three companies under me. Last night I had a narrow escape. I had been inspecting the pickets along the bank of the river and had sent word along the line that I had gone outside so I could get a better idea of what the enemy were doing. After I had finished, I undertook to come into the headquarters of the line, where my own company was stationed. The wind was blowing very cold and made it hard to hear. As I came up the hill from towards the river I saw the form of the vidette and his horse against the sky, which in the moonlight clearly showed up. I heard him say, "Halt!", and I responded. I thought he replied as he should have done, "Advance friend, and give the countersign," and hence I rode forward. When about ten feet from him he fired directly at me. The bullet passed through the lock of my hair above my ear and the powder stuck in my face. Before he could fire again he discovered who I was and thought he had killed me, and I never saw such suffering. It was a long time before I could make him understand I was not dead. He then bound me over not to tell the men about it, but before he had finished the whole company came up at gallop thinking the enemy were at hand. I made the best story to relieve him I could, much to his gratification. The man was Virginius Dunnington, but I do not want you to let it be known at home as he is very sensitive about it.

Linden Station, November 10th.

Here I am on picket. Yesterday we made a scout of great length and reached this place late at night without supper and are this morning practically without breakfast. The army will, I think, move very soon, but continue to direct to me at Winchester though I am so far from that place and have the outpost of my command at Markham Station, in Fauquier County. Good-bye, I must start off now, as I have a long ride ahead of me inspecting the outposts.

November 12th.

We have moved east of the ridge and my headquarters are now in Fauquier. We are daily in contact with the outposts and pickets of the enemy. I called to see Mr. Ed. C. Marshall's family at Markham yesterday, your relations, and was most cordially received. They are one day in our line and the next in the enemy's. I am glad to say they have not suffered much from the yankees. I suppose Mr. Marshall being the son of the Chief Justice protected them somewhat. They seemed quite cheerful and were glad to see me and wanted me to stay awhile, but the enemy was too close for me to go into the house. Many of your Marshall relations have suffered very much from the depredations of the enemy.

November 13th—Same camp.

I was sent yesterday with my company to "feel" for the enemy's position and strength at Barker's Crossroads where they are known to have a considerable camp. I took a circuitous route through the mountains, stopping to make inquiries at "Happy Creek" where some of the Marshall's live, and came within a half mile of the main force without being perceived by the pickets, then suddenly with a few men, I reached a hill just above them from which I could make observations with my glasses and gain all the information I wanted. Leaving my men in a glen I rode alone around to get another view, approaching with great caution. I found a good place to make an observation and then turned to leave. Just as I did so a fellow, who had sneaked on me hidden by a stone fence, rose up from behind it at close pistol range and resting his rifle on the fence took a shot at me with deliberate aim. His bullet passed where my body would have been had I not thrown myself out of the saddle upon the side of my horse as he fired. His bad marksmanship saved me. Had our positions been changed there would have been a dead yankee. Before the war to have been shot at in this way would have been quite an incident but now it is nothing unless you are hit. I was smoking at the time and did not drop my pipe or lose the fire out of it. My company, though small, is one of the most efficient in the regiment. I have only three men absent, which is a very small proportion and less than any other company.

I forgot to mention that yesterday I captured one of the enemy's picket-posts and, among other acquisitions, got a fine oil-cloth, which as I have lost my oil-cloth coat, is a blessing. I was entertained yesterday at the house of Mr. Thomas G. Marshall. The family was very kind to me. They gave my whole company apples and cider, and offered to give them all a dinner. They have lost some thirty negroes, besides horses, cattle and all kinds of provender. The people through this section are much more loyal to the South since they were overrun by yankees.

You may let Mr. Early have the bird-shot I have at home but not the powder; it must be saved for sterner duty. I believe General Jackson's army is still in the Valley. I am at a loss to know what General Lee means by dividing his army while the enemy is clearly concentrating his, but I suppose he knows better than I do, at all events I am willing to leave it with him.

I hear Mr. Nancy has sold the house my office is in to Mr. Maurice Moore. Ask Father to see that my right as a tenant is preserved, for when the war is over I shall need it again, I hope!

Your description of the flowers blooming in the garden made me very homesick. I can picture how the place looks and compare it with the chill bleakness of my bivouac; but we must not be cast down, the roses will bloom as sweetly when the war is over in the garden and on your cheeks as now, and will, I trust, bloom for me in peace and happiness, for if the yankees fail on this "On to Richmond" movement I believe we will have peace before next autumn.

Near Fredericksburg, November 30th.

We, the whole regiment, have been through some of the most arduous duty of the war so far. As you know, Lee has moved his army down and our brigade under General Fitz Lee, had been acting as a curtain to keep the yankees from knowing what the army has been doing. Every man seemed to know that General (R. E.) Lee's move must be carried out with the most complete secrecy and did yeoman work driving in yankee pickets and scouting parties, guarding every little footpath and stopping all traffic across the lines. Needless to say it meant every man in the saddle most the time with little in the way of food and rest.

My company is becoming smaller and smaller through sickness, wounds and lack of horses, chiefly the latter. It is, as you well know, difficult for a city company like ours to keep up in mounts. My men do not have farms, or relatives and neighbors with farms from whom they can draw when their horses get killed or disabled, but have to purchase their horses at prices even I hesitate to pay. I believe this is the only army in history where the men have to furnish their own horses and it is the main weakness of our cavalry. To me to lose a horse is to lose a man, as they cannot afford a remount and new recruits with horses of their own are almost nil.

I am fortunate in that I have been sent to Lee's headquarters on some business which gives me a chance to rest a bit and write.

After leaving Lee's headquarters I rode into Fredericksburg and a sad sight it is. The people, as far as possible, are all leaving and are carrying away everything they can possibly get off. A large detail of wagons and ambulances is sent into town every day to help them to move, and it is amusing to see the soldiers helping them. As far as I have heard any expression of opinion the citizens generally prefer the place to be burnt to the ground rather than it should be surrendered to the yankees. Our old home is entirely deserted, and as the fence in the back of the garden is down the lot is open to the depredations of the few cows and hogs which yet wander about the place. Dr. Brodie Herndon, his wife and daughter Betty, and his son Johnny were in town. They had just come up from Richmond to try to save something from their house and carry that which they could back to Richmond. They had gone off

on the first alarm. I also saw Nannie Corbin who was here on
a similar errand from the Bowling Green in Caroline County,
where the Maury's have fled and where they propose remaining even if the yankees do occupy the country. This is the
most desolated land I have ever seen. From Fredericksburg
up the river, the country is as poor as poor can be, and now
that it is subject to the devastation of war it presents the best
illustration of starvation I have ever seen. What the few people
who are obliged to remain are to do for something to eat, it
is hard to imagine.

I left Fredericksburg yesterday evening about four o'clock
for our picket post which is about ten miles from town, but
as night overtook me, I got a farmer on the route to shelter
me, and after spending a comfortable night and getting a
good breakfast, I now spend an hour, which I rob from my
picket duty, in writing you this letter. Mail facilities are so
poor you had better direct my letters to William, care Stuart's
headquarters, and he will send them down through military
channels. Longstreet's army is much better clothed than Jackson's. Longstreet is now holding the hills around Fredericksburg. Where Jackson is I do not know. We hear he is near
Gordonsville.

At Camp, near Spotsylvania Courthouse, December 2nd.

We were relieved from picket yesterday evening, but so
late that we did not get back into camp until nine o'clock,
and we were as hungry a set of men as you ever saw. I was
so hungry that I found my mind reverting back with almost
tearful longing to the tough roast beef about which I quar-
reled so much when I was last at home. I would have regarded
it equal to the most excellent of turkey. We soon filled up with
our rations, and though the flour was dark and the meat
tough, our pangs were allayed. Colonel Watts and myself
rode in front of the regiment as we came from picket to camp
and found ourselves drifting into descriptions of grand dinners and sumptuous suppers, and as neither of us is given to
such style of conversation we attributed it to the natural
result of our condtion, and to test the matter, as the men filed

into camp, we stood to one side and listened to their talk. Without exception, every couple which passed were engaged as we had been, picturing the delights of the table.

We are now camped about two miles south of the Courthouse in a country so poor that even hen's grass will not grow. What little does come is instantly cropped by some wandering pennyroyal stock which live by faith and not by sight. One of my men said, "Crows fly over this district with haversacks and three days' rations." This part of the land, however, is fertile as compared with that in which we have been on picket, extending from "The Wilderness" to Fredericksburg where there is scarcely a cultivated field and many miles of utterly unbroken forest. We got out of rations and found it impossible, for love or money, to procure anything to eat, and hence our starving condition. The regiment which relieved us was well supplied. We are very uncomfortable here in the wintry air and on the frozen ground. We have nothing but the most meagre supply of army rations, no tents, no cooking utensils and only such blankets as each man carries on his person. I am writing now in the open air by the side of a fire, the fickle smoke from which blows one way and then another, but always in my eyes, which must account for the straggling writing. I am so cold I can hardly keep my pen in my hand or my paper on my knee. It is getting colder every minute and the wind is blowing very hard.

This is a wearisome life, and if I am to be appointed Judge Advocate of the first corps, I hope the appointment will come soon, for the place will be very much more agreeable. I would as soon stay here if I could fill up my company, but I find that almost impossible. I can get men enough—the difficulty is about horses. I am very pleasantly situated in my cordial relations with Colonel Watts. We are great friends and I value him much. As a man, a gentleman and a soldier he has few equals. General Jackson has joined Longstreet, but what is to be done now, of course, I do not know. I have never known an army more quiet or fewer signs of a battle but I should not be surprised if one occurs any day. The armies are close to each other, and one would anticipate a fight were it not for the season of the year and the enormous strength of our position. I can scarcely think Burnside can be such a fool as to undertake to cross at or near Fredericksburg and attack Lee's lines. If he does, it is a mere question of how many dead he will leave for us to bury.

Same Camp, December 3rd.

We are still in the wilderness country, with starving horses, and men only half fed with blue beef and black bread, yet, strange to say, I have never seen the men in such fine spirits. I wish I knew where to send your letters. I have been at work today trying to fix me up a sort of pen for a bed, and now comes a rumor we are to move and that my labor will be lost, but we must move somewhere nearer the base of supply or be starved. Don't measure the length of your letters by mine, for I have to write sitting on the bare ground, with the flag of my saddle for a desk, and with fingers so cold the pen will scarcely stay in them, to say nothing of the ever-varying smoke which keeps me in constant tears. I had a visit this morning from John C. Pettus. He is now teaching in a small school and farming in this neighborhood. He is married and has four children. Why he is not in the army I do not know. As I write I can hear Sam Sweeney, brother of the famous Joe Sweeney, playing on his banjo. A man named Taliaferro is accompanying him on a fiddle. It is the finest music I ever heard. We are entirely cut off from the world and hear nothing. Just here I am interrupted by the paymaster with funds, and I must devote myself to the payroll.

Same Camp, December 5th.

Never since I have been in the service have I ever been camped in such a stupid spot. We are twelve miles from the rest of the army, in a pine woods, and even out of the reach of a newspaper. As we have no men on picket we hear nothing even of the enemy. My coat is giving signs of dissolution which warns me I must be making arrangements for another: so have one made for me out of the cloth I sent you by Callahan. I do not want yellow cuffs or collar, but have it braided with gold lace, bars on the collar and knots on the sleeve, of the regulation style. Let the buttons be of the handsomest staff variety you can get. I burned quite a hole in my coat yesterday, and I am in daily dread my pantaloons will not stand much longer the strain of this cruel war. To be breechless in this weather and in the face of the enemy will not do.

Same Camp, December 7th.

I cannot imagine what has become of your letters. I know you have written, but none come. We are still in the desert, doing little or nothing and with nothing to talk about but the chances of the next meal. It is true I have the advantage of some few in the activity of my mind in inventing schemes to hide my nakedness should my garments give way before my new suit arrives. I have neither patch or pin or paste to mend a rent. Possible they may hold out, or yet again a yankee bullet or sabre may render me indifferent to such casualties. We are camped not far from the house of Mr. Oscar Crutchfield. Their house is full of refugees from Fredericksburg. I have been invited there once or twice and have been cordially treated. I fear the brigade being so near makes it uncomfortable for them.

My hand is almost frozen. I am writing on the bottom of an inverted stewpan. I warm it by the fire and then throw an oil-cloth over it, and am only thus able to keep my hand from freezing.

Same Camp, December 10th.

Nothing from you as yet and it makes me low spirited. The letters will come in a golden shower, I suppose, whenever I can strike the place where they are stored. I have not written in three days because it has been too bitterly cold. We are suffering very much. I went by invitation yesterday evening to Mr. Crutchfield's to supper with Churchill Cooke, who sang very charmingly. I wish you could have heard him.

We have no news from any quarter, and until I hear from you I have nothing to write about. I am going to a shoemaker's in the neighborhood this morning who I hear, can make ladies shoes, and will try to get you a pair.

Same Camp, December 11th.

I have two letters from you today; one dated November 30th, and the other December 3rd. The last contained the news the President had appointed me Judge Advocate of the first corps. I was, of course, much pleased, as it will be a more convenient berth and a staff officer is not subject to so many annoyances as the commandant of a company in the line— especially when the company is one of cavalry and from a town where horses cannot be obtained. No orders have yet been published announcing my appointment. My relations with Colonel Munford are very agreeable now, and, though he did me injustice I think, I will let the dead past bury its dead.

As I write I hear a heavy cannonading in the direction of Fredericksburg. What it means we do not know but we fear it is the bombarding of the town.

I was, I suppose, the most astonished person who heard the news of my appointment to the staff. I had little idea I would get the place, as the applicants counted by the hundreds and many were on hand to back their applications by personal interviews with the powers, while I have never left the field a day. I suppose I owe much of my good luck to Kean, who has been a good friend in the matter.

We have been kept in a fever of excitement all day by the terrible cannonading in the direction of Fredericksburg. It commenced about half-past four this morning and there was a continuous roar until about noon, when it ceased, and now (1:30 p.m.) it is quiet. We have been expecting orders all day for the brigade to move, but none have come.

Hamilton's Crossing, December 14th.

I have only a few moments to let you know that by the mercy of God, I was yesterday unhurt amidst the dangers of battle. Our brigade was not actively engaged, but was under fire from the enemy's cannon all day. We held the enemy in check on our extreme right flank. I have heard nothing from William or Eugene and know little of the particulars of the fight of yesterday.

December 17th.

We were drawn up yesterday morning at Hamilton's farm expecting to be ordered to charge the enemy every minute when an order came and we were moved off and are now camped about seven miles above Fredericksburg on the plank road, the enemy having crossed the river into Stafford again.

We are going on a "Grand Round" into Fairfax and Prince William, and will perhaps start today, but certainly tomorrow. I have had no change of clothing for a long time and don't know when I will. Our brigade was only a slight partaker in the fight and lost very few men. As soon as I can get pen and paper I will write you a full account of the battle.

The Battle of Fredericksburg, (written later).

On the 12th of December Fitz Lee's brigade, in which my regiment was included, was bivouacked some five or six miles west of Fredericksburg in a wood. We had left our camp after midnight, at moonrise, the night of the 11th. We rested quietly until about ten o'clock in the morning. We saw nothing portending a battle except a long column of men dragging its slow length along up the railroad near Fredericksburg. We had no tents, the weather was cold, but not bitter,—freezing at night but thawing by day.

Just across the road from my fire was the fire of Colonel Williams C. Wickham, colonel of the Fourth Virginia cavalry. He was then a member of the Confederate Congress but anticipating a battle came up to take command of his regiment. He is a distant cousin of mine and we were on very good terms and spent the evening of the 12th together, and ate our supper out of the same skillet. We parted about nine o'clock and he lay down on the ground by the fire to sleep, with his sword and pistols on and a blanket wrapped around him. I went over to my company, inspected every man and horse to see if they were ready to move on a moment's notice, for I was sure we would be ordered off before daylight. After satisfying myself the men and horses were ready for action, I lay down with my feet to the fire, my saddle as a pillow, the oil-cloth under me and a blanket over me. John Scott undertook to keep the fire burning. The fire was made some fifteen feet long and with a number of men, we lay around it, our heads outward and our feet to the fire. In this way three or four fires could accomodate my whole company, both men and officers.

About 11 o'clock I was awakened by the sound of groans from Colonel Wickham's fire. I went over and found him in great pain, suffering from a wound received during the summer at Williamsburg, the pain of which was renewed by his hard, cold bed. I found him in a very bad humor. He turned to me and said, "Blackford it's a damned shame I should have to suffer so much now and probably be killed tomorrow for a cause of which I do not approve. Remember, Blackford, if I am killed tomorrow it will be for Virginia, the land of my fathers, and not for the damned secession movement."

After doing all I could to make him more comfortable I returned to my fire and was soon asleep again. Long before daylight I dreamed I heard the enemy's cannon firing and strange to say I thought I heard the voices of my dead children calling me from Heaven and telling me I would soon be with them. The dream was so vivid it awoke me, and I found it was not all a dream: from the direction of Fredericksburg came the unmistakable boom of many cannons, so heavy I conceived it to be no ordinary skirmish. I was sure the bombardment had commenced and the enemy was crossing the Rappahannock, and that a general engagement would at once follow. I sprang up and called John Scott, who was dozing by the fire, and told him to cook some rations, then I called the men and told them to feed the horses and get something for themselves, which was done at once.

The horses and men had about finished their scanty breakfast and some had lain down again when, far down the frozen road from Fredericksburg, I heard the clattering of hoofs in rapid motion. I was sure it was orders to move, and I ordered the men to saddle up. The courier dashed into General Fitz Lee's headquarters and in few minutes "boots and saddles" sounded. My men were ready and had the advantage of the whole brigade.

After I had thus been aroused by my dream, and before the

bugle call sounded, I wrote you a letter, telling you of my dream and saying that I accepted it as a premonition I would be killed in the coming battle, and closing with the good-bye and loving farewells such an occasion would justify. This letter I gave to Dick Wade, of Abingdon, who had come from Lynchburg in the ambulance corps, and told him if I was killed to give it to you, if not, destroy it, which I presume he did. I regret it was not preserved as it would prove the superstition of such presentments. Had I been killed it would have been deemed a wonderful revelation of the secrets of the future, for so I regarded it at the time.

Before daylight we were in column and by sunrise we had passed back of the infantry lines by Hamilton's crossing and had taken position on Massaponax Creek in column of regiments, our regiment being at the head of the column. We were thus on the right of our line of battle, Rooney Lee's on our right and between us and the river—the cavalry thus extending from Hamilton's Crossing nearly to the river. When we first took our position the whole valley of the Rappahannock was covered with a dense fog and we could only tell where the enemy were by the sounds which came from their forming lines and occasional salvos from their artillery. As the enemy crossed their pontoon bridges at Fredericksburg and near the mouth of Deep Creek they formed in lines of battle in and near the river road which extends from the town to Massaponax Creek by the farms of Fourneybough, the Bernards, Taylor, Pratt. This road is about half-way between the river and the range of hills which run parallel to the river, upon which Lee had posted his army, extending from the point opposite Falmouth, where the range comes to the river, to Hamilton's Crossing where the hills cease. This range of hills gradually leave the river and thus slowly increase the width of the low ground from Falmouth to Hamilton's. The river road is lined on each side by a ditch, a bank, a watling of fence and a row of cedars, and thus formed a very fair protection for a line of battle against a foe in any other position than one like that selected by Lee, which completely commanded it and from which artillery had almost unobstructed play. If the world had been searched by Burnside for a location in which his army could be best defeated and where an attack should *not* have been made he should have selected this very spot.

Night found the armies just as they were in the morning, but with many a blue-coated man dead or dying on the plain between them. The victory of course was ours, as they had been repulsed at every point many times with great loss. We expected the battle to be renewed the next day and bivouacked on the same line we occupied the day before.

The next day was Sunday. The morning was draped in fog, but by nine the wind and sun had scattered it and disclosed the long lines of martial blue and the fields dotted with their ghastly tenants, many of whom were yet writhing in their death throes, as was shown by the contortions of their bodies. We could not help them, because whenever any effort to do so was made even by one man the yankees would fire at him, and they would not ask a flag of truce to enable them to either bury the dead or aid the dying.

Occasionally a gun was fired from the Stafford hills at our lines, but they were unanswered, and with that exception all day long both armies remained in line of battle inactive.

About one o'clock, when it became obvious that the battle would not be renewed, I got leave, with another officer, to ride up our line as far as Fredericksburg that I might inspect the battlefield and that I might hear something of my brothers, William, Eugene and Launcelot, all of whom I knew had been in the battle. I rode to the top of the hill where our second line was placed behind a breastwork, the first being behind an embankment at the foot of the hill just below. Thus I had an opportunity of seeing everything, and a grand sight it was. From Marye's hill I could look down upon the field of carnage where Meager's men had fought and died. I could see the familiar streets of Fredericksburg, into the house and yard where we had lived and where I was born, and could see the house on Hazel Hill which was built by my grandfather, General John Minor, and where my mother was born, but which was now torn and shattered by shot and shell. Our house, for it still belongs to us, and Hazel Hill were much injured as they were down at the lower end of town and exposed to the fire of both sides, but the town, except for the lower end, had been injured only by the fire of the enemy. It presented a very dilapidated appearance and was a melancholy sight to behold.

The sight of the field at the foot of Marye's and Willis' Hills, and immediately in front of Mr. Rowe's house was extremely ghastly. The havoc of war at that point greatly exceeded any I have ever seen up to this time. We held the top of the hill with infantry and artillery, and just at the foot there is a road sunken below the surface of the plain extending towards town, and walled up with a stone fence. Men in the road could place their muskets on the top of the stone fence and they would be on the plane of the field. The heads of the men would be exposed to the fire of the other side but their bodies would be protected perfectly from both small arms and cannon.

In the sunken road we had men massed, and as the enemy charged across the field which lay between the hills and the town, they had to encounter the fire from the artillery and infantry on top of the hill, and the more deadly discharge from the men in the road. Despite all this some bodies were within twenty feet of our line, showing the gallantry of many of the charges made. Just opposite was what, when I was a boy, was known as Mr. Whittemore's house and garden, and at that point successive lines were formed and hurled madly against our impregnable position. Charge after charge was made, until it looked as if the Gods had made them and that their destruction might surely follow. The field might have been crossed at any point on the bodies of the dead and dying. I say living dying as well as dead, for though our men could hear their agonizing cry for help and for water, they could not get to them, for the instant any effort was made in that direction the sharp-shooters from the rifle pits on the other side would pour a deadly hail of fire upon those who thus benevolently inclined, so there the poor fellows had to lie in the cold until the enemy withdrew on the night of the 15th, when of course, many of them were dead. Many efforts were made by our men at the risk of their lives to give them help and some were killed in the effort.

One of the brigades in the road was that of General Thos. R. R. Cobb. He would remain on his horse, though the men begged him to dismount, and he was killed, much to the regret of everyone, for he is said to have been a young man of great promise. I did not know him.

Our brigade remained quietly in the same position all day Sunday and Monday. The weather was good and the scene was very fine; no such outlook is often had. I suppose the two armies combined contained one hundred and eighty thousand men and not less than three or four hundred cannons, and there never was a battle-field where as many men were to be seen at one time. Usually one sees only the troops immediately around one and those directly in front but here the enemy's long lines could be seen for miles, and from the spot where Pelham's guns were placed, directly in our front, one could see our lines also.

On Monday night the enemy quietly withdrew, leaving their dead on the field unburied. Much skill was shown in doing this, for, as far as I can see, it was done without the knowledge of our generals, and certainly without an effort to interrupt. Of all this I know nothing, but I take it General Lee knows better what should have been done than I do, or than the newspapers who criticize him for not attacking. A night attack would have been a very severe undertaking, and of very doubtful result.

Tuesday morning we were back on our same line awaiting the movements of the enemy, when suddenly we received an order to move, and we at once took up our line of march for this point, up on the Rappahannock River, seven miles from Fredericksburg, near the point at which we did picket duty some two weeks ago. The war is over, I think, for the winter.

Seven miles north of Bowling Green. Undated.

I have not been able to write to you for some days because we have been moving about in great discomfort from pillar to post ever since the battle, and now I write from the ground on my lap, with the thermometer at about 20 degrees and my fingers about frozen. I have so few comforts that I cannot forego the only one the war has not deprived me of; that of writing you.

Mr. Tucker brought me your letter of the 15th, yesterday, which gladdened my heart greatly. I am glad you got the coon skins. I had entirely given up all hope they would ever be sent you. They will make you good, strong shoes and Nannie a pair also. I was delighted, also, to hear you had a good supply of pork, turkeys, and for the knowledge that, for awhile, at least, you have enough to eat is a consolation.

I have been doing all I could for the sufferers in Fredericksburg. I gave one hundred and fifty dollars to relieve some suffering women and children. Besides my subscription the regiment has given about two thousand dollars, which is very liberal for one regiment of poor soldiers. On the 19th, I went into Fredericksburg, and the sight is woeful, but really the damage is not quite as bad as it appears—I mean not as permanent. Every fence is broken down, the doors and windows of the houses broken up and much of the furniture pulled out into the streets and badly used up and scattered. Some twenty-five houses have been burned and almost every house shows the mark of having been struck by some kind of missile, most of them shell or solid shot.

The part of town known as Sandy Bottom was the scene of the most terrible fighting and every house facing Marye's Hill is covered with bullet marks. Mr. Marye's house, Brompton, which is of brick, is raked by musket balls until it looks as if a hail storm had scoured it. The heaviest carnage of the enemy was upon the street which passes by Rowe's house and in the field in front of the house. On one square the yankees left four hundred and eighty dead bodies, though they had been burying their dead during the two days they occupied the town after the battle. The town was full of dead men when evacuated. It seems very strange to see a deserted town, with nothing but corpses of dead men and horses for inhabitants.

Our house was only struck by one cannon ball, and that was a solid shot fired by one of our batteries. It did not go through but buried itself in the brick, but fell out and was lying on the ground just below. A fragment of a shell broke a window-blind. A shell struck a house in the yard known as "Uncle John's Study," went through the wall, knocking a number of books on the floor, then went through the front door, struck the pavement, ricochetted, tore down our front fence, and then exploded as it struck the top of Mr. Caldwell's on the other side of the street, tearing it to pieces very much.

Our house was used as an operating hospital and many yankees were buried in the back yard, one just at the foot of the back steps. In the dining room the large table was used as an operating table and a small table by its side had a pile of legs and arms upon it. I poured them out into the back yard and managed to get the table out to camp and will send it home in a few days.* I also got a large Church of England prayerbook printed in 1745 which had belonged to my grand-father, General Minor. I further found an empty box and packed up a number of old law books which had belonged to my grandfather, and had them put aside to be sent home. The yankees had been up in the cuddy of the house and taken out barrels of old letters which were scattered all over the yard. Among them I found a letter from Light Horse Harry Lee to my grandfather. The whole house was covered with mud and blood and it was hard to realize it was the dear old house of my childhood.

The old Misses Thom, daughters of Mr. Ruben Thom, were in Fredericksburg during the shelling and their house was burned down over their heads while the most terrible part of the shelling was going on, and when they finally left their cellar on account of the fire they had to cross the street under a shower of shot, shell and bullets but escaped unhurt.

From Mrs. Blackford.
Lynchburg, Virginia, December 3rd, 1862.

Oh joy! I have just received a telegram from Mr. Kean announcing your appointment on the staff of General Long-

*Now in my possession. C.M.B. III

street as Judge Advocate of the First Corps. I am so delighted, and I know that you will be pleased. Nannie says I must tell you she is "perfectly glad" that you are "that thing." She does not know exactly what it is but she thinks it is something which will bring you home..

Your father reported this morning that he made enough money from the profits of the sale of your lot in the Presbyterian Cemetery, after paying for the one in Spring Hill, to pay for my pork. Gabe has purchased me nine turkeys at three dollars a piece. I have packed them away and hope to have one for your Christmas dinner, which Gabe claims he bought it for.

December 18th.

I was much relieved yesterday when your letter arrived assuring me of your safety after the battle. I have not been sure that your regiment was in it or I would have been much more uneasy. Thank God that you are safe. I dread very much to hear the results as to our friends. We have already been shocked by the news of the deaths of Mr. Lewis Minor Coleman, David Barton and Randolph Fairfax and of the wounding of Willy Colston. Poor aunt Jane; I fear she is frantic about Willy. Stuart Cabell had his leg shot off and his sister, Mrs. Brown, has gone to Richmond to nurse him.

Father brought me a letter asking me to take Mrs. Matthew F. Maury and some of her family to board. I do not know whether I can do so or not, it is so hard to keep supplies, but I will take the matter into consideration. I am so in need of bed linen and such things that if I do take them they will have to bring their own things of that character. I took the coon skins down town last evening to have some shoes made, and the shoemaker said if I would furnish everything he would make them for $5.00 a pair. I secured a pair of leather boots for you at $50.00 from Grinaldi.

I had a note from Major Jack Langhorne this morning proposing to exchange a barrel of flour for two gallons of the whiskey you have at home. I do not know whether you will like it or not but I made the exchange, for I regard a barrel of flour which we eat much more valuable to us than the whiskey which we do not drink. I hope you will be home for Christmas. Your mother wished us to dine with her that day. She sent to borrow my jelly strainer to get ready, and I will make some too, so you will have a royal reception for these times.

December 20th.

We had a letter yesterday announcing the death of William's little boy, Landon Carter. It would seem that all the children in the family who bear the name of Landon are doomed to an early death. I will write to poor Mary and offer my sympathy, for surely no one knows better than I do how much she suffers.

Our negro, William, is so much opposed to being hired to the Express Company that he shall not go there. He says that it will entail much work for him on Sunday and I knew you would not like that. Blind Mr. William Langhorne wants him to drive a wagon for him, but he offers much smaller hire than the Express Company, but of course the money cannot be considered against the other reasons. I have gotten the clothes for which you wrote from Page and they are awaiting your orders. You will need the coat you have on for everyday wear and for marching so don't injure it any more than you can help. There is no news. I suppose all the fighting is over now until the spring.

From the diary of Mr. William Blackford, Sr.
December 31, the last day of 1862.

Another year has closed and it is a fit occasion to moralize, but I forbear. It has been a year of mercies to me. My sons have all been exposed to imminent dangers on many battlefields, and two of them, (Eugene and Charles) have had serious attacks of sickness, yet all have thus far been spared to us, and all have have done their duty, each within his sphere. I desire to thank God devoutly for these great and multiplied mercies. Public affairs, too, are more promising than they were at any former period, I think. I see indications of a cessation of hostilities, though many months may elapse before peace is established.

The year has been one of momentous interest. In a mere military point of view the campaigns in Virginia have been equal to anything in history. The defeats of the enemy in The Valley, in the Peninsular, in the Piedmont, the invasion of Maryland, the capture of Harper's Ferry and lastly the victory of Fredericksburg, taken all together, are achievements which do not often crown one year. May God grant that the many precious lives lost by us may not have been a vain sacrifice, but that peace and independence may reward the noble efforts our people have made for their liberty.

CHAPTER IX

THE JUDGE ADVOCATE

An introductory note by Mrs. Blackford.

THE year 1862 ended with Captain Blackford's appointment to the staff of General Longstreet as Judge Advocate. After the Battle of Fredericksburg he reported to General Longstreet, was given twelve days' leave and got home on Christmas Eve. For the first time his leave was entirely pleasant. He no longer had the worries of the company on his hands, the necessity of recruiting men and horses, equipment, and attending the hundreds of little personal problems of his men that would be brought to him by the wives, parents and dependents of the men in his company for advice or settlement. For a Captain, as he often said, was a species of dry nurse for his men, to be called on duty or off.

The change in duty removed him from many of the hardships and dangers of the service in the line but on the march he remained an active officer, his duties as Judge Advocate relegated to secondary place so, although behind the front most of the time he still saw service in the great movements and battles. The hardships of the war became greater for the home front during these latter days as the State was over-run and Lynchburg, unconquered, became of greater and greater importance as a base of supply and a haven for sick, wounded and refugees. The grimmer days of the war were about to commence. Captain Blackford's letters resume January 8th. 1863 from the Headquarters, First Corps.

From Capt. Blackford.

Could you see me now you would think peace had been declared and, having returned home, I was busily engaged in my office with the avocations of my profession. I am in a very comfortable room with a carpet on the floor, nicely arranged with all necessary furniture, including a lounge for my bed. I am writing at my desk with a pile of law books at my elbow, as if no war was devastating the country all about me.

I left Dr. Pendleton's in Louisa County, in a pouring rain and soon found the wagon could not reach headquarters that night, so I made for Mr. Oscar Crutchfield's where I was most hospitably entertained and welcomed. I met there Dick Maury who has been relieved of his command on account of his wounded arm and has been assigned to duty as an enrolling officer for the Seventh Congressional District. I left Crutchfield's about ten o'clock on Monday and soon reached General Longstreet's headquarters and found the other members of the court had not yet reported for duty. The General expressed surprise that I had not stayed at home until I heard of their arrival. He told me to secure a room in which the court could sit, make myself comfortable and wait for the arrival of the other members.

I had my wagon driven up, and from the several offers of bed and board for the night selected the one extended by Major Sam Mitchell, the quartermaster of the corps with whom I knew it was advisable to be on good terms, and whose father, Mr. Robert C. Mitchell of Bedford I know very well. After dinner I rode out to seek quarters, but came back at night in despair, finding every little niche crammed with "roughugees" as the soldiers call them. I spent the night with Major Mitchell and shared with him some of my turkey, being joined in the repast by Major Sorrell, the adjutant of the corps, who gave us a very interesting account of the night he had spent on the other side of the river as bearer of dispatches under a flag of truce. He was most discourteously made to spend the night in the kitchen of Major Lacy's house "Chatham" without bed or bedding being offered him, and with nothing to eat but a bowl of soup, which a common soldier offered him. This treatment of General Longstreet's chief of staff, who came on an errand of mercy to their dead and wounded, I consider one of the most outrageous violations of the courtesies of war which has yet taken place.

This morning I went out again to renew my search for quarters, calling to see William, whom I found in good spirits and expecting Mary daily. She will board at Mrs. Alsop's about a mile from Stuart's headquarters. Mrs. General Stuart will board at the same place.

Everywhere I heard the same cry about "roughugees" until, at last, in despair I went back to one of the places where I had been refused the night before. The place was not over one hundred yards from headquarters. After some persuasion the owner agreed to let me have a room, and I now write from it in comfort and style. He also gave me the use of a small room upstairs where I can take refuge when the court crowds me out of this. I have my tent pitched in the yard nicely protected from the north wind and in it is John Scott who will stay for the present, cooking my meals in the kitchen on the premises.

Mr. Hart, the man of the house, now that I have gotten on his blind side, seems very friendly and I think I shall not be chary of his society. If I can arrange it so I can mess by myself, I can make the nice supplies you put up for me last a long time. As may be expected, there is nothing to be gotten in this country but poor beef and flour, so you must keep a good look-out for me and send me things every chance you have, or rather collect things and I will contrive the means of getting them. I can, if necessary, send John Scott with the wagon over to the Central Railroad. To send them to Hamilton's Crossing is to give them away, as every box sent there is pillaged by the men placed as guards over them. Make Gabe look out for potatoes and onions for me especially.

Ask Father to bring me, when he comes, the best record book he can find at Payne's. I want it for the court.* None can be gotten from the Quartermaster's Department. Have the bill made out against the Confederate Government in duplicate and the quartermaster here will pay for it. Father must let me

---

*This book came and was filled up before the close of the war. I gave it to the Southern Historical Society. I think it would have been better to have destroyed it. C.M.B.

know the day before he comes down so my wagon may meet him. He had better make his headquarters with me, as I can make him more comfortable than any of the boys. William is only a mile from me and Eugene about twelve miles. Give a kiss to Nannie and my love to all at Father's.

Headquarters, January 10th.

I went up to Stuart's headquarters yesterday about ten o'clock and William and myself rode to Fredericksburg and over the battlefield again. I enjoyed the trip exceedingly. William knows more of the position of the different troops than any living man, not excepting General Lee, for he has surveyed the ground and gotten the position of each regiment on his map from the brigadier under whom it served, while General Lee only has the general knowledge of the position of brigades and division requisite for a commander-in-chief.

I met General Chilton, General Lee's adjutant-general, who asked me whether my court had yet convened, and when I told him no he said he would put me to work at army headquarters, which I am glad to hear. He was very polite to me, and seems to be well acquainted with the details of his business. William returned and took supper with me.

This morning was dark and gloomy and about nine o'clock commenced to rain, which is a serious drawback to the grand review of Fitz Lee's brigade of cavalry (my old brigade), which is to take place to-day and would have been a very gay affair. Many ladies were to have been on the ground. As it was raining I did not order my horse to attend the review, and supposed it would be postponed. I walked up to headquarters to get some remedy for my sore throat. While waiting for the prescription the Second Regiment came by on the way to the review and I joined my old company and walked along by the side of the men through the mud and rain for about a mile, and then stood during the whole ceremony. The weather was so bad that it destroyed all interest in the sight, which otherwise would have been very inspiring. Generals, Lee, Longstreet, and Stuart were out, who, with Stuart's staff and

couriers, myself and one wagon driver, were the only spectators. It rained so hard we could see only fifty yards ahead of
us down the line. The men and horses had been roused before
daylight, marched fifteen miles through the mud, and then
thoroughly wet and worn had to march back. Could anything
be more foolish, and all for the sake of a "grand review," by
which a parade might be made before a few women? I have
little patience with such vanity, and I think Fitz Lee and his
command agree with me.

My company seemed delighted to see me. I wish I could
have given them all something to eat, for they told me they
had no breakfast and were very cold and hungry. Colonel
Watts, Captain Tebbs and Captain Alexander, of the Second
Regiment, slipped out as the review broke up and came over
to my quarters, and I have never seen men enjoy themselves
as they did. They were so cold they had to put their hands in
cold water to keep them from being frost bitten. I soon made
them comfortable by a good fire and with a stiff whiskey toddy.
I gave them some of your cakes and pipes and tobacco and
started John Scott to cook dinner, which he did much to their
satisfaction by three o'clock. I never had the pleasure of en-
tertaining men so hungry or so enjoyed by viands. They would
have spent the night with me but they had failed to get leave.
Tebbs sends you his love. Try and get me two or three gallons
of chestnuts, I want to make coffee out of them.

January 12th.

I am very busy now preparing myself for my new duties and
hope I will understand them by the time I will be called on
to act. Only one member of the court has been heard from, and
he says he cannot report for duty for two weeks. I am going
to see William this evening and he is to take me to see your two
cousins, Mrs. Grey Carroll and Mrs. Robert Stribbing, who
are on a visit to their husbands. They are at Mrs. Alsop's where
Mrs. General Stuart is staying and William's wife will stay
when she arrives.

Night.

I left off writing and went to see William and found he had

just gotten a lot of oysters in the shell, which, in company with several other officers, we roasted on the fire in front of his tent. After dinner we rode over to Mrs. Alsop's to call on the ladies. I liked Mrs. Stribbing very much.

January 16th.

William and Majors Von Borcke, Fitzhugh, and Pelham dined with me last night, but about ten o'clock William was called off and sent by General Stuart to General Jackson on very important business, which was unfortunate as his wife is expected this morning. I am going to meet her. I am sorry she is coming just now, as there is reason to think the enemy are about to make another attempt to cross the river. Our troops all have three days' cooked rations and are awaiting marching orders. The impression is the enemy will attempt to cross in two places, one at Port Royal and the other above Fredericksburg, one of the movements, of course, being a mere front to divide our forces, while the main force can be readily concentrated at one point. Others surmise that the whole movement on their part is a ruse to attract our attention and keep our forces here while they send troops off to North Carolina, and gradually move upon Richmond from that direction. Our army was never in such condition as to health, spirits, arms and clothing as at present. There are now no barefooted men and the style of their arms has been greatly improved by the acquisitions of the battle of Fredericksburg. I hope father will come with Mary. In case of a move he can take care of her.

The difficulties I have in getting letters through from you stirred me up to write to the Postmaster General. I wound up by saying, "The necessities of the country demand that the army should forego all luxuries and most of the necessities of life, and it submits cheerfully, but it is cruel and useless to rob it of a comfort so priceless and yet so cheap as that of hearing from our families at home."

I hope my letter may stir him up to investigate the causes of the delay, which arises from the neglect of the agents at Richmond, I think. for I am sure the mail bags lay over several days in that city. I went to the train to meet Mary, but she did not come, which is very well, for William may not be back from Jackson's headquarters for some days, and if there is any active operations she would be very uncomfortable. All is quiet today although the troops are still under cooked rations.

January 19th.

Father got here yesterday with Mary and the children. I was at the station accidentally on the arrival of the train and met Mary and Father much to my astonishment, and, as my wagon had not arrived, I took them up to Forest Hill, where Mr. Marye was, to wait while I went for the wagon. About a mile up the road I overtook William, who was riding quietly along smoking enroute to his quarters. He had been to the depot and was there when the train arrived, but failed to see his family. He had returned from Jackson's quarters the night before though I did not know it.

My wagon soon arrived at Forest Hill and William and his family went in it to Mrs. Alsop's while Father took William's horse and rode with me over the battlefield inspecting everything of interest. We went to our old home and all over the town and then back to my quarters for the night where a comfortable dinner awaited us.

This morning we rode down to Eugene's camp to see him, and while there William came in being again on duty at Jackson's headquarters, so we were all three together with Father for several hours. We came back tonight after a ride of some twenty miles and will dine with William tomorrow if he returns.

January 21st.

William did not get back so we had a good dinner at my quarters, thanks to your provident care for my comfort. Eugene had to ride seven miles after dark. Father went this morning much to my regret. They still talk of a yankee advance on our flanks. They publish an account of Longstreet's arrival in Tennessee with thirteen brigades of his army to make their men think we are much weaker than we are and to inspire them with a hope which will make them fight better. Unless they out-general us they will get most terribly thrashed if they do cross, and Burnside is not the man to out-general Lee, Longstreet and Jackson.

I am making my little store of coffee last by using two-thirds rye and I find it does very well. I must soon, however, drop the one-third coffee, as the supply is very short. The gloves you have knitted me will be a most acceptable present, as mine are worn out and have one or two large holes in them.

By Mrs. Blackford.

On reading my own letters during the same period I find nothing especially worthy of record. I was in very bad health and had several of my violent attacks connected with my liver, which in conjunction with other troubles, so prostrated me that my letters were both short and uninteresting. I tell of one of the spells during which Dr. John Minor, who was boarding with me, came home and found me with a maddening headache, my hands and feet cramped and the muscles of my face twitching. He at once took thirty ounces of blood from my arm, which made me very weak but brought instant relief, and I at once went to sleep and slept all night. The Doctor was very kind to me, as kind as a brother, and I have no doubt his constant attention and heroic treatment saved my life more than once.

My niece, Anne Colston was a tender and devoted little nurse during my sickness. My dear little Nannie never left my room, and though only five years old did all she could to help me. The fact that during much of the time of this terrible suffering I was left to the care of these two children is a very good illustration of the condition of society at the time. Private suffering and necessities were forgotten or shrunk into insignificance as compared to the general anxiety and public calamities which oppressed the feelings and occupied the thoughts of everybody. The wail of the individual was not heard amidst the groans which marked the death throes of a nation. When I read what was written to my husband at the time and, I remember how much was concealed from him, I wonder I lived through it.

In one of my letters I mentioned I was greatly interested in having my large garden cultivated and in my efforts was much assisted by our faithful man-servant, Gabe, a slave who had belonged to my father and who, during my husband's absence, showed a devotion and sympathy worthy of all praise. He was more of a friend and a protector than a slave, and guarded the premises and watched over me and my wants as would a father or a brother. I shall ever remember him as a model of fidelity. He has been dead now for many years, and I have no doubt that his entrance into the next world was greeted by the judgment, "Well done, good and faithful servant, enter thou into the joy of thy Lord." Never was there one of whom it could more truly be said that he "did his duty in that state of life in which it pleased God to call him."

On the 11th of February, Mr. Blackford's father wrote my husband as follows:

My dear Charlie:

I sympathise deeply with the sorrow I know this letter will occasion. Sue was taken sick last night, and about seven o'clock this morning gave birth to a finely formed boy, which, however, did not survive more than an hour. I am confined to the house and could not go over to your house. I hear Sue is getting on very well. She sent for your mother this morning about eight and she is still there. The funeral will take place tomorrow at eleven o'clock. Possibly your mother may have written you. I pray God to give you strength to bear this sorrow.

Launcelot will reach Hamilton's Crossing on the 17th, and wishes to add hearty sympathy in this affliction. I am not able to use my eyes and have to use Launcelot's pen.

Your affectionate father,
Wm. M. Blackford.

On the 18th I wrote from Lynchburg:
I know you will be surprised and delighted to get a letter

from me once more, and I assure you it gives me infinite satisfaction to be able to write. Oh, my darling, I have indeed passed through a dark and dreary time since I last wrote. So fierce and terrible was my agony that it produced the premature death of our child. I never felt anything approaching it before, though from the first to the last it was less than one hour. The child was perfectly formed and very large. Its eyes and hair were black. I was so happy when told it was a boy and would bear your name. No one but you and my God can know the anguish of my sorrow when I found it could not live. I had taken more pleasure in making preparations for it and preparing its little clothes than I had ever done before under like circumstances. The thought of it had buoyed up my spirits and enabled me to bear my long months of agony, but now when I think it was all in vain and that it is lying in the ground by the side of the other two my heart is almost broken. It brings back my other great grief with terrible force. My dear sister's [Mrs. John B. Minor] being with me was a great comfort. It was so sweet and kind of her to come over and stay with me and I know it was a great pleasure to you to know she was here.

I thought you would like to have the child buried in the same grave with the other two, and I had it done. I think it would be well to have inscribed on the little tombstone over them, "Also our little baby boy who tarried with us only an hour."

*   *   *

From Capt. Blackford.
Longstreet's headquarters, January 24th.

Your feeble little letter of the 20th inst. reached me this evening and made my heart sad, for I could see from the tremulous lines how very sick you have been. My heart bleeds for you. I value the letter all the more when I think what pain it gave you to write it.

Two of my court reported today, Colonel L. W. Spratt of South Carolina and Colonel Hill, of Mississippi, a brother of my friend D. H. Hill. I find them to be gentlemen with whom my association can and will be most agreeable, and as they seem to be favorably impressed with me and my qualifications I take it we will get along together very well. I know you will be shocked when I tell you we will all mess together, but there is no helping it. In some respects it is better. It is more economical and more social. They at once elected me head of the mess and gave me an unlimited drag on their pockets. They seem to think it will cost us sixty dollars apiece each month. I think half that sum will answer. I fear it will add to your labours, as you must be our disbursing commissary. I nominated Launcelot to them as clerk, and I was glad to hear they had no one in view and thought I should have the selection. He will get $120 a month and have quite a snug berth, much better than being a private in the Rockbridge Artillery. I received two letters today in answer to mine to the Postmaster General. He says the delays have been incident to the overpress of work in Richmond which is the distributing office for the whole Army of Northern Virginia in its present position. The trouble will all, he says, be corrected in a few days. So I will have done a good thing for the whole army if I have the evil cured.

Mrs. Arthur Goodwin passed through here today to take the cars for Ashland, whither she goes to try and keep a boarding house. Her husband was cashier of a bank in Fredericksburg and quite well to do, and they had a happy and comfortable house two months ago. Since then she has been made a widow, has lost her oldest daughter, and all her property down to her last bed and barrel of flour, has been destroyed. She has five small children and has to commence her life anew at a time when the strongest and best find it hard to maintain the struggle for existence.

February 1st.

Tomorrow the court will commence its work trying Colonel G—— of Norfolk, against whom are charges of a serious character preferred by certain officers of his regiment. There is much feeling and bitterness in this case, and I doubt not I will come in for a share of it before I get through. I have had sent me a large number of cases, some twenty of which are for capital offenses, so we will, I fear, hold a "bloody assize." William's wife has gone to her cousin's, Mrs. Guest's, to spend a few days. William has been paying board at the rate of $100 a week which he could not stand.

I sold my horses this morning to the Government for $635 which is what I paid for them, and drew them back on requisition from the quartermaster for the use of the court. I shall dispose of my wagon the same way.

Headquarters, Longstreet's Corps, February 2, 1863.
Dear little Nancy:

Your funny little letter came to me today while I was in court trying a colonel who had been making a bad boy of himself and using bad words to his men and officers. It made me laugh out loud as I read it. I wish I could see the snowman with the pipe in his mouth. I expect he did "look like a ghost" sure enough. I wish you could have seen the great snow-balling we have down here in the army since the snow was so deep. The soldiers fought great battles like real battles, four or five thousand on a side. Generals were in command, with their staffs, leading brigades and colonels and majors leading regiments, keeping up a line of battle several miles long. It was as exciting as a real battle. Generals and colonels riding about everywhere amidst the thickest fighting, cheering on their men, and of course as they were officers the balls came down on them like hail, but they stood them manfully and in good nature though they hurt very much, often drew blood. My friend, General Jenkins, of South Carolina, and his brigade, were surprised by a brigade which came three miles under General Law to make the attack. Jenkins and his men were right badly used up. They had no ammunition prepared, while the others made their balls the night before and let them freeze. They carried them in their haversacks. Each man had some six or eight balls to start with and it gave them a great advantage in making a sudden attack. The next morning, however, General Jenkins had his men up by daylight, each with a good haversack full of frozen balls, and leading them himself moved upon Law's brigade while it was cooking and eating breakfast. They were very close before the alarm was given. Then the long-roll beat and the men fell into line and were very gallantly rallied and formed by General Law and his officers, but they had no ammunition and could not stand Jenkins' terrible charge. The Jenkins men gave the rebel yell and drove the other brigade out of their camp, and taking possession of their huts used them as places of safety while they made up snowballs and ate up all the breakfast they could find also. Law's men hated it very much but they had to stand it. Part of the fight was just outside General Lee's headquarters. He came out to see it and found much difficulty in protecting himself from the balls, which made the air white. He was struck several times.

It has been one great snow battle all through the army. Regiments fought regiments, brigades fought brigades and even divisions fought divisions. The funniest part was, when the battle was over, both parties would join us and go through camp and every man they found who had shirked the fight they rolled over and over and covered him with snow. Wouldn't you have liked to see the fun?

Same Camp, February 5th.

Captain John L. Cochran and his old man servant, Tarleton are great acquisitions. The old man is a perfect specimen of an old-fashioned Virginia gentlemen's body-servant. Grey-haired with side whiskers, very courtly manners and a fluent vocabulary, but with a flow that has little respect to the order or meaning of the words; their length being the prime consideration. He is a good cook. Yesterday he supplied us with soup, fritters and cherry roll, all of which seems to be of the highest grade of gastronomic excellence. Cochran is a treasure, I had no idea he was such a man: intelligent, active and brave, faithful and obliging, he makes a charming addition to our social life and a most useful officer.

Mr. Guest has several hundred gallons of fine wines in his cellar, which he proposes to sell at thirty dollars a gallon, fearing it will fall into the hands of the enemy. I shall get you some for use in case of sickness. He says it is thirty years old.

He imported it when he lived in Baltimore.

You can always ship me things by old John F. Tilden, who comes down every two or three weeks with boxes and parcels for the soldiers, and will at all times take pleasure in bringing me a box or barrel.*

Richmond, Feb. 20th.

We have just finished one of the most terrible marches in history. I was detailed to staff duty and marched with the army although the rest of the court went by train. The roads were without bottom and the weather beyond description. The only thing that made it bearable was the fact that no enemy attack was apprehended.

Near Ashland, as we dragged the slow length of the corps through the slashes of Hanover I was riding by the side of one of Kershaw's regiments, I noticed a stripling of about eighteen tramping on but with uncertain step, which, with his weary look, excited my pity and I offered him my horse. In a very refined voice he declined, saying he would not desert the rest of the men and that he thought he could stand it. I could not prevail on him to accept the help, but I remained near enough to him to be able to give him the aid which I knew he would soon want. It was obvious that his strength was deserting him rapidly, though I thought him only broken down, as each step seemed to be the result of expiring energy. He was obviously a gentleman though only a private. Though covered to the knees with mud the upper part of his dress was soldierly, neat and attractive. His arms and accoutrements were clean and ready thus marking him alert and faithful. He grew more haggard as each half-hour passed, though his eyes kept bright and he continued to struggle on with the constancy of a true soldier. Suddenly he seemed to stumble, and staggering forward, fell prone upon his face. I leaped from

*Mr. Tilden was a very good man. As long as he was able to do so he made a species of express of himself for the benefit of soldiers from Lynchburg. Anyone wanting to send anything to a soldier could put it under his care. When he had gathered quite a number of packages he would ship them and then go along as guard and distribute them on arrival. C.M.B.

my horse and with many others ran to his aid, but too late, his manly spirit had fled and left only a smile on his gallant face to tell how noble the parting. A burying detail was made, and, shrouded only in his uniform, without rite or coffin, we laid him to rest in the oozy ground, a martyr to duty, a priceless sacrifice to his country. From his comrades, gathered around to do him the poor honor of this scant ceremony I heard many heartfelt words of praise. He had first proved his manhood on the bloody field of Second Manassas, had followed Gregg in his famous charge at Fredericksburg, was faithful on picket and ever cheerful in camp. By the men in his company he was petted, by the women at home beloved. A tall pine marks the head of his grave and a laurel bush its foot. No pictured or storied bronze will mark his resting place or tell the legend of his heroic life, but God, who notes the fall of a sparrow will not forget the gallant boy who crowned His image with a life so faithful and a death so heroic.

I wish you could have seen Hood's division as it passed through Richmond. They had marched three days through the mud and slush, but had stopped just outside the city and cleaned and scraped up, and after a good rest they commenced the march through the town. I was at their head with General Hood by invitation. I had never seen men look so well or in such high spirits. It was refreshing to see how joyous they were after such hardship. Their bands were playing and their flags, soiled and war-worn, were flying, their arms shone in the sun and they kept perfect alignment and rhythmic step as they moved with rapid swing along the streets, the sidewalks of which were crowded with spectators. They laughed and shouted amongst themselves and guyed the people on each side with rough jokes. As they passed the Spottswood Hotel, on Main Street, a great many officers were standing on the porches and around the doors. As the troops passed in front they made great miration over what they were pleased to call the "Officer's Hospital." As we passed that point I heard one of the men shout out to a dapper little quartermaster, who with spotless shoes and faultless uniform, was on the sidewalk enjoying the sight: "Howdy-do Major!" The Major was delighted to be recognized by any one of the gallant force and started out as if to embrace his friend, when the same voice said: "Oh, don't come out in the mud, Major, you'll soil your shoes! Is you drawed your bounty yet? If you is just fall in, Major!" The Major retired amidst a derisive shout from the regiment.

I heard a story about my friend, Major John C. Haskell, of South Carolina, who so distinguished himself in the battles around Richmond and lost his right arm. He was in Richmond when the troops passed through and was out on a porch with some girls on Franklin Street, very handsomely dressed and with a short military cloak thrown over his shoulders. As the troops passed by the men began guying him about his fine dress; he suddenly wheeled and faced them and threw back his cape showing his empty sleeve. The effect was electric. The men took off their hats and one continuous cheer greeted him as the whole corps passed, each regiment catching the inspiration from the one ahead of it. I wish I had seen it but I did not. It was told me by one who did.

The citizens displayed great hospitality as the men and officers passed and everything available to eat and drink was brought out to the sidewalk and freely distributed. The officers of Pickett's brigade were the special recipients of the hospitality of their many friends,—a hospitality which, in many instances, was almost too much for them. They were very excusable for losing their heads under such circumstances. After months of danger and hardship they were called upon by beautiful women to pledge their love or friendship in sparkling wine. Colonels Mayo, Otey, Williams and Floweree and others were put under arrest by Pickett. Such an offense, under such circumstances, like Uncle Tobey's oath, should be blotted out forever.*

*It was not blotted out however. They were brought to trial under my court martial and were convicted on their own evidence. They were still under arrest the night before the battle of Gettysburg when they came to me in a body and asked me to secure their release and restoration to their commands. I saw Longstreet and he directed me to issue an order in his name restoring them, which I did, and they led their regiments in the great charge of Pickett's division on that bloody day. Williams was killed and all the others wounded. C.M.B.

A note by Mrs. Blackford.

The court was set up in Petersburg where Captain Blackford made arrangements for me to visit him at a rate of $250 a month for room and board. In the meantime he had been speculating in tobacco to add to his income which was entirely too small to support the large house and servants in Lynchburg. His profits amounted to $3,800. He sent John Scott up to Lynchburg to get his roan horse.

From Mrs. Blackford to Capt. Blackford.
Lynchburg, March 1st.

I am beginning to look forward with great pleasure to my proposed visit to Petersburg and hope I shall be well enough to go before you are ordered off. It seems to me now that it would have been a great pleasure had it been willed I should have had the care of my little baby boy. It seems like a dream that I had one which came to bless me one brief hour and then went to God who lent it to me. I am glad it lived even that short a time to receive the heritage of a soul to rest on the bosom of the Savior and join our other dear ones in Heaven. But I cannot trust myself to write on the subject.

John Scott arrived yesterday but, poor fellow, found his wife had been dead a week. Your father telegraphed you about her sickness while you were in Richmond but you failed to get the telegram. John does not seem so inconsolable and Annie Colston sagely remarked that as white men get over such things so easily and so quickly it is not to be expected that black ones should be any different. He says your roan is very well and fit for service again. Jack Alexander was taken prisoner and your company has now, I am told, no non-commissioned officers. Gabe, and O'Brian, our Irish gardener, are hard at work preparing the garden, setting out lettuce, planting peas, etc. Mr. John T. Smith had the smallpox but now is well and not disfigured.

I am much interested in having my servants clothes woven and I am also having some homespun dresses made for myself and Nannie. I do not suppose I shall get the cloth you engaged for me last summer in Loudoun. Mrs. Minor brought Nannie a nice new calico when she came over, which was a grand present. It costs $2.50 a yard. If the war lasts much longer I do not see what people will do. The poor will not be able to get even rags to cover them.

This is a sad day for me—the anniversary of our darling boy's death. I dreamed last night and I saw him distinctly and thought I had him in my arms, but on awaking found it was Nannie I had folded closely to my bosom and was covering with kisses. The great sorrow seems more sometimes than I can bear. It seems to rise up in my throat and choke me.

I am thinking seriously of renting the house and boarding somewhere nearer you. If we could rent it by the month for enough to pay our board Nannie and myself could follow the army. We will talk it over when we meet.

March 6th.

I have engaged you a pair of fifty-dollar boots for which I pay only thirty-five dollars. You had better buy yourself four yards of cloth from the Quartermaster Department if you can. Buying it from the government that way you can get it for seven dollars a yard, I am told. I am going to send Frances down to Richmond to see her mother. I want to give her this trip in token of her faithful service to me during the winter and all the time I was sick.

Tell me candidly if you can stand the expense of our trip to Petersburg. I know your means are running short and I will not be hurt if you tell me not to come. I will be very economical, I would not take Mary with me except that I have nowhere to leave her and I am not strong enough to look after Nannie. I do not expect to stay over two weeks, indeed I cannot, as Annie Colston will be here and I must be here to look after the garden, which will be our principal source of support this summer.

☆ ☆ ☆ ★ ☆ ☆ ☆

CHAPTER X

TO GETTYSBURG,–AND BACK

☆ ☆ ☆ ☆ ☆ ☆

Mrs. Blackford writes:

THERE is little of interest in the actions of Captain Blackford until the next May when I joined him in Taylorsville in Hanover County. He secured a room for us in the house of a Mr. Hackett. It was a mere loft, the steps up to it little better than a ladder. The ceiling was so low that Mr. Blackford could not put on his coat without striking it. The food was very plain, much of it cooked at his campfire. I remember we ate as salad the young sprouts of the poke-berry and found it very good. It was hard to get because the soldiers who were camped all around us watched every stalk and gathered it as soon as it was out of the ground. We also ate, more to give relish, the small wild onion which abounded in all the fields around and gave its flavor to all the milk we could get.

The fare and lodgings were very hard, but I was with my husband and that gave joy to the visit both to Nannie and myself. We rode about among the camps on Mr. Blackford's fine roan and Nannie rode his black with old Tarleton riding at her side keeping her horse in control with a check rein. She was a great pet and constantly cheered by the soldiers when she rode out among them, and would return their cheers with a smile and a bow which would produce more applause. Capt. I. F. Lucado, the quartermaster of Pickett's brigade, was very kind to her and she would spend most of the day at his quarters, where she was the pet and the admiration of everyone.

On one of the Sundays we were at Taylorsville we all went up to "Old Fork Church", a colonial edifice where all the old families in that part of Hanover County had worshipped for a hundred or more years. This neighborhood was particularly dear to my husband who in his boyhood spent much time at Edgewood, Dewberry, Airwell, Oaklands, Ragswamp and a number of other places owned by the Minors, Cookes, Pages, Nelsons, Berkleys, Fontaines and others, all of whom are his relations.

On this particular beautiful Sunday I rode horseback accompanied by a cavalcade of officers from Pickett's staff and division. At the church, besides a large number of soldiers, we found the neighborhood people in great force and among them many of Mr. Blackford's friends and relations. I never enjoyed a service more nor saw a more attentive and devoted audience. There were many Generals, Colonels, other officers and private soldiers. As Mrs. Judith Nelson, of Oaklands, came into the door she ejaculated loudly and with much unction: "Lord, I thank Thee that Thy house is filled!" She is the widow of Mr. Thomas Nelson, son of General Nelson of the Revolution. She is "Aunt Judy" to everyone in the neighborhood.

The ride to and from church was very delightful. We went at a rapid gait, but owing to the high qualities of my roan, I outstripped all my escorts, much to my delight.

I remember a charming visit to Dewberry, the residence of Mrs. Edmonia Cooke, whose son, Churchill, later married Mary Blackford, my husband's sister. The house was full of company, principally of young ladies, only one of whom I now remember: Miss Lucy Fontaine, who was very pretty. Of the many military beaux whom we found there, visitors from Pickett's division, many were to be left dead upon the field after the glorious charge that division made at Gettysburg.

I can ever remember the simple elegance of the house, the cordial hospitality, the delicious dinner served, and my recollection, sharpened doubtless by my scant fare in camp, especially recurs to an elegant quarter of mutton dressed with drawn butter, eggs and green pickle. I am sure there never was such a delicious piece of meat. I remember also the lovely face and gracious manner of old Mrs. Cooke and how she made us feel the sincerity of her welcome. Surely there was a charm, a grace, an elegance in the Virginian hospitality of those days which have no equal. The abolition of slavery and the poverty of our people have rendered such a life almost impossible. Life in the country, in Virginia, would not have been distinctly Virginian without the old "mammy" who had nursed all the children, or the grey-haired old butler under whose guardian care they had all developed into young men and women. His courtly bow, his patronizing instructions to his subordinates were very awe-inspiring. So, too, the fat cook in the kitchen and the jolly scullion were essential to the cheer. All are now gone, and with them the luxurious living and the genial hospitality.

Just when my visit ended I cannot tell. I returned home slowly visiting along the way while my husband, and the army moved forward towards the crest of its endeavors. I return to his letters:

From Capt. Blackford.
Mr. Rode's house, Orange County, June 11th.

I always like to send you a letter when I am moving to let you know where I am. I did not do so the first night I was out because I was too tired. I went from Taylorsville to Edgewood where I took dinner and spent two hours. Then I crossed the North Anna at Reid's Mill and joined my party at Cedar Fork and went to Rehobeth where we spent the night. Yesterday we came about thirty miles to this place which is about seven miles from Raccoon Ford where Pickett's division camped last night. I am quite unwell and travelling makes me feel worse. We learn there was a great cavalry battle on Tuesday in which we were entirely victorious but the loss was very heavy on both sides. Several of Stuart's staff were wounded but I have not heard that William was hurt.

Camp near Mr. Ewell's, Culpeper County, June 12th.

We left our camp in Orange County about nine and came on here, a point three miles from the Courthouse, with Pickett's division. I received yesterday an expression of approbation from General Longstreet which was agreeable to me and I know to you. General Longstreet's headquarters are near the

Courthouse today but I will remain on duty at present at Pickett's. The cavalry fight at Brandy Station can hardly be called a *victory*. Stuart was certainly surprised and but for the supreme gallantry of his subordinate officers and the men in his command it would have been a day of disaster and disgrace. My old regiment distinguished itself greatly, and I hear much well-deserved praise for Captain Thomas Whitehead and Col. Watts. Stuart is blamed very much, but whether or not fairly I am not sufficiently well informed to say. The country around here is looking very green and pretty, but there is nothing growing but grass. It looks strange to see miles of land and not an acre of sod broken for grain. What will the people do for bread? It will be a serious question next winter. No fences, no wood, no grain. Such is the desolation of war.

June 13th.

I was up at General Longstreet's headquarters today and was most cordially received by him. I am entirely well now, but have very little to do. I do not know how long we will be here, but I suppose for some time as we have too small an army to advance as long as A. P. Hill is at Fredericksburg with his corps. Ewell has gone with his corps into the Valley, and we have only Longstreet with three divisions at this point, not numbering more than twenty thousand men. I do not feel that our position is a strong one. If Hooker concentrates rapidly and advances upon this corps he could overpower it before the other corps could come to our support. However I take it that General Lee knows more about this than I do; at all events I leave it to him without my advice and without losing much sleep about it. If General Lee can carry out what I believe are his designs he will achieve the greatest victory of the war. At all events this army cannot be routed, and will hold its own against any force which will be brought against it.

Camp at Yowell's Tavern, June 14th.

Your letter came and was most welcome. Yesterday all the camp was broken up and all the wagons packed and the troops ready to march, but they did not move. I moved my camp up to

Taylor Scott's tent, and there spent the night and most the day. It is now late at night and I have just gotten a place and time to write. The unwonted movement was caused by the enemy moving two regiments across the Rappahannock and then going back again, like the King of France. Our troops all seemed prepared to move backwards, from which I suppose it is intended to make the Rapidan our line of defense, which surprises me. We are all in suspense and anxiety to hear from Ewell and his operations in The Valley. We have a rumor that Milroy has evacuated Winchester and Ewell reached there yesterday. I saw Major Fitzhugh, of Stuart's, today and he told me that William and his horses escaped without a scratch. Eugene is with Ewell but I hear nothing from him. He will delight in this trip as he has never been in the Valley before. I went to church today and heard the Rev. General Pendleton preach a very good sermon. His avocations were curiously mixed in his apparel. The gown covered up his uniform entirely except for the wreath and stars of a general on his collar which peeped out to mildly protest against too much "peace on earth" and the boots and spurs clanked around the chancel with but little sympathy with the doctrine of "good will towards men." I think it would have been better if he had, like Ireton and Cromwell, have preached with no garb but that of a soldier. I do not much approve of mixing the two professions, except for the duties of a chaplain. Generals Lee and Longstreet, and a considerable number of little brigs were present, not to mention a host of stars of less magnitude. A few ladies were there, but only those who felt that in the case they fell into the hands of the enemy their looks would insure their safety.

June 16th.

The army is on the move. It started at twelve M. today, we hear to join Ewell in the Valley, but I know nothing about it. I will write you as often as I have time and space.

We marched only eighteen miles today. We reached here at two o'clock and I am bivouacked in a Mr. Fletcher's yard. Various rumors from Winchester. All agree we have had a victory and captured many prisoners, wagons and supplies. That corps always gets the plunder. Ewell won his right to Jackson's mantle at Jackson's game on Jackson's ground. This success will give the corps more confidence in Ewell. We are as yet all in the dark as to what all this movement means. We have heard cannon this evening but cannot tell in which direction it is. I hope to get this letter to you by someone going back, but I am in dispair about hearing from you again. Who should I find today on the roadside, in the corner of a fence but Mrs. Grey Carroll. She had been over to Fauquier and sold her husband's sheep and was returning with the money. She had started with an old man and a small one-horse cart which was so uncomfortable she had undertaken to walk ten miles, but Captain Whitehead sent a member of his company back with her and he made her take his horse and upon it rode here where, to her surprise, he met her husband with his battery. She has shown great resolution and she reminds me of you. I like her very much and I am sure you will. I wish you would invite her up to see you. I am, of course, anxious about Eugene but I suppose he is safe as I have heard nothing to the contrary.

Berry's Ferry, June 19th.

I wrote you from Gaines Crossroads on Tuesday or Wednesday and gave it to an old gentleman by the roadside who said he would give it to someone going to Culpeper Courthouse so possibly you got it. The evening of the day after we camped at Piedmont not far from Major James Jones's. The day was very hot and the troops suffered greatly. Some died on the roadside from the effects of the heat. I met much kindness from your Marshall relations as I passed through Fauquier. First I was hailed by Mrs. Barton, who had come out to the roadside with her mother and sisters to bring supplies to their friends. I went to their carriage and took a slight lunch and renewed my acquaintaince with them. Going a little further I was stopped by Dr. Cary Ambler and his wife, with whom I took a more substantial meal and drank a very good glass of home-made wine. They, too, were on the roadside with a large stock of supplies for the soldiers: buttermilk, ham, bread, pickle, etc., and where deemed advisable, something more, stronger than milk. At Markham I went to see the family and was pressed to stay for dinner, but as I found General Lee was to dine there, and I had already eaten two dinners, I declined and went to Mrs. Stribling's to call. I spent several hours there in compliance with the demands of their hospitality and ate what might, I suppose, be called a third dinner, dining with General Pendleton and many other officers. After dinner I went to Piedmont to camp and yesterday came on to this place. Pickett's division only got as far as Paris, in Fauquier, last night. Hood crossed the Shenandoah about a mile from here. Rain last night made the fording very deep but not impossible. I fear it may yet rise and give General Lee some trouble. What Lee's plans are no one knows, of course. Even though I am on the staff of the second in command I know nothing. I passed yesterday in sight of your old home, "Snowdown" at the foot of the ridge, and pictured myself how you once looked as you ran about the yard in short dresses and bare feet. I wished you were there then, only I should have preferred that Nannie was your substitute in the short dress and bare feet performance. As I passed by your brother's old place near Paris I wondered what you would have thought, when a girl, had you been able to lift the veil of the future and see your future husband ride by covered with dirt, with sword, pistol and uniform, and surrounded by thousands of fierce looking soldiers, all weary and sore-foot. Such a vision would have puzzled philosophers and prophets and all speculation would have been baffled.

As I write two hundred and sixty yankee cavalry are passing. They were captured yesterday at Middleburg by some of Jones' brigade. Their horses and equipment will do much to make our cavalry more efficient. This will balance our loss at Brandy Station. One of Hooker's aides was captured yesterday bearing a dispatch from Hooker to Stoneman ordering him to advance to Snicker's Gap. If he does it will be bad for him, as we have a large force of infantry on this side of the river;—I mean the Loudoun side as I have not yet crossed. Hooker is moving towards Leesburg with the intention, it is thought, of crossing the Potomac at White's Crossing into Maryland to prevent Lee from crossing at Williamsport. We find it hard to get any accurate information as to the amount of captures made by Ewell but I hear it is some seven thousand prisoners and vast stores of everything needful to the comfort of an army including guns, wagons, horses, corn, wheat, bacon, &,&. and also great stores captured at Martinsburg, Berryville and Charleston. I rode up to Millwood, in Clarke County yesterday, stopping to inspect Mr. Burwell's beautiful place, "Carter Hall." The country is beautiful but no crops but grass are growing. What the people will live on I cannot tell, yet, at the first blush of their joy at seeing us they are hospitable in sharing their small stock of provisions as they were lavish in their welcome of the first soldiers who passed down The Valley. Everywhere we hear the same talk of oppression and cowardly cruelty of Milroy. How I wish we could have captured him! But the infamy he will live to see heaped upon his name and fame will impose a heavier punishment upon him than any we could inflict under the laws of war. His course in shamelessly abandoning his men in time of danger, after getting them into the trap, is in keeping with his cruel oppression to the helpless and unprotected people of the lower Valley. He seems to be brave only when his opponents are women and children. He flies when armed men approach. Milroy threatened to burn the town of Winchester if Ewell attacked him. Ewell replied that if he did he would raise the black flag and put the garrison to sword without mercy. Not a house was burned.

Clarke County, June 20th.

I have nothing much to do. I carry an occasional message for the General or get some information, but, as a rule, I merely go along the road with the rest of the army. My anxiety about Vicksburg is very great. If success crowns our efforts both there and here it will be the beginning of the end. If otherwise the war will be greatly prolonged. I find it very hard to control a burning desire for revenge when I hear the piteous tale of wrongs which these people of Clarke have suffered at the hands of the yankee soldiers. It is scarcely fair, however, to call them yankees, for nine-tenths of them are foreigners sent as substitutes for the native-born patriots who thus would bleed vicariously for the Union. The people of this country are very noble, and I trust they will never again be exposed to the depredations of these vandal invaders. Were I to tell you all I have heard of their sufferings it would at one and the same time sadden and anger you, and all for no good. I trust that our own beautiful home may never be subjected to such desolation, or you and Nannie to such insults.

Berryville, June 21st.

We were to have moved this morning but so far no orders have come. Pickett's division is all around me. I am utilized, as we move, as a guide and scout for General Longstreet, as I know the country well. Pickett's division was yesterday thrown into line of battle just at Egmont, your old home in Loudoun. We do not know yet where we are going nor have I any conjecture as to General Lee's plans. General Lee has not consulted me, strange to say, and I am left to vain speculations. We have many rumors afloat, mostly derived from yankee prisoners, amongst them that Johnston has given Grant a good thrashing. I am almost tempted to believe it. I would do so if it were anyone but Johnston in command on our side. He is a very able man, I doubt not, but seems to so doubt the ability of his troops to carry out the plans his skill devises that he will not test it. No victory has ever been won without bringing about a fight.

Monday night, June 24th.

Tomorrow morning at three o'clock we take up our line of march for Maryland and Pennsylvania. We will cross the river at Williamsport. I wish it were to be at Shepherdstown, that I might see the country that is so familiar to me from your descriptions of your early life there when at school and which is associated in my mind with you.

Old Tarleton has just caught up with us. He says you have gone to Lynchburg but will return to Albemarle on Monday, General Jenkins sent one thousand head of cattle, gathered in Pennsylvania, which will help our cause greatly. Tell

Nannie I shall try to get her something pretty in Pennsylvania.
However General Lee has given orders there is to be no pillaging except by systematic process under the control of the quartermaster and commissary. All supplies to be taken that way
are to be paid for in Confederate money. Does that not seem
strange? Especially when we consider how this country we are
now in has been treated. But Lee is right. Only thus can he
maintain discipline in his army and mitigate the horrors of
war. He sets an example to the world in not making the wrong
of his enemy the measure of his right. Private pillaging soon
demoralizes an army. My prayers will be for you and General
Lee tonight.

Maryland, near Williamsport, June 25th.
As I crossed the Potomac today I felt a great gulf was fixed
between us, and the thought saddened me. The head of our
corps struck the Potomac about noon today, Pickett in front.
The rest of the corps, I suppose, will cross tomorrow and proceed at once in support of Ewell, who is said to be at Chambersburg. A. P. Hill crossed at Shepherdstown last night. I have
never seen the army in such fine condition. We marched from
Berryville here with scarcely a straggler and the report from
every division is the same. Of course I feel anxious about the
result but I never have been so confident of success before,
provided we are not cut off from our line of supplies. But about
all these matters I need not trouble you. General Lee will look
after them all without my aid or interference. I started early
yesterday morning, about three o'clock and camped at a place
called Darksville. Launcelot and myself went to Martinsville
and dined with Mr. Conrad, where we were kindly welcomed.
We had the usual amount of smiles and joy from the loyal and
sour looks from the disloyal, though the latter class were somewhat over-awed, at least the women did not curse us as they
did last year. I tried to be very conciliating to a little girl who
reminded me of Nannie and said, as I looked at the depot we
burned last year:
"How do you do, little girl? I can see that you had a fire here
lately."

She turned very sharply upon me and said with a decided yankee twang: "Don't speak to me!"

"Why, you must be a rebel!" said an officer near me, with a pleasant smile.

"I scorn the name!" She answered, turning up her nose in the most defiant and acrid manner.

. . . Just here this letter was interrupted by a servant bringing me a waiter with some nice butter and milk with the compliments of a Mrs. Finley, who lives in the nearest house to our camp. She is the niece of the Rev. George W. Carter, who was the Methodist minister in Lynchburg at the Court Street Church. She had spent some time with him, and therefore knew who I was. I at once paid my respects and was charmed with her, and, by invitation, spent a very pleasant evening at her house.

The crossing of the river by our troops was very picturesque. General Lee was on the bank on the Maryland side surrounded by ladies who came down to see the sight and to admire him. The soldiers waded into the water without stopping to roll up their pantaloons and came over in good order as if on review, cheering at every step. One fellow, as he stepped on the Maryland shore, exclaimed: "Well, boys I've been seceding for two years and now I've got back into the Union again!" Another said to the crowd of ladies he thought were Union in their sentiments: "Here we are, ladies, as rough and ragged as ever but back again to bother you."

The joy of the day was marred this evening by a military execution which took place in this division. I heard the death-march but fortunately did not hear the firing. It was not the victim of any trial of which I was judge-advocate, I am glad to say. There were four like executions, I was told, in Rodes' division. Horses are becoming quite plentiful as they are sent back by our vanguard. We need them much, but they are too heavy and too clumsy for either cavalry or artillery. Unless they are kept well shod they soon give out and go lame on these well paved roads.

Greencastle, Penn. June 26th.

I crossed "Mason's and Dixon's Line" to-day and am now some five or six miles within the boundaries of the Keystone State, surrounded by enemies and black looks, Dutchmen and big barns. Night before last I slept on the sacred soil, last night in "My Maryland" and to-night I will sweetly slumber in the land of Penn and Protection. This is a very large change of venue for so large an army. When I awoke this morning the rain was falling in torrents and has continued all day, much to my discomfort, for I have been wet to the skin since two and a half this morning, and as I have a bad cold, I am none the better for it. The head of the army was detained in Hagerstown about four hours to-day and I had a good chance to inspect the place and did so as far as the rain would permit. The people are greatly divided in sentiment, but far the greater part are Unionists. The minority, however, are very large and very enthusiastically Southern and very bold in expressing their sentiments. One little girl, about sixteen years old, struck me particularly. She was a Miss Dodge and first cousin to the unfortunate young man whose candy so nearly overcame your affections as to give me great uneasiness some eight years ago. She lives near Honeywood, but on the Maryland side of the river. Many ladies gathered around General Lee and seemed overcome with their emotion. The state of society in that part of Maryland is terrible. With them Civil War really exists, and the different elements of society are arrayed against each other with great bitterness. So far as I have seen since crossing the Pennsylvania line, there is not much to indicate that we are in enemy's country. The people, of course, are not pleased to see us, but they are not demonstrative in their hatred or very shy in their treatment to us. As no maltreatment is permitted, and no pillage of other than their stock, they are so favorably disposed towards us that they almost seem friendly. Private property is respected and men are not allowed even to go into a yard to get water without permission of the owner. The orders even go so far, and they are strictly enforced, as to prohibit the burning of rails for firewood, a rule not enforced in Virginia and one I must say I think unnecessary here. Of course there will be some pillaging and even more violent robbery, for it is hard to strictly enforce any rule in so large an army, but such acts will be exceptional, as every possible means are taken to enforce General Lee's order, and the rule meets the approval of the army generally. I think the citizens have remained at home. It is reported that Ewell has captured a large number of militia a few days since and turned them loose with the admonition to go home and tend to their business or he would treat them very badly. I doubt whether the report is true.

To-morrow we march to some point beyond Chambersburg. We have Richmond papers of the 23d. and Baltimore papers of the 24th. but no news except the accounts of the excitement of the yankees created by the invasion. General Lee looks well and seems to be in fine spirits. He is handsomely dressed and the grandest looking man I ever saw today in Hagerstown. The feeling of the men for him is that of blind devotion. Our army is not costing the Confederate States much at this time. Our Northern brethren are supplying us very freely with both bread and meat.

In camp, three miles north of Chambersburg. June 28th.
On the march I have little to do; nothing indeed but act as aide and carry messages along the column, which is not laborious and gives me a fine opportunity to know all there is to be known. We are now in the Cumberland Valley, and a fine country it is, that is as the yankees count fineness—small farms divided into fields no larger than our garden and barns much larger than their houses in which live their owners, their families and laborers. The land is rich and highly cultivated, much more highly than the men who own it, among whom, while I note physical comfort, I see no signs of social refinement. All seems to be on a dead level, like a lot of fat cattle in a clover field. Except in the towns I saw no signs of social distinctions and a common dollar mark seemed to place all on a common plane. In Chambersburg there are some beautiful places which tell of taste, culture and refinement, but in the country around there is nothing but the same tasteless houses and the same

immense barns, each the counterpart of the other.

The people of Chambersburg are very loyal to the "old flag" and keep it displayed everywhere possible. I rode through the town with General Kemper, at the head of his brigade. The windows and porches were filled with women who were covered with flags, and each one had a flag, waving it over our troops as they passed along the street, often giving them a sharp bit of their tongues in addition. The men exercised forebearance and seldom replied, but occasionally hit a sharp lick in reply. We heard one of the 7th. Virginia say to a very bold looking girl who was standing on a porch with a great flag pinned and hanging over her shoulders and over her bosom: "Look here, Miss, you'd better take that flag off!" She replied with some asperity: "I won't do it. Why should I?"

"Because, Miss, these old rebs are hell on breastworks."

Not a very refined joke, but the woman brought it upon herself, but did not seem to be the least abashed by it. General Kemper and myself were much amused, and we made a comment, which is certainly true, that where men are thus herded together there is formed a confluent wit which may find its flash, like that from a Leyden jar, from the dullest knob in the regiment. This I have seen often, as has every officer who is a close observer.

The stores in Chambersburg were generally open to the quartermaster and commissaries, but generally closed to soldiers. By some little persuasion they could get in. Yesterday some articles were purchased with Confederate money. I have thus far only purchased a hat, for people generally were very unwilling to sell for the currency. Strong as my feelings are towards the yankees as a class I find they melt when they come to the individual.

The town of Chambersburg has six or seven thousand people but the streets are lined from one end to the other with young and able-bodied men. A conscription, such as is in force with us, I am sure, would have garnered five or six hundred good soldiers from the curb-stones along the line of our march through town.

Our corps stopped here to-day, for what purpose I am unable

to tell. Orders are issued preventing anyone from going to a private house for any purpose, and we are thus shut down to our commissary department for rations. It is obvious that these people are as much surprised as delighted by the treatment they are receiving.

Same Camp, June 30th.
You never saw a country so densely populated as this. The farms are small. One of ours would make twenty of these. General Lee's orders have been enforced and obeyed with greater rigor than I had supposed possible. Of course such things as are the supplies of war, such as forage, cattle, horses, and such are taken by the duly constituted officers but such devastation as the yankees practice on our people is not known. Chambersburg is as quiet and orderly as if there was a con- tinuing Sunday, and the ladies and children may and do walk about everywhere without the least disrespect, or indeed with- out a word being said to them of any kind. So, in fact, can the men who literally swarm the streets. Our men take great pleasure in saying to these men: "We don't come to make war upon women and children as your men do in our country." Of course some acts of violence will take place. Where there are so many men it is hard to keep watch on all. Some chickens, sheep, onions and pigs will be taken, but I challenge the world to show an instance of an invading army behaving with such consideration, good order and propriety. I have seen men, whose homes were ashes from a yankee torch, eating the hard- est rations and without the commonest necessities even for a Confederate soldier, when the least show of violence would have secured every luxury the heart of a soldier could wish.

I have not spoken to a citizen since I crossed the line nor have I been under a roof, nor do I intend to do so. Never in my life have I seen so many ugly women as I have seen since coming to this place. It may be that the pretty ones do not show themselves but the ugly ones parade around everywhere. The men are not remarkable either way. They have an awkward, Dutch look and the analogy between them and horses and barns is perfect. Men, women and children are all afflicted with a yankee twang that grates against my nerves and ear-drums most terribly. I have heard nothing from Eugene, who is with Ewell, or from Stuart. Ewell is much in advance and Stuart's whereabouts is unknown.

Near Gettysburg, July 3d.

I left Chambersburg yesterday at two o'clock in the morning and we made a march of twenty-three miles by twelve o'clock without a single straggler, I believe. On the road we heard that on the evening before (July 1) General Lee had met the enemy about two miles from Gettysburg and drove them back several miles, capturing some five thousand prisoners, without any serious loss on our part. Soon after we reached this place yesterday a very terrible battle began, which raged until nine, the particulars of which I have been unable to gather, except the two wings of the enemy were driven back with great loss, but their center stood firm. We captured some two thousand prisoners and, it is said, fifteen guns. All this, however, is but a rumor, and even at corps headquarters we know little. Hood is said to be wounded, Barksdale killed and Archer captured. The fight commenced again this morning about four o'clock and has been raging at intervals and in different quarters ever since, until now, at ten o'clock, as I write under the shade of a tree, a terrible cannonading is going on. General Longstreet is a little to my right, awaiting orders I suppose. His men are not yet engaged except the artillery. I have heard nothing from William or Eugene. This will be a great day in history. I wish I could see more and know more of what is going on, but I suppose our lines under the cannonading are preparing to charge.

(Continued July 4th.)

The battle so increased in violence that I could no longer write. I knew it was a terrible battle but how terrible I did not know until it was over. The results of the day even now are not accurately known. We were the attacking party,—that is Pickett's division was, for I can only speak of what I saw, and we were not able to drive the enemy out of his fortified lines on top of the hill except at certain points which we were unable to hold. They vastly outnumbered us, and though our men made a charge which will be the theme of the poet, painter and historian of all ages, they could not maintain the enemy's lines much less capture them.—The might of numbers will tell. Our loss in men and officers exceeds anything I have ever known. The loss is especially great among the officers, and those from Virginia particularly.

Your cousin, Jimmy Marshall, was killed leading a North Carolina regiment. I am ignorant of the fate of either William or Eugene. I was in the bivouac of the Eleventh Virginia and saw Kirk Otey and all our friends who survived the charge. Kirk is wounded in the arm by a piece of shell. Jno. Holmes Smith has a bullet hole through his thigh but was lying on the ground as bright and happy as any of the boys around him. From what I can learn there were six killed from the Home Guard in the charge and five wounded.

Williamsport, Md., July 6th.

Well here I am again in sight of dear old Virginia. I was sent back here on some duty. The wagon trains have pretty much all arrived and the troops are but a little way behind, all marching in perfect order and without molestation by the enemy. There are only two regiments of infantry here at this time, but all the wagon trains, and they are crossing the river quite rapidly. Lee has fallen back and the campaign has failed, but nothing could be more orderly. There is not the least resemblance of a retreat except that we are counter-marching. The counter-march is as orderly, and Lee's orders about depredations are as well obeyed, as when we were advancing.

The charge of Pickett's division was the historic feature of the battle. General Lee sent word to General Pickett that his troops had made a name in history; that they had done all they could do and the blame rested on him, (Lee), for ordering them to do what was an impossibility.

Val Harris is unhurt, tell Mrs. Spence. He covered himself with glory. When the color-bearer of his regiment was shot down he siezed the flag and, with it in his hand, led the regiment over the breastworks from which they had driven the yankees. General Armistead fell, waving his hat on his sword, on the enemy's breastworks twenty paces ahead of his men. Your cousin, Robert Fisher was wounded in the leg but not seriously. Berkley Minor was wounded in the hand and Samuel Henry Early in the foot.

Same Camp, July 7th.

The rise of the river prevents the wagon train from crossing. William joined me yesterday, and we were sitting talking at my tent door when we saw some very handsomely dressed cavalry come out of the woods on a hill just opposite us. We supposed they were our men, but their handsome dress made us somewhat suspicious and we were getting our glasses out to inspect them when a battery of guns came dashing out of the woods, wheeled into line on top of the hill just opposite, unlimbered and in an instant opened up on the mighty camp in and around the town. The first shell burst over John Scott's head while he was putting on the bridle of my horse, but it no wise disturbed him, and in a second or two he had both William's and my horse bridled and saddled and we were off to aid in the defense, while he went on getting supper. Quite a number of disorganized troops, wounded men and others assembled as soon as the first shot was fired and as soon as they showed themselves the guns limbered up and the whole party started off at a rapid rate without waiting for our charge. They were followed by a small body of organized cavalry. The force of the enemy had come up the river and had gotten in the rear of the army without being noticed. William and myself got back in a short time and John had a good supper for us. I cannot keep myself from believing the fall of Vicksburg, a rumor which comes to us through the yankee lines.

I am in somewhat better spirits this morning. I cannot say why, for the outlook is very far from bright, and this looks much to me as the turning point of the war. As we were the invading party at Gettysburg and made the attack, our failure to carry the enemy's lines amounted to defeat, though we held our own, slept on the battle-field and remained there for twenty-four hours without molestation, showing that we had so punished the enemy that they were incapable of an advance.

If the rumor from Vicksburg is true the Confederacy has been cut in two and our supplies from Texas cut off. So great is the disparity in numbers and resources that any loss to us is a great loss, and our losses at both places have been heavy.

I grieve deeply over Pickett's division, in which I had so many friends. Three of its brigades were absent but the three brigades remaining lost thirty-nine hundred killed, wounded and missing and almost all their officers. Poor Virginia bleeds again at every pore. There will be few firesides in her midst where the voice of mourning will not be heard when the black-lettered list of losses is published. The residue of the army did not suffer proportionally, I am glad to say, and is in good fighting trim.

What our loss was in the late battle I cannot tell but not less than sixteen to eighteen thousand men have been withdrawn from the active, available force.

July 12th.

Vicksburg has fallen! I trust I over-estimate its importance. The fact that it has been so long and so gallantly defended against such fearful odds may make us do so. I will try to get you a copy of General Lee's address to his troops after the battle. It is beautiful and compares most favorably with the apologetic bombast the yankee generals pour out to their own troops after a repulse. He does not claim a victory, takes all the blame upon himself and tells the troops the same valor displayed by them on the field of Gettysburg will assure their success in the future. He thanks them for their gallantry. There is now a pontoon bridge at Williamsport, and by tomorrow there will be one at Falling Waters, below this point. It happened there was a large amount of timber at Williamsport and out of it we built twenty boats and on them built a pontoon bridge in four days. I do not know whether General Lee will recross without a battle. One is certainly imminent now. It seems strange when one reads the bragging reports of the battle of Gettysburg published in the Northern papers, and is told by them how demoralized and depreciated is Lee's army, that nine days have elapsed during which it has awaited an attack from the exultant foe, with all its baggage on the banks of a swollen river behind it, and yet not a hostile gun has been fired at my part of it except by the lost and nervous little company which broke up our supper nearly five days since, of which I wrote you.

CHAPTER XI

OUR SKY IS DARK

Camp near Falling Waters, July 13th.

HERE I am in dear old Virginia and I am very thankful that is so . . .

I was interrupted here and had to postpone writing for a day, and I may have to stop again at any moment and move my headquarters further from the river, at least out of range of enemy shell.

The wagon trains commenced fording the river yesterday morning and most of the men were safely over by night. Our wagon and the rest of headquarters wagons crossed at Falling Waters on the pontoon bridge. One bridge was built at the place while we were advancing. It was made from boats captured at Richmond last summer, but a very insufficient guard was placed there while we were in Pennsylvania and the yankees destroyed it. Twenty more boats were built at Williamsport, as I have already written you, and of them a first-rate bridge was built, over which most of the army crossed on yesterday. This morning Ewell's force forded the river at Williamsport. The rain last night raised the river somewhat and made the wading very deep. Eugene has just left my camp, where he stopped while the regiment was passing, to get something to eat, and I never saw anyone enjoy a meal so much. He was very hungry having been in line of battle four days without the chance of cooking anything and having anything but hardtack and water. He had quite a handsome skirmish yesterday evening and he says his regiment nearly destroyed a regiment of cavalry which had the audacity to charge our infantry line. He is greatly distressed at leaving Maryland and thinks we should have fought the enemy there at all hazards,

I do not concur. General Lee had tendered them battle for a week and as they did not accept and were being reinforced hourly he very wisely, I think, recrossed the river. To do so in safety in the presence of so great an army without the loss of a man or of any property was a great military feat. That he should have been permitted to do so shows how hard a blow he struck. Still, with such an army as Meade has, upon its own ground, it ought to have forced a fight. Had the conditions been reversed no one can doubt the result. I suppose now that Lee will make his line of defence at Martinsburg and Bunker Hill, as he did last year, keeping the cavalry near Martinsburg and the infantry on the Opaquan. I crossed the bridge with General Longstreet. We were nearly the last to cross, all but the rear guard, and the enemy were keeping a very sharp cannonade upon us. After we crossed, our rear guard, under the command of General Pettigrew, of South Carolina, was sharply attacked and the General was killed. He was one of the most brilliant men of the army and his loss will be greatly felt. Captain Thomas J. Kirkpatrick called to see me this evening. His wagon, trunk and servant have all been captured and he is in a very uncomfortable condition.

Bunker Hill, July 16th.

I was quite sick yesterday but had been in the saddle many hours. I am better now and much cheered by a letter from you. The men are enjoying the rest here very much and they will be benefited by it. They are washing and dressing up again and repairing the ravages of the campaign upon their scanty wardrobe. They are in fine spirits and not the least depressed by the results of the invasion. I could not get anything for you in Maryland or Pennsylvania without doing things of which you would disapprove and which were against General Lee's orders. Launcelot purchased in Maryland a few spools of cotton thread, etc. and Eugene secured by purchase in Pennsylvania some other articles but as his headquarters wagon was captured he lost them and all his baggage besides.

I was shocked to read the account of the mode in which Mr. Kinckle has stripped himself to aid the suffering poor. Be

sure to send him a barrel of flour to aid him aid others. I have
no sugar and can get none from any source, and rye coffee
without cream or sugar. It is not enticing and makes one long
for peace.

Same Camp, July 18th.

Raining, still raining and with a south wind blowing up
fresh banks of clouds; so no immediate prospects of cessation.
The campaign we have just finished will be a valuable lesson.
We will not attempt another invasion beyond a cavalry raid.
An invasion can only be made by an army fully equipped
and with numbers much in excess of those opposing. To keep
open communications with the base of supplies and to protect transportation and exposed flanks requires large forces
detached from the main body, and unless supplies of food and
ammunition are plentiful there is always danger of their giving out at the time they are the most needed. The mere want
of horse shoes would have prevented us going far into Pennsylvania. We have no adequate supply of either shoes or portable forges, and as soon as a horse casts a shoe and has to go
barefoot on macadamized roads, of which there are plenty in
Pennsylvania, he becomes lame and of little use. Indeed has
to be abandoned unless shod very soon. I picked up a very
fine large horse near Chambersburg and intended substitut-
ing him for one of our wagon horses, but he cast a shoe, and
within five miles became so utterly useless I had to give him
to a Maryland farmer.

Few people have an idea of the extent of a column of ar
army. If General Lee had seventy thousand infantry, twelve
thousand cavalry, one hundred and seventy-five guns and the
usual impedimenta his column would extend over sixty miles
Thus:

The 70,000 infantry with ambulances . . . 20 miles.
      12,000 cavalry . . . . 12 "
        175 cannon, caissons, forges, etc. . .   8 ".
      1,500 wagons . . . . 20 "
        Total distance on a march . . 60 "

Of course, this would be, if possible, divided into at least three columns of twenty miles each, but still you can see, from these estimates, that a big army takes much space. I am pretty sure that my figures are nearly correct, for the distance occupied on a march is much more than would be requisite to move the same number of men on a parade. I think I have underestimated both the number and space of the wagon trains of the army, but I have no data except my observation of them. Sometime one balky horse will make a gap in the line of half a mile, and I am trying to average.

To protect those long lines in enemy's country used up much of the effective force of many men. When among our own people such protection is little needed. A lady finds it hard enough to manage her train in a ballroom and to protect it from the threatening feet about her. How much harder is it for General Lee to manage his.

This letter, I fear, has bored you, but as we proposed to keep a species of diary I must put down my thoughts and theories, and one of them is that we have never been strong enough, or well enough provided with munitions to justify an invasion. The enemy has a better chance of invading us because our land is much more sparsely inhabited and because of the information they derived from the negroes; but with these advantages, in Virginia at least, they have always been defeated.

General Stuart is much criticized for his part in our late campaign, whether rightfully I cannot say. During his many reviews in Culpeper he was said to have twelve thousand cavalry ready for duty. He crossed the river with six thousand, but they played a small part in the great drama either as the "eyes of the army" or any other capacity. In his anxiety to "do some great thing" General Stuart carried his men beyond the range of usefulness and Lee was not thereafter kept fully informed as to the enemy's movements as he should have been, or as he would have been had Stuart been nearer at hand. I was much amused to see Stuart pass through Martinsburg with a large cavalcade of staff and couriers and two bugles blowing most furiously. Lee, Hill, Ewell and Longstreet respectively passed the point at which I was standing, each with one or two persons with them and not even a battleflag to make their rank. Launcelot, who was present, says he rode up to The Bower, (Mr. Dandridge's), with the same pomp and show. I scarcely like to write this of so gallant an officer, but all of us have some weaknesses and should be very liberal to each other.

Same Camp, July 19th.

I fear you grow weary of my long letters but you know I can never be idle and I have no other way to work off my surplus energy but in writing to you. Hence you will have to bear it as best you can. They may some day be interesting as the story of my experiences during the war. If I live through it I intend writing from them a diary commencing with the very first of the war. I do not mean to have it printed, but in manuscript. You and Nannie will enjoy it much even ten years after the events have all passed. General Lee has just issued a very wise order cutting down the regimental transportation to one wagon for every three hundred men. This gives rise to a rumor that we are to go back into Maryland, a rumor which, in my opinion, has no foundation. Were I organizing an army I would not allow more than one wagon to a regiment for regimental purposes only during a campaign and that to carry a box for the adjutant, a few axes and cooking utensils, no tents or clothing for men or officers beyond what they carried with them on their backs or horses. Of course there must be quartermaster and commissary and ordnance trains but they should be confined to their legitimate work.

I think you had better sell the mare. I fear she will never get well of her lameness. She will bring you two hundred and fifty or three hundred dollars and I will send you as much or more soon. I think you had better buy seventy-five pounds of common brown sugar and twelve barrels of flour as soon as the new crop comes in. You had better, also, get about a hundred and fifty pounds more of bacon. The money I will send you and what you will get for the mare will, I think, pay for the things and I will feel better satisfied that you will have enough to eat at least. I am anxious about your fuel. I have not heard from William for two days. He was quite unwell with a cold in his head, but in good hands at The Bower.

Culpeper C. H., July 24th.

After a very laborious march we are here. We broke camp at Bunker Hill on the 20th. The troops are very tired and so am I. The weather is so hot the troops suffer much in moving.

Same Camp, July 26th.

Longstreet and Hill are here, camped side by side. I do not know where Lee is but it is rumored we are soon to move towards Fredericksburg or Richmond. I think the campaign is pretty well over for the season, in Virginia anyway. Both armies are in need of rest and recuperation after the mighty contest of Gettysburg. I send you $300 enclosed, two months pay.

Same Camp, July 28th.

With a sad heart I write this evening, for one piece of bad news follows another in quick succession and, though I am usually hopeful I feel much depression now. Our sky is dark and the worst feature is that our people seem to be letting down. We have had only our first reverses, yet many people have gone into a fainting fit. The press seems to take infinite delight in publishing everything to increase the depression and chill the enthusiasm of the army. The Richmond "Enquirer," I observe, speaks of the present as comparable with the darkest days of the Revolution, and, with apparent glee, quotes the price of gold as an indication of our condition. The language of the "Enquirer" I regard as treason.

Same Camp, July 29th.

No letters, and constant rain and the two causes are depressing. Last night, in spite of ditching, the rain ran through my tent and the floor is muddy this morning. It is twenty days since I had a letter, and I only presume you and Nannie are alive. What is being done to secure you against next winter? Ask Father to try to get you three or four hundred bushels of

coal, cost what it may. Coal you must have, if it can be bought.
I hear that William is sick and has gone to Lynchburg.

Same Camp, July 30th.

Two letters, directed to Winchester, reached me last night.
They gladdened my heart. First to business. I do not like the
idea of borrowing to pay my taxes. I must try and make something outside my salary; it will not feed us two months in the
year. We must, however, have money, and it must be ex-
pended on the necessities of life, taxes being among them I
suppose. I will send you a power of attorney to sign my name
to a note, and Father will raise the money with ease, and then
you will lay in at least an eighteen months supply of flour,
coal, bacon and, if possible, some sugar. Don't let other people
persuade you not to do this. It is important. Such articles will
continue to rise in price and the debt will remain stationary;
so even if you do not use the articles yourself you will be
perfectly safe in buying them. I am living as economically as
possible, but, with all care and buying at government prices
from the commissary department, it costs me forty dollars a
month to pay my part of the mess bill, and we have only poor
and poorer beef interspersed with fat bacon, rye coffee, no
butter and no sugar. Still we get on very well and are very well.
If we are to stay long I want you to join us. I have no doubt
you would improve our fare very much, especially vegetable
dishes. We find it impossible to get the commonest vegetables,
as the army all around us eats up everything green as soon as
it is up out of the ground, but I believe you would soon open
the hearts of someone who has a garden to let us have a cabbage or some beans or anything which would break the monotony of the bill of fare we are now using.

If you do come bring very little baggage, but don't leave
your side-saddle, as it will enable you to visit all places of interest around here.

The court is working very smoothly now and we are clean-
ing up all the business of the corps and emptying the guard-
houses in every division, which is an infinite relief to the army.
General Longstreet appreciates my work and loses no oppor-

tunity to compliment me. Mr. Eugene Davis, of Charlottes-ville, will spend the night with me. He has rejoined the army as a private, I believe, not having been re-elected. Is not that a high example of devotion to duty and patriotism? A man of his age and tastes, of fortune and education, who could easily bring influence enough to secure him some office, has entered as a private soldier, and there will be none in the army who will more gallantly or faithfully discharge every duty, from policing the camp to charging the breastworks.

From Mrs. Blackford. Lynchburg, August 1st.
My Precious Husband;

I received your charming letter by Mr. Kinckle. You say nothing about my going down, which disappointed me much. I will send you a box of vegetables by Mr. Vandergrift on Monday. I hope you can get off for a few days and come home, as your affairs here sadly need your attention. I bought Nannie two plain dresses yesterday for which I paid $61.25. I also got some brown cloth for a cloak for her, and I will make them up myself. I shall make my old cloak last through the winter. I went to see John T. Smith and he promised to sell me 150 lbs. of bacon at $1.50 a pound and also some wood, and have it corded. He says it will cost about $20 a cord delivered. Mr. Robert Davis bought a whole boat load and paid $21 a cord for it. Everyone says it will sell for $50 a cord during the winter. I have eight barrels of flour on hand, and Mr. Smith says he will get me some new flour when it comes into the market. He will not charge me any profit and is as kind to me as possible. I will not starve. I have potatoes enough to last all winter and you may not be uneasy about me.

I thought yesterday I had bid farewell to the grey mare as the press-gang took her from me. She was, however, sent back to me later, as, on inspection, it was thought she could not pull the artillery. They pressed Mr. Flood's and Mr. Warwick's horses. You ask me to have my likeness taken for you. It will cost $15 and I think it would be extravagant. But if you want it I will have it taken.

From Capt. Blackford.
Headquarters, Hood's division, August 16th.

We left our camp at Roger's Shop on the Plank Road in Orange on Friday morning at nine o'clock, and made twenty-three miles, camping that night two miles this side of Chancellorsville. I was, of course, much interested in the battle-field, though, outside the results, there is not much of interest in the locality. The relics of the fierce encounter were strewn about everywhere, and at one point, judging from the marks on the trees, I am sure our batteries poured a rain of shell such as has never before been emptied on one spot in the history of warfare. Fragments of shell, broken wheels, dead horses, vast quantities of torn clothing, knapsacks and many bones attest to the carnage of the field. In the ruins of the Chancellorsville House we found the charred remains of many human skeletons showing the truth of the rumor that many wounded perished in the flames when it was burned during the battle. After the house caught fire a sick lady who was in it, and who was unable to walk, had to be carried to some safe place by the officers of General Hooker's staff, one of whom offered her his horse. As the negro was bringing up the horse for her to mount, a shell burst and killed both negro and the horse. Another conical shell passed through her skirts while she was waiting for another horse to be brought up. She describes the scene as very terrible. All but those unable to walk got out of the house. They were left to their fate. As the flames reached their rooms they made heroic efforts to escape and many crawled out of the windows and threw themselves out only to be mangled anew or roasted on the ground against the hot walls and scorching pavements. The charred remains of the men can still be seen. Why the yankees did not save the men from this fate I cannot imagine. I suppose the shot and shell were too destructive. They put up a yellow flag on the house, then placed their batteries all around it, all actively engaged. Of course ours had to reply and could not respect the flag.

The people in this neighborhood are in the most deplorable condition. Before the desolation incident to the battle and the presence of two armies they merely existed. Now their fences and outhouses are destroyed and not a pig left to drive away the wolf of hunger. Many must starve to death. At the house where we camped I do not believe the old man had a mouthful to eat when we got there and his wife had not been out of bed for six months. At the next house they had had no meat of any sort for three months. Our visit was a godsend to the old man and his wife, for we were able to do much for them.

We started yesterday morning. I rode with Cochran, Col. Wood and Launcelot through Fredericksburg and sent the rest of the party on with the wagons to Mr. Hart's house near Hamilton Crossing. We went to our old house where we found Lewis with his engineers camped and we took quite a good dinner with them. I noted little change in the town since our last visit. The erection of some fences had somewhat improved the outlook. A good many people had returned. Lewis, as usual, is very comfortable. Eddie Fisher is with him as rodman. He seems to be a very intelligent boy. We spent last night at Mr. Garnett's, near Mr. Hart's, camping in his yard, and came over this morning to a place where a house called Eastern View used to stand, but which is now burned. It is in full view of Mr. Marye's house and Hamilton's Crossing.

Mrs. Blackford resumes the narrative.

On the 14th of August I wrote a long letter to Mr. Blackford detailing in full the treatment I had received from my boarders, to whom he had written a letter saying that hereafter he desired me to cease taking anyone to board with me, as my health was not good and he desired me to be free to visit him whenever the army was quiet. They took great offense and I was made to feel their indignation deeply. I much regretted the necessity for the step, for they had difficulty in finding another place, and no such desirable home was open to them. But there was no reason I should be so rudely treated in exchange for the months of kindness I had shown them, except, possibly, the trait in human nature which destroys all sense of human gratitude when there is no "lively sense of future favors."

One of the reasons why these boarders took such offense at our refusing longer to keep them was the opinion, not an unnatural one, entertained by most of the refugees from the territory occupied by the enemy, that they were the only sufferers from the war and that it was the high duty of every one who had a home inside of our lines to throw it open to them. The truth was that the people inside the lines were little, if any, better off than those outside. Provisions were very scarce, the usual avocations by which the people were supported were largely suspended, and, owing to the combination of scarcity of provisions and the depreciation of the currency, the vast majority of our people barely had enough to eat to sustain life. What they did eat was of the plainest character. We had few clothes and seldom anything which was new. Ladies' dresses, which long since had been laid aside as past the wearing point, were brought out, refitted, brushed up, turned and required to do duty as "something entirely new." We made our own bonnets and our husbands' hats, and most ladies made their own shoes. Could we have an accurate picture of the dress of that period, both male and female, it would be a valuable contribution to history, for I know nothing which would so accurately tell the story of the privations to which our people were subjected or the self-denial they were impelled to undergo.

Strange to say, with it all there was a degree of gaiety which was wonderful. If people in these "piping times of peace" would be willing to submit to the same self-denial and reduce social gatherings to the same degree of simplicity, many a family would be independent where there is now debt and distress, and yet it would be found that real pleasure would not be curtailed.

There was, however, a dash of chivalric romance in the social life amongst the younger people especially, during those days, not found in times of peace. Where every man under sixty was a soldier and the life of every woman was devoted to the duties incident to his welfare in the field or his comfort in the hospital, it was the legitimate outcome of nature that there should be a heroine for every hero. The man who endured hardships without a murmur, and followed the flag of his regiment to victory was proudly conscious that far away a loving heart beat in unison with his tread, and many a girl who watched over the couch of a wounded hero beguiled a lover as well as a soldier back to life.

The battlefield, the camp, the hospital and the home were in such close proximity that all were soldiers without regard to sex or age, and heroism became so common a virtue that in its universality the hero was almost forgotten. Now that a whole generation has passed [written in 1896] and that there are children whose parents have been born since the war closed, this forgetfulness has naturally been increased. Amongst the class now turning the hill of life there is many a modest veteran whose empty sleeve, halting leg or still aching wound tells of heroic deeds, of battles fought and victories won. In their poverty they are still free and independent, faithful and uncomplaining. Few monuments perpetuate their mighty deeds and no pensions mark the scale of their patriotism. They are carrying these honorable scars to their grave in testimony of duty well done, but with no reward but the consciousness of duty well done and the love and veneration of the land for which they fought and bled. But to return to my letters:

August 26th, 1863.

The city bell has been ringing all day to summon the old men of the town and convalescents from the hospitals to go up the Virginia and Tennessee Railroad to repel a threatened attack by the yankees. Oh the cruel war! Will it ever stop? I feel sometimes in perfect despair about it. It is so doleful for me to sit here alone day after day that I think I had better make arrangements to take Nannie and, with Mary as a nurse, follow the army. I can get somewhat near you and when the army moves I can fall back to the nearest town and wait. The rent of the house will nearly pay my board, for I can live very plainly, on army rations if necessary,—anything to be near you.

The courthouse bell has sounded again since I commenced this, and I can hear the bugle calling Shaner's company of old men to arms. Mr. J. R. Davis has sent over to me to get some

bread to put in his and Mr. Whitehead's haversacks as both
of them have to go out in the party. They are ordered to New
River Bridge, as an attack is expected at that point. Both their
wives are dreadfully distressed, of course, and I know very
well how to sympathize with them. This is indeed an eventful
and exciting age, and one which will be better understood or
realized by our greatgrandchildren if we have any.

I went down to the stable just now to look at your horse.
I think it has improved very much just now in strength and
health but its ankles are still sore, as also are the hips, which
seem to have a sort of eruption. I hope, with the careful management Gabe is giving it, he will soon be well. I got some
beautiful calico to make your collars. I did not buy any linen,
for it is twelve dollars a yard, so I got calico at four dollars
and a half a yard. A dozen linen collars would cost you more
than a month's pay.

From Capt. Blackford.
At Camp, near Fredericksburg, August 18th.

As I write I hear a heavy cannonading in the direction of
Culpeper. It has continued all day. Here it is quiet, though
we are anxious to know what it all means. The enemy has a
picket force at Falmouth, and occasionally a squadron of their
cavalry show themselves opposite Fredericksburg, but it is a
harmless amusement. I went up to Mr. Marye's on Thursday
evening and there met a young lady, whose name I must not
mention for fear this letter may fall into the hands of the
yankees and that she may get into trouble. The story connected with her is this:

When the yankees were trying to carry their pontoons to
the mouth of Deep Run, to cross before the battle of Chancellorsville, being then in Stafford County, she discovered their
movement and about dark she slipped out alone to the river-
bank opposite our picket post, attracted the attention of one
of the guards. She then displayed upon her white dress a black
cross and pointed to the mouth of the run, up the river. The
officer in command of the picket was called and he took in
her meaning immediately, and, in a low tone said, "cross

above?" She waved her hand to give assent, and then made her way back to the house where she was staying, avoiding the yankee pickets. The officer immediately sent a courier to General Lee, and he was thus apprised of the movement as soon as the enemy commenced to move. The girl is only seventeen. This girl seemed to regard it as an inestimable privilege to see a Confederate flag or hear a Confederate band, yet she had lost everything. South of the James there are some people, as we know, who have made more money than ever before, who complain of everything done by the government and regard their soldiers as a necessary nuisance, though they most willingly appropriate their glory as "ours."

August 24th.

On Friday evening Cols. Hill, Wood, Cochran and myself with John Scott as body servant and forager, started down river to Port Royal on two days' leave of absence, on horseback. The distance from our camp to Port Royal is twenty-two miles, but the road passes through only some eight or ten plantations, that many persons owning the intervening land. These fine plantations lie on the low grounds between the river and the bluffs some mile or more back. On those bluffs Jackson's corps was camped last winter, making one unbroken line of rifle-pits from Port Royal to Fredericksburg.

The first residence we reached was Mansfield, owned by Mr. Arthur Bernard. Nothing but bare stone walls, however, is left to tell of the grandeur of this old seat of the Bernard family. It was accidentally set afire by our own soldiers after being completely dismantled and shelled by the yankees. Next came Smithfield, Mr. Pratt's beautiful estate. This is a large brick house without anything remarkable but its fine yard and spring. Next is Mr. Dickerman's, a handsome house, then Belvedere, Mrs. Taylor's old home. Next Prospect Hill and Santee belonging to the Gordons; Judge Brooke's St. Julien's; Hayfield, Mr. W. P. Taylor's; and Moss Neck, one of the handsomest houses in Virginia, which belongs to our old friend, Dick Corbin.

All the houses except possibly Santee, St. Julien's and Moss

Neck are deserted by their owners and held by their overseers and negroes. We inspected each place as we passed. Opposite those, immediately on the river, we always found a squad of yankees on the look-out. On the road near Moss Neck we met Richard and Welford Corbin, who pressed us to go home with them, but as their houses were something out of our line of march we could not accept their invitation. The next farm is Gaymont, the seat of another branch of the Bernard family. This is an old, very old place surrounded by shrubbery and trees and is situated upon a very high hill, which commands a most magnificent view of the river bottom for twenty miles and all of the country seats on both sides of the river and the beautiful old village of Port Royal. Close to Gaymont is Hazelwood which is surrounded by a 'live fence' made of growing cedars intertwined into each other so as to turn either a horse or a pig. The fence is now near twenty feet high and encloses several thousand acres.

Just opposite Hazelwood, on the other side of the river, is Cleve, one of the seats of the Carters. It was owned and built by my great-great grandfather, Charles Carter, (from whom my name descends), and was the home of my great-grandmother, Landon Carter, and there my grandmother, Lucy Landon Carter, was born. Cleve is a very large estate, which is stretched out in full view of Hazelwood. The house is of stone, octagonal in form, and surrounded by extensive grounds. I much wish I could have gone over and inspected it, but the yankees had its possession and I had no way to get across the river even if I had not feared capture. There were no yankees there at the time but their cavalry was patrolling all that side of the river. I was glad to get a glimpse of the old place; for me the traditions of my childhood were all connected with it. I have heard my grandmother tell of the English ships shelling the house during the Revolution, and I remember the indignation I felt when she told me of the Continental press-gang stopping her coach, to which there were four horses and two outriders, in which she was en route to join her father, who was a member of the House of Burgesses. In that coach were only her sister and herself, both children, and their maids. They made such an outcry that they were permitted to proceed, after being shorn only of the horses of the two outriders, who had to walk back to Cleve. The present owner, Henry Byrd Lewis, is now lying in Caroline County Jail awaiting trial for murdering my old college mate, Dr. Rose, of King George.

We found Port Royal crowded with soldiers of Law's Alabama brigade which was stationed there. It is an antique and pretty village, all embowered with flowers. The streets are well turfed and the people look as if neither they nor their ancestors ever had anything to do. But the people have a refined look and everything is neat and clean, though time and yankee shells have given it an air of desolation. The yankees wantonly shelled the town last fall though they knew that its only inhabitants were helpless old men, women and children. I say they knew there were no troops, for a detachment from one of the gunboats had just visited and inspected the little hamlet. We spent the night at the house of Mrs. Pratt near the town, a place called "Camden." When the yankee gunboats came up the river last winter one of her children was very ill. The Captain of the gunboat "Freeborn" came ashore and assured her she was in no danger and seemed to sympathize with her anxiety about her dying child. Then he rowed back to his gunboat and instantly opened fire on the house. The first shell passed through the chamber in which her child was lying and very close to her as she leaned over the cradle. In her alarm she caught the child up in her arms and, followed by her servant girls, ran out into the yard. As soon as they were seen from the gunboat a load of canister was fired at them, but fortunately they all escaped. They fired seven shells through the house. I was shown the holes made by the shells, and especially the one which came so near killing Mrs. Pratt and killed the child through concussion.

Mrs. Blackford takes up the narrative.

There is a gap in our letters as I was able to get to Fredericksburg and did not reach home again until September 14th while Longstreet moved his division into Tennessee. We stayed at Mr. Hart's and as the weather was fine we had a very pleasant stay. I rode much on horseback and on one occasion rode all over the battlefield. Nannie also learned to ride and I well remember how she looked dressed in a little Garibaldi red flannel jacket trimmed with black, and a little riding skirt, which I made for her before I left home. Her escort was old Tarleton. She was seven years old and as she rode her father's beautiful black horse through the troops the men would come out and gather around her and vie with each other in their efforts to make themselves agreeable, and when she did not stop, but rode by at a canter, they always cheered her as they did Lee.

I remember one occasion when Mr. Blackford was sent for to go over to Hood's old brigade, and when he got there he was told he was wanted as judge-advocate to prosecute a lamb for straggling. He found a court of subaltern officers already organized and several very clever lawyers on the spot waiting for him. The court and lawyers were all from that brigade, which was made up largely of Virginians who had gone to Texas, and among them were some of the highest lawyers of the state. The culprit was a very fat lamb, fully grown and very tempting to a hungry court. Mr. Blackford prepared the indictment and the trial commenced. Of course I did not see it but he described it as one of the most brilliant he ever heard. The court, witnesses and counsel were all very clever and the speeches were exceedingly bright. The trial lasted all day and wound up with the foregone conviction, followed by instant execution; the court, counsel and witnesses sharing the tempting carcass of the prisoner and the victim.

The order to move came one night and we started to move early the next morning. Launcelot, with Mary and Nannie started for Lynchburg by rail while I rode with the army for a day; then Mr. Blackford and myself branched off and continued on to Lynchburg by horseback. Mr. Blackford was ordered to follow in the rear of the corps, receiving instructions by telegraph and keeping the general posted on the trains carrying the troops. I continue his letters from the time he reached the army in Tennessee.

CHAPTER XII

★ ☆ ☆ ★ ☆ ☆ ☆

THE RIVER OF DEATH

☆ ☆ ☆ ☆ ☆ ☆

From Captain Blackford.
Chickamauga, Tenn., Oct. 1st, 1863.

H<small>ERE</small> I am at last, after much wandering in the
Army of Tennessee and about as uncomfortable
as a man can be. I sit in a box-car, with some dozen other
men, awaiting the arrival of a wagon to take me to the headquarters of our corps. It is raining hard and very cold and
the General is about eight miles west of this point; he occupies
the left of our line near Bridgeport, wherever that may be.
I got here at nine last night and it is now ten in the morning,
and I see no chance of getting anything to eat. The rain is
coming down in such torrents that it not only puts out the
fire but washes the wood away. We look for the wagon about
twelve and we will start at once, but as the roads have no
bottom there is no telling when we will reach headquarters.
I ate the last of your provisions last night and thus severed my
last tie to Virginia. It is hard to keep up one's spirits with an
empty stomach and wet clothing and nothing to do. I left
Augusta day before yesterday evening and came up on a troop
train containing the last of our corps. There was a car attached, and by Willy Waller's good auspices I secured a seat
in it, but only kept it part of the night, giving it to some ladies
escorted by some soldiers enroute to the army. The girls
were dressed in homespun and were quite pretty though un-
refined. I had a seat on the floor at their feet and became
smartly interested in them until, to my horror, one of their
beaux offered them a drink of fresh apple brandy out of his
canteen, which they accepted and drank, "by word of mouth"
without water or cup. I have no doubt they then took to dipping, but I stretched out on the floor and went to sleep.

We reached Atlanta yesterday morning and after an hour's delay I got a place in this box-car and got here at nine o'clock. I hear no news except that our corps, from the head down, wants to get back to Virginia. The men have no transportation or any, even, of the comforts of a Confederate soldier, and in this long rain, are, of course, uncomfortable.

Longstreet's headquarters, Oct. 3d.

This is a beautiful, quiet Sunday morning and I find my heart going back to you every hour. This camp is not attractive. It is in a low, flat meadow, about one hundred yards from the Chickamauga, which in Indian tongue means, we are told, "The River of Death"; and a river of death it certainly has become, not only because of the bloody battle fought on its banks so recently but because of its capacity to breed chills and fevers and other dire maladies which are beginning to send many a brave man to the hospital and the grave who did not flinch in the hour of battle. The roads are without bottom, and every night, and until nine or ten in the morning, we are enshrouded in a pestilential fog.

I went to the top of Lookout Mountain, and well did the glorious scene repay me for the tiresome journey. The rock upon which I stood is upon the extreme eastern end of the mountain, almost overhanging the Tennessee River. The yankees were camped a musket-shot away on the other side. From it I could see into seven states, seeing, of course, only points of each, viz: Virginia, (and I strained my eyes to see even an outline of her dear blue mountains), North Carolina, (Mount Black), South Carolina, Georgia, Alabama, Tennessee and Kentucky. The distant view is not very striking as it only gives a continuity of peaks which fade into infinity, but the view at the foot of the mountain is very imposing. In the bend of the Tennessee River there is the town of Chattanooga, around which the yankees are camped, making the earth white with their tents. Their line of fortifications extends across the tongue of land made by the bend for about a mile and a half, and in this little pen the whole vast yankee army is camped with the exception of a brigade or two thrown across the river to protect the bridges. They draw their supplies from some point on the Nashville and Tennessee Railroad after it has crossed the Tennessee River at Bridgeport, which is lower down the Tennessee in Alabama.

While Bragg cannot advance now that the fortifications are made, he has Rosecrans in a very tight place. Our fortifications are within less than a mile of each other and there the two armies lie, each afraid to advance and Rosecrans, for the present at least, afraid to move in any direction. The position of each army as against an attack from the other is very strong though I think we might be able to shell them out of Chattanooga, if anything is to be gained by that, for our position commands the whole town. There are some who talk of this being attempted.

It is rumored that Rosecrans is receiving heavy reinforcements from the army in Virginia. If that is so there will be no fighting in Virginia this fall, and Lee may come here and take command. He is much needed. Bragg is much overcropped, the mere knowledge that Lee was at the helm would be worth untold reinforcements. The belief that most men have in his infallibility of judgement makes them invincible.

By Mrs. Blackford.

I now return to my own letters. I do not think them so interesting as his but he, on the other hand, claims there will be many persons well describing what sights he saw and the incidents of which he tells while there are few contemporaneous accounts of what took place at home during the long, dark days of that dreadful war.

While we were together we decided to sell all our furniture and rent out the house. We were almost bankrupt, possessing only our house, household goods and servants. We could hire the latter out for enough so they would be of little expense, if not some profit; but few people nowadays realize the slave laws were very strict and their owners were responsible for their wellbeing. They had to be fed, clothed and housed whether useful or too sick or old to be of any value. My next letter is dated

September 30th, 1863.

I have not been able to have the sale of household goods as I am not quite ready to break up housekeeping yet, and William's family is still with me, and I have been trying to get all necessary sewing done for Nannie and myself before we take the house from over our heads and take wing. As soon as I am ready I will rent the house and have the sale. I cannot stay here and see our sweet home occupied by strangers. Uncle George Fisher wants one of the book cases and offers three hundred dollars for it, and a cousin of William's wife offers two hundred and seventy-five dollars for one of the old bedsteads. From these indications I think everything will sell very well. I have attended to the feeding of your horse personally and he is improving rapidly. I took your father out to the stable to look at him and he was much struck by the change for the better in his appearance. I had a letter from Delia Willis asking me to take care of her piano. I want to go to Albemarle as soon as possible, but I cannot go to sister's as Henry Trueheart is there badly wounded. I may board at Miss Leaton's.

October 6th.

I dined at your father's yesterday. The house is full of agreeable girls and I was very hilarious and spent a charming day. Patty Minor, of Albemarle, was one of them. The Mercers' are renting the house but won't want it until about the first of November, so I have concluded not to break up housekeeping until nearer that date, as I would for the present have to go to your father's. His house is always crowded with people, many of whom impose upon his hospitality. As the time for breaking up approaches I look around at all the things in this house, so associated with you and the happy hours of our life before the war, and my heart sinks within me to think that in a few weeks they will be scattered and in the possession of strangers. I could stand it if you were here to cheer me but to break up all alone is doubly hard. I hope you will not wait until the campaign is over before you let me come to see you or come to be near you. Your people are all as kind and affectionate as possible, but I have no right to crowd them or add in any way to their many burdens. I feel very lonely now that you are away. I lay awake last night and had a long cry in the darkness. I weep in my loneliness as thousands of other women weep. Even this letter, as you can see, is blotted in tears. I cannot cloud Nannie's bright soul with my sorrow, and there is no one else in whose ear I can pour them. So you must help me to bear them.

From Captain Blackford.
Longstreet's headquarters, October 5th.

It is quite quiet except for a constant shelling which has been going on ever since ten without producing the slightest result on either side. The men on both sides sat out on the opposite breastworks watching every shell as they passed to and fro over their heads.

It was announced last night that the enemy were to be bombarded today so we adjourned court and betook ourselves to General Bragg's headquarters to see the sport, but so tame did it seem to the ears that had heard the deep-toned thunders of Fredericksburg and Gettysburg that I returned to my tent and to the more grateful pleasure of writing you. From the point I occupied I could see the batteries of each side and the place where each shell exploded. Though many hundreds were fired I do not think anyone was hurt on either side. Col. Alexander had charge of the bombardment and his battalion did most of the firing. Young Mercer belongs to that command. He was at my tent just now, tell his mother he is well and in fine spirits.

The country around here is one of the most unhealthy in the world. I have been dreading chills and fever ever since I came. A great many of our corps are sick. I suffered much last night and am now under the influence of opium. I hope cold weather will mend things, we had a hard frost last night. My horse is much crippled and I must get another before I move again. I can get one to serve my purpose for seven hundred dollars I think.

We can make no arrangements for your coming out here until we know that Bragg and Rosecrans are to watch each

other all winter, which, I think, is the most probable outcome
of the campaign. Besides a cannon shot or two every day we
have no sign of war at present.

I sympathize with you much in the strain put upon you by
giving up our house, but I see no other solution to our prob-
lem. We cannot afford to keep it, and there is no reason why
you should be so tied down that when opportunity offers you
cannot come to see me. Wherever you go I want you to pay
board, even at Father's; he is so imposed upon by those who
have no claim on him that we must not add to his burdens. I
do not, however, approve of your suggestion of going to board
at Miss Leaton's, in Charlottesville. If you are not with your
brother or sister, why leave Lynchburg, where you will be under Father's care and protection, even if you are not at his
house? I think that you had better reconsider the plan. The war
has so demoralized the people that a woman as young as you
are must be very careful to keep under the guardianship of her
natural protectors.

Same Camp, October 8th.

When you get ready to come down here be sure and get all
the powder, shot and caps you can find. Game is very plentiful
just outside the army lines and we can get a shot-gun very
easily. Col. Alexander, whose camp is close to ours, has part-
ridge every day. He makes his own shot by cutting up bullets.
I think you might still find some shot for sale in Lynchburg.
Every thing is quiet, but I begin to doubt whether it will so
remain. As I write the enemy are shelling our lines, but none
of their shells have been aimed at us, which surprises me, for
they could reach our camp as well as any other. I am glad they
do not, as it does not add to the domesticity of a camp to have
a shell or two explode every day in its midst. Your letters are
very slow coming; they are the great pleasure of my life and
I feel refreshed for several days after getting them.

Same Camp, October 10th.
My Darling Nannie:
The mails bring me letters very slowly, and I have been

nearly a month in this strange land amongst strangers—almost a thousand miles away—and have only one letter to tell me whether you and your mother are dead or alive.

In North Carolina I saw people making turpentine, which is the juice or gum which runs out of a pine tree when the bark is cut. It is used for many purposes, some of which you know, for from it is made an oil which you have often seen in lamps and which gives a light almost as bright as gas. To get this gum large chips are cut from the sides of the trees and as it runs out it is scraped off and put into barrels and sent to market. I saw along the railroad many thousands of these barrels full of gum which is called resin. At Wilmington, which is quite a pretty town in North Carolina, I saw six or eight large steamers, which had come in from foreign countries laden with all kinds of supplies, especially articles necessary for the army, imported by the Confederate States Government. They had run the blockade. When we say a place is blockaded we mean that the enemy has put their ships of war all around the mouth of the harbor to prevent any vessels from going in or coming out. The yankees have ships near all our harbors for that purpose, but in spite of that a great many ships come and go from Wilmington. They run by the enemy's ships on foggy mornings, and that they might not be seen in the grey mist they are painted white, their hulls, chimneys, masts and rigging are all white which looks very strange as vessels are usually painted black.

In South Carolina I saw many lovely wild flowers and I thought as I looked at them what a delight they would give you if you could see them. The swamps, through which the road runs, are very curious. They are filled with tall cypress trees, from the branches of which long streamers of grey moss hang down like flags, some thirty or forty feet long, swaying backward and forward in the wind like ghostly draperies. These swamps, thus decorated, are very solemn, and at night when the great owls give their mournful hoots one feels as if they were attending the funeral of nature. The cypress trees put up what are called "knees." They are a growth which rises up from the roots of a tree sometimes twenty feet high covered with bark like the tree itself, and yet without limb or leaf and rounded on the top like a knob.

While I was writing just now I heard a great shouting a long way off, so I got my horse and went over there and found it to be Mr. Jefferson Davis, the President of the Southern Confederacy, and the soldiers were cheering him. He was riding at the head of a column of troops. He was dressed in a black coat and was riding a very fine black horse, and behind him was a perfect regiment of generals. I noticed especially Generals Bragg, Longstreet, Hill, Breckenridge, Preston and McLaws, all dressed in their handsomest uniforms and riding fine horses, each with quite a numerous staff. All this, with the shouting of the troops and the music of the bands made quite a handsome sight which I wish you could have seen. My wagon driver, who is a regular Georgia Cracker, named Lucky, caught a crane yesterday. You would, I know, have been delighted with it, for I remember how you liked the one at Mr. Clemens'. The servants killed and cooked it but it was nothing but neck and legs, we could not eat it; possibly they did.

You would be much amused if you could hear the various sounds which strike upon my ears as I sit in my lonely tent. Close around me the horses are munching corn with a will that marks its scarcity; nearby a prayer meeting is being held in an artillery camp, whence I can hear the singing and praying; on the other side there is a concert, with a banjo and a violin, with singing and dancing, and still further off two bands are playing very sweet music. Is that not a strange medley? Yet amidst it all my heart is straying far away to Old Virginia, where my fair-haired "bonnie lassie" is nestling close to her mother's side, dreaming of me.

When you go to your grandmother's to stay you must be very good and kind to them and cheer them up, as you know so well how to do. Remember that all their boys have gone away to the war and that they are very desolate and love you very much. Think what your mother would have felt had Willey lived and grown up to be a big boy and gone off to fight, when a bullet might have killed him at any moment. When you think how she would have felt you can understand how they feel now, and your love can soothe them very much.

The old roan came out safely all the way in the cars. Whenever I look at him he reminds me of the rides you used to take on him, and I almost think I can see you again with your little hat and riding skirt, as, with old Tarleton as a guide, you rode through the troops at Fredericksburg. When you come to me you will ride him again.

A letter from Mrs. Blackford.
Lynchburg, October 10th, 1863.

I went over to your father's house to see William's wife. She is well and enroute to Abington. Your father has a letter from Lewis. He missed seeing you at Wilmington by about five minutes. His box from Europe, which ran the blockade, has arrived in Richmond, but he has not yet received an invoice of its contents.

With regards to your tobacco speculation, I think it will turn out all right; but if it does not we must bear the reverse cheerfully. Remember how many people are worse off than we are, even if we lose it all. If you think best, I can try and get a small school with which to eke out our small means. I am sure I can make enough to meet my own wants. Let me hear from you at once. I know that at first you will be shocked at the idea of your wife going to work to support herself, but you are so situated you can do nothing more and I should bear my share of the burden. I was much interested in your account of the position and doings of the two armies. I understand it perfectly.

I think I shall have the sale of the furniture next Thursday. I do not know what to do with William and Dick [slaves], they are both so delicate they cannot stand any exposure either to wet or cold weather. Write and tell Mr. R. J. Davis what you will take for Fanny and her children. He owns her husband. They will all thus be together on his farm and a good home secured her. If poor Jack gets well Mr. Flannigan wants him on his farm, which will be a good home for him; and the purchase money from both sources will help hold your tobacco. If I do not join you you I may get a position in one of

Dr. Davis' hospitals in Charlottesville which will give Nannie and myself comfortable quarters and sufficient rations to keep us alive. This is hardly such a letter as I should write on Sunday, being full of business, but I am so anxious to do something to relieve your mind of its many burdens and make me feel that I am not, as Eugene says all wives are to their husbands, a millstone around your neck. Nannie says to give her "particular regards" to John Scott and Tarleton.

Lynchburg, October 13th.

I cannot commence the sad work of packing up without the comfort of pouring my sorrows into your sympathetic ear. Next Thursday will be the day of the sale of the furniture, and then I must leave to a tenant this delightful home, where I have been so happy and which is endeared to me by a thousand tender associations, and become a homeless wanderer, without even the cheering hope of seeing you. I would not mind it so much if the house was to be shut up, but the thought that strangers are to wander through it, and that the roses are to bloom only for others, makes me very sad. I ought not to write thus, but I have no one else with whom to weep,—and weep I must or my heart will break. I begged your father not to let a red flag be brought up here. I could not bear the thought of strange men tramping through our house and inspecting furniture and places most hallowed by its association with the past. I still think it wise we should break up housekeeping; indeed we are shut up to that course, as starvation is the only other alternative, and this necessity gives me nerve to bear it.

The McKinneys' are offered $25,000 for their home and will sell it. They break up in a few days. There will be few of the old neighbors left. Mr. John D. Holt will buy their place. Your father sold your office safe for $500 and the carriage for $450. The latter is not a good sale, for though it is not new it is sound and well built.

Lynchburg, October 17th.

Your father has just come in and says I must tell you all our belongings brought high prices. The carpet in the room over the parlor sold for $400; the parlor chairs $30 apiece, the sofa in the dining room $187, the French bedstead $260. I am now at your father's. I went home this morning to get some things, among them the powder and shot for which you wrote. I also got some candles for my own use while I am here, for gas is so high I must economize in light. Butter is now two dollars a pound and cheese is higher. I am laying up as much of both as I can.

From Captain Blackford.
Same Camp, October 11th.

This is a very beautiful Sunday morning, and, except for the occasional boom of cannon, very quiet. Everything remains *in statu quo* out here and will continue so until Rosecrans has so reinforced his army as to be able to come down upon us with a crushing force. The suicidal policy which Bragg has adopted has rendered futile the victory which Longstreet won for him at Chattanooga. If Lee had been in his place with such an army we would be now chasing the shattered yankee fragments out of Tennessee. This is a fine body of men, and with the confidence they would have in Lee they would be irresistible. Bragg is so much afraid of doing something which would look like taking advantage of an enemy that he does nothing. He would not strike Rosecrans another blow until he has recovered his strength and announces himself ready. Our great victory has been turned to ashes. I am still at work in spite of a constant dull headache and pain in the back of my neck, and I am all right so long as the work holds out, but as soon as I have nothing to do I am sick. I am dreading chills and fevers very much. Thousands of men are laid up with such attacks and the death rate is large because of want of hospital accommodation. I wish you would send me a common bed-tick which I could fill with straw when we are in camp and empty when we move. Make it three and a half feet wide with a long slit in it with buttons, through which I can put in straw.

I had to stop writing at the end of the last sentence because

I felt so badly. I had a chill, followed by a high fever, from which I am now suffering. As soon as we get to some better camping ground I hope I can bring you down, and I want you to have as nice a wardrobe as you can secure. There are many Virginians amongst the troops and you will be a belle with them, to say nothing of the South Carolinians and others at Kershaw's headquarters and in his brigade with whom you are already a favorite.

Same Camp, October 15th.

There is a tradition amongst these flats that there has been a time in the past when it wasn't raining, but saving and excepting one or two days I have seen nothing to make me give credence to such a belief. It has rained almost incessantly and the ground is knee-deep in mud and slush and the air so dark and dank that it may be cut with a knife. My chills and fever continue, and this locality and surroundings offer but little chance for me to get well; yet, strange to say, I am better, or think I am. I have no bed and water runs through my tent, as the ditch only gathers it so it can creep through my floor of dark mould, which is literally spongy with moisture, and my poor oilcloth does not keep the dampness off me. Each morning as I wake I am stiff and cold and every joint is painful with aches and suffering.

We improved our condition somewhat by a change of location yesterday but the pall of the River of Death still hangs over us. I have not been able to get out of my tent now for three days. It is a terrible feeling; one would court death when in my situation, for life seems robbed of all charm. I have heard people describe this disease, but I never believed their accounts until now.

The rain, General Wheeler and General Bragg are the main topics of conversation out here. I have told you of the rain, now for General Wheeler. You know there is a railroad from Nashville to Chattanooga, but owing to the mountains it is not a direct line. It comes first to Bridgeport, some fifty-four miles below Chattanooga, and then comes up the Tennessee River. That road is the principal source of supply of the yankee army. Their depot is at Bridgeport, whence they haul everything in wagons, as the railroad is on our side of the river after passing Bridgeport. General Wheeler, with eight thousand cavalry, crossed the river and fell upon the railroad north of Bridgeport, burning many bridges and destroying vast stores of supplies, trains, engines, etc., which were between Nashville and Bridgeport. At one place he was twenty-four hours engaged in the work of destruction. He captured and destroyed seventeen hundred wagons and thousands of horses and mules, many of which, however, he had to kill, as he could not get them away. A more successful or effective raid has not been made by anyone. It is said, however, that he lost many men from want of strict discipline; for, in many places, his men got hold of whiskey, and many of them, and, in some cases, his officers, got so drunk they had to be left behind, so that his loss appeared heavy. It is thought that many of those reported missing will yet come in. It is altogether a creditable feat for General Wheeler for which he may be proud.

Now for General Bragg and his snarl. Of course I do not vouch for my statements. I give only the *on dit* of the camp; but as I am part of the headquarters of a corps, I have quite a fair chance to get what is said—even if what is said is not true. You know the President has been out here to see what is the matter—who is to blame and so forth. He sent his aide, Col. Chisholm, first, but he telegraphed he must come in person, and he came. He looked around, made some fine speeches to the men and finally summoned General Bragg and all the prominent generals and required them to give their opinion about General Bragg's capacity to manage his army. Old Pete (Longstreet) was the first called upon to express his opinion. He told the President, Bragg being present, that he had not been out here a half-hour before he saw that General Bragg was incompetent to manage an army or put men into a fight; that his intentions were all good, but he knew nothing of the business, and wound up by saying that if the army had been properly handled it could have destroyed Burnside before he knew he was near, then forced Rosecrans out of Nashville into Kentucky, and that after the battle of Chickamauga he should have followed up his victory and not allowed the enemy to make his position at Chattanooga impregnable. This is only an outline of what he said. He was respectful but crushing. He was followed by all others, who expressed practically the same opinion. The President heard them through, took time to consider, and wound up by sending a circular letter, in which he sustained Bragg and chided them for want of confidence and harmony, and putting upon Longstreet the duty of reconciling differences and bringing about harmony. All the officers whom the President placed in this most unpleasant position at once asked to be relieved of duty with this army, on the ground they could be of no use out here, but the applications were all refused except that of D. H. Hill, who, with his staff, is ordered to report to the adjutant-general in Richmond. This is a mess very different from anything we ever had under Lee.

I hope that our people know that Pleasanton's raid that Stuart frustrated was intended for Lynchburg. So, at least, Major Clark, of the Engineers, tells me and he is fresh from Lee's headquarters. This only confirms what I told the council of the city in my letter to Mr. Doane, and of which Mr. Daniel thought so lightly. I have no doubt you are tired of army matters but I have so little else to write about. I am enclosing my first commission as Captain. It is from the State of Virginia, and, of course, I value it more than the one I hold from the Confederate States, which I received when I accepted my present position.

I am not surprised at you being gloomy at the outlook for we will have a terrible struggle for mere bread and meat, but we will pull through, exactly how I do not know. We would regard things now as luxuries which three years ago we thought necessities, and we have learned to accommodate ourselves to changed conditions, and as long as we are not actually hungry we need not complain. We are much better off than thousands of others. When the war is over we will, if I am spared, at least be together, and I have no fear but that I can make a living. I never was lazy, and since the war I believe my energy has no limit except my physical capacity to endure. That, barring chills, is daily improving. I have learned to look *facts* in the face and to regard nothing impossible.

If Lee had this army there is no limit to what he could do with it. Both men and officers would, with the confidence he inspires, be vastly improved, and the raw material is first-class now, only badly mangled by Bragg's incompetency. He is a good and brave man, I believe, but he ought not to be over-taxed with such a burden, all because General Taylor, President Davis's father-in-law, said to him: "A little more grape, Captain Bragg."

Same Camp, October 22nd.

We are working very hard now. I tried twenty cases today which is no easy business, I am also engaged in preparing a new edition of the "Articles of War" which I propose to get the Secretary of War to approve and recommend to Congress for adoption. Those we have are the same as those which for many years have prevailed in the United States. They are crude and need pruning. Thus you see even when I am off duty I am by no means idle.

Same Camp, October 25th.

As I wrote you I have been engaged in the preparation of a short hand-book for the use of our corps in all matters connected with courts-martial and breaches of military law. I have finished it now and General Longstreet has sent it to Macon to be published. He ordered eight hundred copies to be printed for the use of the corps*. In it I give the forms of the various papers, and especially for charges and specifications. I got off a little fun in it when I came to forms against quartermasters and surgeons by saying in a note that as quartermasters and surgeons in the service of the Confederate States never did anything wrong I would make the forms in their cases apply to United States officers, and then proceeded to give a form against a quartermaster for "neglect of duty" setting forth some of the most common complaints against them by way of specifications. The form against a surgeon is for "mis-

*This pamphlet became in general use throughout the whole Confederate Army but at this time (1892) no copy is known to be extant. C.M.B.

applying government stores" and specifying his having given a dinner party at which three gallons of Bourbon whiskey and two of French brandy, belonging to the hospital, were consumed.

The army is very badly generalled and the result is there is much demoralization and want of confidence. Bragg ought to be relieved or disaster is sure to result. The men have no faith. The difference between this army and Lee's is very striking: when the men move in the Army of Northern Virginia they think they are doing the proper thing, whether it be backward or forward, and if all the success anticipated is not secured, at all events it is not Lee's fault. Down here the men seem to feel the wrong thing is being done whatever it be and when success is secured they attribute it to anybody else than Bragg. Thus they give the whole credit of Chickamauga to Longstreet, though he commanded only a part of the line and his troops did not fight any better than the others.

By the way an incident occurred at the battle of Chickamauga which I must tell you. I got it today from one of the actors. Kershaw's brigade was hotly engaged driving the enemy back when a major of one of his regiments, which had two majors, was struck by a cannon ball that killed his horse and cut off one of his legs. His friend, the other major, saw him fall but had to go on with the advancing line. As soon as it halted he rode back to where his friend was lying and found the leg was shot off just above the knee, but was still attached by a strip of flesh. He had tied his handkerchief about the stump to cut off the bleeding and was stretched out on the ground waiting for a surgeon. His friend, from whom I got the story, at once put a knapsack or two under him to raise him up, then he called for his pipe and tobacco and calmly began to puff away as if nothing was the matter. He then borrowed his friend's knife and with his own hands severed the injured leg from the stump and, with the aid of his friend, got the boot off the discarded leg and fastened it to his sword belt, for the purpose, he said, of trading it to someone who had lost the other leg. After his friend had made him as comfortable as possible and had filled his tobacco pouch afresh, he drew a book from his pocket and commenced to read, telling the other major to go back to his duty. Such men are hard to kill.

A letter from sister Nannie received today tells the sad news of Jack's death. I did not know he had run away with the yankees until I was in Fredericksburg nor that he had returned until I heard of his death. Nannie did all she could to save him, and it was like a negro to try to return to his master when sick and neglected by those who "freed" him. Although he could not get back to us in Lynchburg he went to the first member of the family he could reach, well knowing he would receive all sympathy and attention.

An amusing incident occurred at Longstreet's headquarters this morning while he and his staff were at breakfast. An old woman, dressed up in an ancient silk dress and very remarkable bonnet, approached the table, and stopping a few paces off, asked if General Longstreet was there. He replied: "Yes, is there anything I can do for you?"

"Is there any harm to come here?" she asked.

"None," the General replied. "Come and take breakfast with us."

She said she had walked eight miles since her breakfast and she did not have up in her "settlement" what she used to have and she believed she could take a bite. While at breakfast she was very lively, telling of her adventures during the war. She spoke of the cavalry as "Mr. Forest's critter company" and a line of battle as a "string of fight." After she had breakfasted she informed the general that the object of her visit was to get him to give her a little tobacco to smoke. Her pockets were filled with "Lone Jack" and she was sent home in an ambulance.

Same Camp, Oct. 29th.

My troubles in the matter of health have finally developed into regular chills and fever. Yesterday was my chill day and a good shaking I had of it. Today I am dull and stupid from the effect of quinine. Several of our party are under the baneful influence.

The social conditions of the country in which we are camped are very strange. There are no gentlemen nor gentlemen's houses; the people all live in cabins with little cultivated patches of ground around them. As to patriotism there is none. Fully one-half went off with the yankee army when it retreated. The people down in these states are not as much enlisted on principle in this war as we in Virginia. They regard it as a war to protect their property in slaves and when they are lost take no further interest in it. In Virginia we are fighting for the right to govern ourselves in our own way and to perpetuate our own customs and institutions among our own people without outside interference. This feeling being universal no loss of property or temporary defeat affects our people and they remain true. In East Tennessee the people are about equally divided and there rages a real civil war, which causes great misery. Its horrors are greatly increased by the conduct of such fiends as Brownlow and Maynard.

There is some movement to our left. The enemy has crossed the Tennessee River about six miles below here and driven off two regiments placed to annoy their wagon trains on the other side. Whether anything ever will be done I cannot say, but the whole of our army has been in partial line of battle for several days. All believe that whatever should be done will be left undone and whatever should not be done Bragg will do.

Same Camp, Nov. 4th.

After the lapse of a week I return to my pen with joy. I hope I am on rising ground. I had my first chill on the 7th of October and though I did not go to bed until last week I have not had a well day since. I have not suffered many privations, as a good many delicacies have come to me one way or another. A poor woman close by sent me a pot of butter and another a chicken and some eggs were sent Richmond from his home in North Carolina which he shared with me. The butter and chickens were priceless gifts. I do not know when I had either before.

Night.

The corps is about to move towards Knoxville and thence into Virginia. I cannot tell you what will become of me. I am unable to get off the bed, much less to mount my horse. The court has been dissolved for thirty days, Launcelot has been very kind to me and a most excellent nurse. I could get a furlough now if I desired, but I do not want to leave the army now if I am able to move.

Camp in the mud, East Tennessee, Nov. 6th.

We moved thus far yesterday through mud, the like of which I have never seen. I was carried in a wagon and stood the trip better than I expected. It is inspiring to feel that we are moving towards Virginia, though there is many a dreary mile between here and there. We will go by rail to Loudoun, which is the point where the East Tennessee and Georgia Railroad crosses the Tennessee River. Where we go from there I do not know.

The mud today was terrible, and the constant rain made it worse. We stalled every half-mile. I am stiff, sore, feverish and have a headache; indeed anywhere but in the army I would be in bed and surrounded by an anxious family. I am inspired by the thought every step brings us nearer Virginia.

Mrs. Blackford adds:

This closes Mr. Blackford's letters for six or seven weeks. When he reached the railroad he was so sick the surgeons sent him back and Longstreet contrived to get him sick leave to go home. He wrote the following account of his return afterwards:

By Captain Blackford.

I remember very little of what occurred after I was sent to the rear. Somebody had me in charge, I remember, as far as Atlanta. Then I was put on a train and I remember nothing until after we passed Augusta, except at various stations where the train stopped ladies came into the train and ministered to my wants by giving me dainty food and bathing my face.

After we passed Augusta I was put out at a station where we had to await the train from towards Savannah. I was laid on the hard floor of the platform with only my overcoat as a pillow and with nothing under or over me. While in this condition, in which I was suffering much and in which my only comfort was the partial delirium of fever, a lady stooped over me and commenced bathing my face with bay rum and to cheer me with kind words. She was one of an organization of ladies in Columbia, S. C., who sent a committee down to the junction to meet and nurse the sick and wounded who were there transferred. As soon as I spoke my thanks she said, "You are a Virginian, are you not?" Upon receiving the affirmative she asked me where I lived, and upon mentioning Lynchburg she at once replied: "Then you know my friends, the Blackfords?" Which, of course, made us friends at once. She was originally a Miss Knox of Fredericksburg. I remembered her when as a boy she sat in a pew directly in front of my father's, in old St. George Church. She had married a Mr. Thomas A. Ball, whose firm engraved the notes and bonds of the Confederate States. Her husband was near and they took charge of me as if I was their nearest kin. When we reached Columbia their carriage took me to their elegant home. It seemed to me the most palatial spot I had ever seen. I was taken to a room with a bath-room attached, and as I got rid of my camp-worn clothes, washed in the warm water most copiously supplied to the ample tub, put on one of Mr. Ball's linen nightshirts redolent with the odor of lavender which every Eastern Virginian kept in the bureau drawers, and then went to rest between linen sheets in a bed a queen might envy. I thought my troubles were at an end and I was in Heaven. I fell asleep a little after dark and slept until the next morning at eight. In a very few days I was able to resume my journey homewards and reached it on the 13th of November.

Mrs. Blackford continues the narrative.

For those who are interested in what happened after Mr. Blackford left the army I give the following extracts from his father's diary touching on the movements of Longstreet and Bragg:

November 13th, 1863.

Just as Charles Minor was leaving the house at 5 A.M. my son Charles came in. He has been very sick with chills and fever and had suffered much on his way back from Chickamauga and looks very badly. He was detained in Petersburg and speaks very gratefully of the kindness he received in the hands of Mr. and Mrs. Thomas A. Ball, of Columbia. It will take some time to put Charles in working order again. . . . About eight o'clock (that night) Eugene came in. He had been sick in camp and the surgeons sent him home. He has been broken down by recent hardship and exposure.

November 19th.

Charles spent a sleepless night. We have rumors from Richmond that Longstreet has whipped Burnside in East Tennessee and from Abingdon that he has occupied Knoxville. They may prove true but they have not been confirmed.

November 20th.

News comes very straight that Longstreet has occupied Knoxville, whether after a battle or not is doubtful. Charles is very unwell.

November 24th.

Yankee accounts admit that Knoxville is invested and Burnside has sustained losses. I fear an attack on our lines at Chattanooga. Thomas' army has been reinforced and Bragg's lessened by the withdrawal of Longstreet. A battle must yet be fought for that position and it will be very bloody.

November 25th.

A dispatch from Bragg is ominous. He says the enemy were assaulting Lookout Mountain. I don't like the tone of the dispatch.

November 26th.

Much distressed at a dispatch from Bragg which says the enemy has carried Lookout Mountain. Our loss is considerable in one division. This deplorable news will tend to the retreat of Bragg. Fresh and more detailed accounts of Longstreet's success at Knoxville.

November 27th.

Nothing from Chattanooga, which is ominous. Nothing from Longstreet. Charles is better but is still very unwell.

November 28th.

Details of Bragg's disaster at Missionary Ridge. His left center was carried by overwhelming masses. His left, on Lookout Mountain, gave away. His right repulsed every assault and inflicted heavy losses, but when the enemy held the mountain they enfiladed the right and the whole army fell back.

December 2nd.

Rumors were rife that Burnside had surrendered. There is no doubt that Bragg has been relieved at his own request. Bragg telegraphs that the yankee army that followed in his rear has met a severe defeat.

December 7th.

There is little doubt that Longstreet failed to take Knoxville.

December 28th.

Roused at four o'clock by the porter coming for Charles' baggage. Charles left at five with Captain Pleasants. He leaves with restored health.

*   *   *

Mr. Blackford was eight days returning to the army. It was so cold that he had to walk at times to keep from freezing, as he returned by horseback. The army was still in East Tennessee, headquarters being in Judge Barton's house, near Russelville.

CHAPTER XIII

EAST TENNESSEE

From Captain Blackford.
Longstreet's Headquarters, January 7th, 1864.

BETWEEN us I am much afraid there is a want of energy in General Longstreet's management of a separate command. I would trust him to manage men on a battlefield as implicitly as any general in the Confederacy, but when not excited his mind works too slow and he is almost too kind-hearted to have control of a department. In my judgment there are many things left undone which should be done to increase efficiency in the army and advance the cause. For example those railroad bridges should have been finished long ago, and it would have been done if Col. Robert Owen had been put in charge. I am perhaps a little extravagant in my ideas as to what energy and perseverance can do, but if I was a skillful engineer I am sure I would have had them completed. The word *impossible* has not been sufficiently stricken from the vocabulary of our leaders. There is too little of the *terrible earnestness* of a revolution. Lee and Jackson are the only men who seem to rise to the height of our occasion. Longstreet is too phlegmatic to be efficient except when much aroused. General Lee, you will remember, told Mrs. Page that it took three rounds of the enemy's canister of the battle-field to rouse him to action, but that then he was terrible.

Don't forget to look out for a present for John Scott. I told him you would have one for him when he goes home. I think I shall send him to bring you and Nannie down here. He has taken most faithful care of my things, and the horses look better than I have ever seen them before. The roan is so frisky I can hardly ride him. My driver, Lucky, I found with-

out shoes, so are so many of the men on active duty, so the pair
I brought him were very acceptable.

January 9th.

Ask Father to get you ten dollars in silver or greenbacks,
which will do just as well except for the difficulty in making
the change. Bring it out with you when you come. We shall
want it to keep our table supplied, for Confederate money
will buy nothing here. Butter can be had for eight cents a
pound if we pay for it in silver, gold or sugar, so if silver can
be bought twenty to one it will be more economical than
using Confederate money.

January 18th.

We are moving again, toward our beloved Virginia and the
yankees don't seem to be inclined to fight. They retired very
hurriedly after a slight skirmish, giving up about thirty-five
miles of territory to our foraging parties and opening up to us
a vast supply of provender for our horses. We captured about
one hundred prisoners and three pieces of artillery; though
of the last I am not sure. Our cavalry out here is in a horrible
state of disorganization and needs an efficient officer to command them very much. They commit all kinds of depredations
on the citizens and I have been constantly engaged in preparing charges against them under the laws of Tennessee. All
such complaints are referred to me for investigation and ad-
justment. I don't know which are the worse, the cavalry or
the people. I never ride out into this beautiful land that I am
not reminded of the line of Bishop Heber's missionary hymn:
"Every prospect pleases and only man is vile."

The question of supplies for the army is a serious one out
here as in Virginia, but I think we are safe for two months.
Major Moses, our chief Commissary, and a very able man, as
soon as he got here procured from the owners of the thrashing
machines a list showing who had threshed wheat and how
many bushels. He then issued an order that when supplies
were concealed he would confiscate all, but would otherwise
take and pay for in Confederate money only so much as could

be said to be the surplus crop. This stopped the habit of hiding everything by the Union people and gave us a very safe supply. We have to adopt the mode of foraging here that we did in Pennsylvania, sending a guard with every wagon train for its protection and to enforce the collection of supplies from unfriendly parties. The mountains are filled with deserters from both armies, who are banded together for the purpose of robbing trains of both sides as well as all citizens.

January 22nd.

The bridge across the Watauga is completed and an engine passed over it yesterday, and there seems to be no doubt the cars will be running regularly by the first of February, so you may make your arrangements to start out here near that time. The enemy has retired to the other side of the Holston, burning the railroad bridge they had just completed and retiring to Knoxville, with our cavalry close on their rear. General Jones took four hundred prisoners yesterday near Strawberry Plains, which make eight hundred men and twelve hundred horses he has captured in three weeks which is pretty well for a small brigade. The retreat of the enemy, which was forced by Longstreet, gives us a large area of country. So you see we have done something out here, although they say in Richmond that Longstreet is too slow. The effect of the movement is to give us food for our men and horses besides freeing a large section of the country from yankee rule.

My stock of reading matter is nearly finished. I have read Bourienne's Napoleon and am now deep in Napier's Peninsular Wars, the latter being also read by John Scott; very curious literature for a negro servant. Alexander's battalion of artillery is camped close by us. You will enjoy the company of its officers. Col. E. P. Alexander, Frank Huger, Poindexter, Haskell and others—all elegant gentlemen, who look forward with pleasure to your coming. Don't forget to bring twenty pounds of sugar. We have not a grain, and finding wheat coffee without sugar is very unattractive we have taken to water.

January 24th.

I wrote an article for the "Lynchburg Republican" styled: "An Appeal for Hood's Brigade." Texas is further off from Virginia than Louisiana and the ladies should work for them as much as for Hay's brigade. The soldiers of Hood's original brigade were among the first to come to Virginia, and there was never a finer body of men or more gallant soldiers. They have fought on our soil and spilled so much blood they are practically Virginians, as their fathers were with rare exceptions. They have been campaigning out here on frozen ground, many of them with bare feet, leaving bloody footsteps on the snow and ice. Try to get the ladies in their knitting club to do something for them. Shoes are very scarce. The men get pieces of raw hide from the butchers, and, after wrapping their feet up in old rags, sew the hide around them, making a clumsy ball, which they wear without yanking off until it wears out. I rode behind Robinson's Texas brigade a few days ago on a reconnaissance and it was most pitiful to see the poor fellows struggling along, so many of them with this improvised shoe and others with none,—yet there was not a murmur. Their progress, however, was slow; but when ordered into line of battle they were quick as if shod with the best and as if there was no snow, ice and briars to make their cold feet bleed.

I stopped writing here to take a long walk which came near making you a young and charming widow. I was alone and was walking along a very sequestered road, deeply thinking of the times and you and Nannie, when I heard the sharp report of a rifle and a minnie ball whizzed by my head so close the windage was very perceptable. I turned and discovered the shot came from a hut on the hillside about a hundred yards off. I was unarmed, so I walked calmly on, trying to make the people in the house think I thought it was an accident. In a moment I heard a cap snap and all was silent. It was obviously, I think, an effort to kill me by some of the many disloyal people with which this land is full. I had the house investigated but it was deserted.

I have ordered a box of chewing tobacco to be sent out to me to use in the purchase of supplies from the country people. It has a regular purchasing power. Thus for one plug we get one gallon of sorghum molasses, a turkey, three chickens or three dozen eggs, etc. Everybody here uses tobacco—men, women, girls and boys all smoke, chew or dip snuff or all three. "Dipping" consists of taking a piece of dogwood and chewing on the end of the stick until it forms a brush, then dipping it into a mug of snuff and rubbing the teeth with it. The mugs, with the dogwood brushes, are set about the house and are used indiscriminately by anyone of the ladies (?) who desires a mild stimulant. The effect is shown in the complexions and about the mouths of all women over fifteen.

Today I got the rare luxury of a hot bath and feel like a new pin and am, therefore, more worthy to write you, and have proved my estimate of my fitness by this long epistle. This reminds me of a young man I knew at the University. He was engaged to be married and on certain days in the week always got a letter from his girl. On these days he shaved and bathed and put on his best suit and then went to the post-office for the precious missive. Our party, Fenner, Jackson, Malone and myself, noticed that three times a week he dressed up that way and became curious to know why. He was exclusive and we were not acquainted with him, though he roomed near us. We detailed Malone to get acquainted with him and solve the mystery. This he did with the above result. But if I only wrote you when I could get a hot bath our correspondence would cease.

Same Camp, January 28th.

Longstreet moved his headquarters up to Morristown today but as I am nearer the troops here I shall not move unless ordered. I am looking forward to your arrival with much pleasure. You will have to rough it, however, very greatly. For example you will get no sugar. Longstreet has only wheat coffee and that without sugar. You are well used to wheat coffee but you have never yet, I suppose, been completely without sugar.

Longstreet did a thing a short while ago which was very wise and had good effect. He captured a train at Bean Station with a large amount of coffee in it. Some of his staff put a guard around the coffee, intending to distribute it around amongst the different headquarters. The General, however, ordered that fifteen hundred pounds be kept for the sick and wounded, (which, of course, the surgeons and nurses drank for them), and the rest be distributed to the private soldiers,—allowing nothing for his own or any other staff mess. General Longstreet has been doing many things to increase his hold on the men, such as visiting the sick and wounded and inspecting the hospitals and other like personal attention. This will be a very full corps and a very efficient one before the spring campaign opens. When you come down don't cumber yourself with baggage or supplies, except possibly some sugar if you can procure any and some condiments.

From Mrs. Blackford.
Lynchburg, December 31st, 1863.

Mr. Irby has sold fifty boxes of your tobacco at $1.50 (a pound) making a profit of $3,000. He will sell more during the week. I have commenced teaching Nannie regularly, and can see her improvement from day to day. You would be surprised to see what a good notion of sums she has. She does them very well and proves them.

Belleview, Bedford County, January 11th.

You see by the date of this letter that I am at Mr. Holcomb's, a most charming and comfortable country home, where I was made most welcome Sunday morning. The weather was very cold and the ground covered with snow. Robert Minor, Nannie and myself had to get up at five A.M. and walk down to the depot where we waited in the cold for an hour for the belated Richmond train. The conductor was your friend, Mr. Harmeling, and I supposed he would of course stop and put us off at the switch, where Mr. Holcombe's carriage awaited us. But he said he was behind time and could only stop at Goode's, so we were carried a mile and a half further and were dumped on the railroad track before it was light, with a piercing cold wind coming straight from the snow-clad mountains, almost cutting the flesh as it blew on our faces. Fortunately the mail boy from Bellevue was there and offered to pilot us back. Had he not been there we would have been in an even more forlorn condition, for it was dark and not a human being was moving. Under his guidance we started down the railroad track, slipping on the ice and stumbling in the snow. All this was, however, nothing to what we experienced when we reached a long, open trestle, which is very long and twenty-five feet high. The mail boy stepped out boldly to walk across but I dared not, knowing I would soon lose my head or my feet and fall off. So I crept down the frozen embankment, crossed the half-frozen stream and climbed up the other side on my hands and knees. Poor little Nannie followed me and was crying from the bitter cold and her torn hands as she fell from side to side in the ice and snow. After reaching the switch we found the carriage gone and we had to continue our march up the steep hill to the house, through the bitter wind, which had a clear sweep there equal to a mountain top. I often put my hands to my cheeks to see if they were bleeding, so sharp was the pain.

We were over two hours making the journey, so when we finally reached the house the family was done with breakfast, as they supposed we did not start, due to the cars not stopping. They gave us a most hearty reception and there was soon a delicious breakfast ready for us, which included a cup of strong, *real* coffee! There were three girls staying there: Alice Smith, of Alexandria, who is related to us through the Jacqulins, Sally Robertson, of Charlottesville, and Lucy Landon Minor. I sold the dress Mrs. Callahan made to Mrs. Holcomb for two barrels of flour,—enough to last Mrs. Callahan a year.

Your father has succeeded in getting eight barrels of flour. For three he paid $100 and got the rest for $70. I hope the flour I have stored away will not spoil. It is of a grade that cannot be gotten at any price now.

Lynchburg, January 18th.

The ladies are all very much interested in the knitting society, which is now in an embryo state. We were to have had a meeting yesterday, but the weather was so bad we could not do so. We wish to enlist every woman in town and have appointed ladies to canvass. Our object, of course, is to get socks for the soldiers who are suffering so much on the field. I am sorry I am to be away just now, as Mrs. Spence and myself have been the prime movers in the scheme. I shall see whether I can do anything in Richmond towards getting materials from the government. We hear sad accounts from the army, especially Longstreet's corps, as to their ragged and barefooted condition. Dr. Smith says many men are brought into the hospital with their feet badly frozen and frostbitten. I cannot help being much depressed by the outlook in public affairs. I hear there are twenty thousand yankees in Winchester who will probably march on Staunton, as there is no force to oppose them, Early having gone back to Orange Courthouse. Charlottesville and Lynchburg will then fall into their hands and Richmond be cut off from its supplies.

Richmond, January 20th.

Here I am at last, in Richmond, after a terribly fatiguing journey down. There was a very young looking soldier on board who had ridden on the platform for a long way, and got so cold at last he crept into the car through the window. He looked so young and boyish I felt much interest in him. The stewardess told him she intended reporting him to the conductor. I called to her and asked her to let him stay. At first she refused but on further persuasion consented. I then called him, and got into a conversation with him. He was only seventeen years old, and had joined the army when a little over thirteen, from Alexandria. His name was Coursey. He had just been released from the yankee prison camp at Point Lookout (Md.?) where he had been a prisoner for five months. I was much pleased with him and gave him my address. He asked me if I would accept a ring he had gotten hold of while in prison. It was of some black material inlaid with gold. When Nannie came over he offered it to her. She said, "Oh mama, you are flirting with a soldier!"

Mrs. Blackford in Tennessee.

My stay in Richmond was pleasant although I did find my baggage had not been transferred with me when I changed cars at Charlottesville. There were many gay parties and I attended the Governor's Ball. Then came the word for which I was waiting. I hurried back to Lynchburg and was soon on my way to East Tennessee. The road had been opened up to Russelville and I was escorted by Captain Whaling. I remember little of the long, tedious hours other than the fact I was on my way to rejoin my husband. Mr. Blackford joined the train at Russelville with the word that the train had been ordered to take us two miles further down the track to Judge Barton's where we were to stay. Nannie and her nurse, Mary, were with me. We were there two days, then the army moved to New Market. Longstreet was just about to advance when he received orders to send a large force to Johnston to take the place of the troops Johnston had sent to reinforce Polk in repelling Sherman's raid into Mississippi. Longstreet had to fall back to Greenville to protect his base of supplies and communications. On the 21st of February we got orders to move to Greenville. In the morning we started out. I rode the roan while Nannie and Mary rode in the forage wagon on top of the shucks and Mr. Blackford stayed with the wagon while I rode with the other members of the court. The weather was fine and we made twenty miles, camping in the yard of a Mr. Shields near Blue Springs. Mr. Blackford, Nannie and myself got a room in the house but took our meals with the mess. We arrived in Greenville the next day while Richmond, Mr. Blackford's courier, rode ahead to find quarters for us. Nannie rode behind Mr. Blackford eighteen miles. Behind us we could hear cannon but there appeared to be no serious fighting as Longstreet and his staff rode near us. Richmond secured a snug little cottage with two rooms belonging to a Mr. Stewart. We made ourselves very comfortable, Mr. Blackford and myself occupying one room and Captain Cochran, Launcelot and Richmond the other. That room we also used as a dining room, office and sitting room.

A few days later we went to a party at Mr. Link's, some four miles away. I was asked to be chaperone. Mr. Link seemed to be a man of means whose wife was an invalid and whose daughters were fresh from school. We went out on horseback with General Kershaw and his staff: Cols. Alexander, Huger, Walton, Costin and many others. We took a band in a wagon and had music all the way. We spent the night. The supper was very bounteous and the hospitality without limit. It was, however, strictly a war affair, swords and pistols being laid about everywhere as the men took them off to dance or discharge the more civilized duties of the occasion. We enjoyed it. A very nice room was given me and Nannie. Mr. Blackford slept on the floor which was covered with men in blankets. I found a sword and pistol in my bed when I went to retire. Someone had put them there for safety before retiring. An early breakfast was given us and we went back to our quarters with a band playing and colors flying.

That Saturday there was a grand review of McLaw's division, Kershaw commanding. General Longstreet had division drill. I rode on Mr. Blackford's horse with quite a number of beaux attending. Little Nannie was on the black and rode about everywhere with old Tarleton as her groom. He had a white rein fastened to the horse which he held as he rode near her to prevent the horse from getting restive as the troops cheered the different generals and the salutes were fired. She was as much cheered as Old Pete Longstreet himself. Her face was beaming, and she looked very beautiful to my eye. She had on a red body and a black skirt, and as the troops would cheer her she would bow over until her golden curls mingled with the mane of the beautiful black. The horse would arch his neck and seem very proud of his precious freight. The day was a grand gala, and after it was over a number of officers came to our house and had refreshments,— not very grand but much relished.

About the 24th of March we moved back to Bristol. We rode on the cars with the staff while the horses returned with the troops. We got comfortable quarters at the hotel for myself, Mr. Blackford and Nannie and Mary for only sixty dollars a day. A few days later we got quarters in the house of a Mrs.

Wibber where we were very comfortable. Nothing much occurred as we waited for the army to catch up with us. About all we did was wonder where we would be sent next. Everybody wanted to go back to Virginia, including Longstreet, who told Sorrel that while it was more honorable, possibly, to have a separate command, he preferred to be under Lee, as it relieved him of responsibility and gave him assured confidence.

On April 11th we received orders to move without delay to General Lee which delighted everyone. Our brigade left that day by train for Lynchburg just at midnight. We were in the car reserved for Longstreet and his staff. I was the only lady on the train of mixed passenger and box cars all full of happy, cheering soldiers. We reached Lynchburg the next afternoon to find that Mr. Blackford's father was very dangerously ill. Mr. Blackford and Launcelot were given a leave of absence by General Longstreet, so we remained in Lynchburg while the troops passed on.

Two days later he died. Fortunately all his sons were able to attend the funeral. The five were dressed in their full Confederate uniforms with swords and sashes as they acted as pall-bearers. Never was a father borne to his grave by more loving sons, nor did sons ever lay a father to rest whose love and life had been so absolutely devoted to them. His death was as much a result of the war as if he had been slain and left stark upon the battle-field. He had high duties to perform for his country, his family, his friends and to the community around him. To those duties, from the outset of the war he devoted every energy of his nature and to which willing testimony will be borne by all who knew him and the hundreds who shared his hospitality and were recipients of his kindly services. For three years his frail body had borne against the many burdens placed upon his shoulders, until at last, oppressed by anxiety and worn down by labor and responsibility, exhausted nature found rest in the grave.

CHAPTER XIV

GRANT COMES TO VIRGINIA

MR. BLACKFORD remained home for his leave then returned to the army. His first letter upon rejoining was dated

Mechanicsville, Louisa County, May 1, 1864.

This corps, I think, will be held in reserve, so far as there will be any reserve. I think we shall move towards the front tomorrow. Burnside's army has come around to Manassas, thus settling the much-mooted question of what he would do when we left East Tennessee. His arrival, I doubt not, is the prelude to an active move on the part of Grant, who now commands the Federal troops in Virginia. All the artillery in Hill's corps is camped in this neighborhood, and has been here in winter quarters ever since the middle of December. They will move to the front tomorrow.

Same Camp, May 3d.

Grant is certainly concentrating a large army against ours. If we defeat him the military strength of the enemy will be broken, and we must have peace. God, in his mercy, grant us a victory! Officers and men are confident of success. I am so also, but sometimes I find my fears giving away to the force of numbers. Their army is twice as large as ours. They can replace every man killed and wounded. We, on the other hand, are using up our reserves. Grant can afford to have four men killed or wounded to kill or disable one of ours. That process will destroy us at last, by using up our material. What a terrible period of anxiety and bloodshed the next ninety days will be! Our very existence may be at stake in a single battle. If we fail, we cannot carry on another campaign. Our supplies of men and munitions will not permit it. If we succeed we will have peace in less than twelve months.

May 4th.

The enemy are crossing at Germanna Ford and all his army is in motion towards our right flank. Our corps moved today about twelve o'clock, Longstreet about five, and we move in the morning, easily catching up with him. This movement will precipitate a fight, I doubt not. What momentous interests, public and private, are bound up in the result and hang on the issue! Peace follows victory and subjugation defeat. Let it terminate as it may, many of our best and bravest will be killed and many thousands more be made widows and orphans without anyone to guard or support them. Your large acquaintance amongst the First Corps will give you a new interest in the lists of killed and wounded which must soon be on the bulletin boards. General Kershaw and Major Costin send you their love and say they will write you after the battle to thank you for the presents you sent them.

Longstreet's headquarters, The Wilderness, May 5th.

We started from Mechanicsville about nine o'clock having sent Col. Wood to Charlottesville with a fever. We then came on and camped that night at Mr. Ellis' on the North Anna in Orange County and reached headquarters about two o'clock today. The troops had been moved forward some two miles and had been hotly engaged this morning. Yesterday Ewell's and Hill's corps and Rosser's brigade of cavalry had a fight in which they drove the enemy back several miles capturing four guns and two thousand prisoners. Major Latrobe has just come in wounded in the thigh. Sorrel is missing and it is not known whether he is killed or captured. Thompson Brown is mortally wounded and Cols. Nance and Guilliard of South Carolina are killed. General Jones and Stafford are killed and General Benning wounded. Kershaw is thus far unhurt though he acted like a lion and exposed himself most recklessly. The terrible anxiety of the present is hard to estimate. We are fighting in a boundless forest and the artillery plays no conspicuous part. The enemy occupy very nearly the same position they did at Chancellorsville last year, when Jackson outflanked them. Our troops are behaving most gallantly and thus far they are confident of the result. The whole line of the enemy has been forced back about a mile today, and they have made four or five successive charges on our lines, and have been repulsed at great loss. At one time Generals Lee and Longstreet were talking and came near being captured by a charge of the enemy. I do not know what General Longstreet will do now he has lost both Latrobe and Sorrel, two of the most efficient staff officers, and two of the most gallant.

In one of the charges today the enemy broke through our lines, and the men fell back in some disorder. General Lee, seeing it, dashed forward to rally them, calling on the Texas brigade to follow him in a charge. They gathered around him and told him they would not charge unless he would go back to a safer place, and he had to do so. They then, under his eyes, made one of the most gallant charges of the war and swept everything before them.

The following was written in pencil on the back of the letter:

5 *P.M.*

General Longstreet severely wounded in the left shoulder, not mortally. General Jenkins, of South Carolina killed. Enemy retiring.

May 6th.

Up to noon today William and Eugene unhurt. There has been little fighting today. The result of the last two days has been decidedly in our favor. We have thus far captured four guns, three thousand prisoners, including three brigadiers. We have driven the enemy from the battle-field some two miles and hold all his dead and wounded. On our side the loss has been heavy, of course, not so much as in a general engagement. None of our staff hurt except Latrobe; Sorrel escaped and returned. Kershaw exposed himself most daringly and showed much skill in putting his men into action and managing them under heavy fire. Longstreet says he fell in the very achievement of victory but his plans were frustrated when he fell. General W. C. Field takes command of the corps as the senior major-general in command.

Corps headquarters, Spotsylvania C. H., May 19th.
This is the eighth day of rain and the fifteenth in which our troops have been in the line of battle. The great days of fighting were the 5th, 6th, 8th, and 12th. Also yesterday morning. The intermediate days there has been no general heavy engagement, but skirmishing has been going on all the time, with occasional more severe attacks on some point on our line. Thus far, with the exception of the partially successful attack on Johnson's division, (the "Bloody Angle"), on Thursday morning in which we lost some fifteen hundred prisoners and some guns, the enemy have not, in a single instance, been successful. The fight on Thursday inst. was, with the exception of the trouble on Johnson's front, the most one-sided affair possible. They made repeated and very gallant attacks on our breastworks and were as often driven back again with great loss of life to them and none to us.

Our corps lost only fifty men killed and wounded, while I am satisfied from what I saw with my own eyes that the enemy left unburied in front of our troops alone at the very least one thousand dead, and they buried as many as they could reach and all killed behind their lines. This represents a loss of killed and wounded and many thousands, almost as many as we have in the corps. There is no exaggeration in this statement. Others make this number larger, but I make my statement from what I saw the day of the battle and from a closer inspection of the field since. Only at Fredericksburg have I seen so many dead on one line. The enemy's loss in front of the other corps was greater than the loss in front of ours, I am told. I have good reason, I think, for saying the enemy's loss was between twenty and thirty thousand killed, wounded and captured. Ours from the same causes cannot exceed six thousand of whom fifteen hundred were prisoners of Johnson's division. After the battle the enemy abandoned his line on our front, leaving his dead unburied and some twelve hundred of his badly wounded on our hands, eighteen caissons and twenty-one gun carriages, the guns of which are supposed to be buried in some of the many graves with which they have dotted their field. They have now taken position on our right, and on yesterday, at daylight commenced a general attack on our lines. The cannonading was terrible for some half an hour, but as the infantry lines would come out from under it, our men would open up on them and they would fall back in great confusion. This was repeated several times with the same result, when, about twelve o'clock, they gave it up. Their loss was considerable, yet, as far as I can learn, we had not a man killed and few wounded, yet at times the cannonading was second only to that of Gettysburg.

The enemy's men would not charge, and from our lines we could distinctly hear the officers vainly urging them forward. Prisoners say they will not charge our breastworks again. Thus far Grant has shown no remarkable generalship—only a bulldog tenacity and determination in a fight, regardless of the consequences or the loss. If it required the loss of twenty-five thousand to rob us of six thousand he was doing a wise thing for we yield our loss from an irreplaceable penury, he from super-abundance. Ultimately such bloody policy must win, and it makes little difference to them, as the vast majority of the killed and wounded are foreigners, many of whom cannot speak English. Our men delighted in firing from behind breastworks; they have had but little experience in such work. Our corps behaved splendidly and has excited the admiration of the whole army. I wish Longstreet was with us. He is a tower of strength and the men have confidence in him. Eugene's superior officers were wounded and he is therefore in command of his regiment. I hope he will be promoted if he gets through this safely. General Field gives satisfaction. Kershaw, of course, is grand. Costin is unhurt.

I hope you will show all possible attention to General Longstreet and Major Latrobe while in Lynchburg.

May 20th.

Our headquarters are in the yard of a Mr. Herndon. To-night the regimental band gave him and his family a sere-nade. We also had a "negro-show," the actors of which were soldiers blacked up. The music and the jokes were capital, the latter entirely confined to the army. I wished for Nannie very much. With them was a boy of seven who danced better than anyone I ever saw. His father was a member of the 49th Virginia Infantry, and was killed at first Manassas, and this, his only child, having no house or friends, was adopted as the child of the regiment, and has never left them. He has never been sick and, what is more remarkable, has been in every march and has never broken down or been heard to complain. The officers often offer him their horses, but he will not accept any such lift. Is it not wonderful?

Headquarters, First Corps, Hanover Junction, May 23d.

After a march of all night and half a day our army is con-fronting Grant again, from the south bank of the North Anna River. Grant, being foiled at The Wilderness, slid off by his left flank towards Spotsylvania Courthouse, Lee moving in a parallel line by his right flank. Again a battle was fought and the advance stopped and a movement by the left flank was again made towards Milford Depot, on the north side of the Mattapony. General Lee then, instead of making his line on the south side of the Mattapony, made it on the south side of the North Anna River, and there we are now placed. We made a forced march on Saturday night and on Sunday morning were all occupying this strong position right across Grant's march to Richmond. I was on the march all night guiding a column. We crossed the river at the island ford by Dr. Thomas B. Anderson's where I breakfasted with him. He was much distressed that he was to be left in the enemy's lines. He had no notice to move and naturally is in great trouble at the thought that his house will be in just the position to be blown up by our shells as it will be in the enemy's line of battle. His farm is looking very beautiful and his crops are fine. Mt. Airy, the adjoining farm owned by Mr. Dickerson, is in the same condition.

Near Taylorsville, Hanover County, May 26th.

It is raining hard and the men in the trenches are suffering very much. It looks as if it will rain for a long time to come. Our line is extended from Hickory Hill (General Wickham's) on our right to Beaver Dam on our left. The enemy has not yet made himself felt. He is resting on the banks to the Mattapony. I have been to Ridgewood and Dewberry, and had a very pleasant visit at both places.

Yesterday I was sent by General Field to inspect and report on the various crossing places on the Little River above Edgewood down to its mouth. When near the mouth I found William with a detail from his regiment repairing a bridge. We rode together until I had finished my errand, then we went to Mrs. Jane Winston's to dine with the fair Rosalie, whose weeds are very becoming. We found the young widow's face as beautiful, the old lady's hospitality as boundless, the dinner as bountiful, the grass as green, the roses as bright as when we were at the same place last year; only the charm of your presence was wanting to make it a paradise.

Dr. Cullen and Dr. Post have returned from Lynchburg where they went with General Longstreet when he was wounded. They both say they saw you and that you were very busy with the wounded.

Near Richmond, May 28th.

The enemy are moving and have gone back over the river. We received orders to move and have been moving ever since by uncomfortable marches. We are now camped near Mechanicsville, about four miles from Richmond. Where the army is, except our corps, and where the enemy is I do not know. The yankees left their line in front of us on Friday morning and commenced moving towards Hanover Town, on the Pamunkey River. Lee shifted his position by the right flank, and is now awaiting Grant's advance, but where he will form his line I do not know. Everything is quiet and no cannon are heard. I am camped in a very nice spot, on a bluff overlooking the Chickahominy bottoms. I went last week to see my old company and was, as usual, most cordially received. Every officer has been disabled and young Gilmer Breckenbridge was put in command but was killed a few days ago. The men want me to publish a list of their losses from the beginning which I will do. They have behaved most gallantly and have lost heavily.

I am much in want of a pair of pantaloons; I wish you would tax your ingenuity to get them for me. I want you, also, to get that Mr. Seay, who lives in the alley which comes up from Main Street by the Washington Hotel, to make me a pair of shoes. He has my measure and he can make them out of the piece of leather you have. The sole leather is at Father's. See that the leather is returned as soon as the shoes are cut out, for when that is gone I do not know where I will get more.

May 30th.

Received two letters from you this morning, much to my joy. They are not in as good spirits as usual. General Lee did not fall back twenty miles. He only followed Grant as he changed front. In this changing, Grant, it is true, got nearer Richmond by making a detour, but when he got in his present position he was where he could have been at first without seeing a Confederate soldier or losing a man. As it is he has lost fifty thousand men and Lee and his army are before him, full of fight and unconquerable. The truth is he has entirely abandoned his plan of campaign, and that plan, which was to march straight forward upon Richmond along the line of the Richmond and Fredericksburg Railroad, has *failed,* and he is now making for a new position which McClellan held, and which he could have reached by coming safely up the James under the cover of his gunboats. In one respect only has his campaign been a success: to kill and wound so many of his men required a loss on our part at least one-fourth of his, and he is a hundred times better able to stand it. We are being conquered by the splendor of our own victories, and Grant accepts defeat with that consolation. The Federal army is greatly demoralized, and I do not think Grant will subject them to the test of another general engagement for some time to come. They will get behind breastworks in their old lines extending on both sides of the James from Chickahominy to Petersburg. I wish our Generals were all well. Longstreet is absent wounded and Lee and Ewell are both sick though both on duty.

June 2d.

There has been a very heavy skirmish this morning in which I am proud to say Kershaw gained fresh laurels. With his division he covered the disorderly retreat of some North Carolina troops, and drove the enemy back inside their entrenchments. Col. Kiett's regiment behaved badly yesterday when he was killed, but recovered their character today most handsomely under Kershaw. I went to Richmond yesterday and called on Mr. John Randolph Tucker and his wife. He is quite unwell. She told me she had seventeen persons in the white family and ten in the black, making twenty-seven in all to feed besides an innumerable host of straggling connections who find a square meal under their hospitable roof. They have no supplies laid up and buy bacon at ten dollars a pound and flour at three hundred and fifty dollars a barrel. It is a wonder to me how they stand it. He has nothing but his salary as attorney-general and his practice which is not much at such times. How vast must be the suffering in Richmond, not merely amongst the poor, as the term is usually applied, but amongst the class which is generally the happiest, those who have neither poverty nor riches. Why people do not move off into the country I do not see. They certainly could get them something to eat and fuel. Butter in Richmond is twenty-five dollars a pound.

Corps Headquarters, McKay's farm, June 4th.

Today has been one of excitement. The enemy attacked Lee in his entrenchments at four o'clock this morning and continued the fight until midday, charging time and time again against our breastworks, and as often hurled back with great loss. All agree that the loss to the enemy was as heavy as it ever had been on any field. Our loss was not one hundred men, killed, wounded or missing. We cannot ascertain the loss of the enemy but I believe ten thousand would not be an over-estimate. I never saw anything like it. Terrible musketry is going on now, at ten o'clock at night, but not, I presume, in front of our corps as the general and his staff are all quiet. General Kershaw distinguished himself again today and it is rumored at headquarters that General Lee has recommended him for promotion to Major-General. The world, our world, is making history now. During all our lives the histories which will be written will be partisan and the truth will not be in them. It is hard to get the truth of what happens now and happens just in our front, and of course the difficulty will increase.

Same Camp, June 7th.
My Darling Nannie;

Your letter, and the one from your mother, has just come, having been sent out to me by Col. Wood. Your handwriting has improved much. I am delighted to know that you and your mother are doing so much for the wounded and sick soldiers. You have received so much attention and kindness from them you ought to love them very much, especially those from Longstreet's corps. There has been some fighting with this army now every day for thirty-two days, and every evening some poor wounded men are carried back in ambulances and stretchers to hospitals in Richmond where, like in Lynchburg, they are kindly treated by the ladies and little girls too. We are camped on the farm of a gentleman named McRae, who has some daughters, one of whom is just a little bigger than you. They go out every evening to the breast-works to watch the firing of the cannon, and though the enemy shells come near they do not run away, but seem to enjoy the excitement. Do you think you could stand and see a battle as close as that? Many of the houses about here have great holes in them which were made by the yankee shells two years ago when General McClellan commanded them. A general named Grant commands them now, but neither of them are to be compared to Lee.

I suppose Lynchburg is in a great state of alarm now because the yankees are in Staunton, but I do not think there is any danger. General Lee is going to send General Brecken- ridge up there with two brigades. Did you see General Long- street while he was in Lynchburg? I am sure he would have been glad to see you. I wish you and your mother were down here, but it would have been too dangerous. Lee published an order just as the campaign opened asking all the ladies to leave the army, as they prevented their men from doing their duty. Don't you think he was hard on the ladies? And not very polite to them either. I hope you take care to comfort your grandmother. Your uncle Eugene is well and is much rejoiced at the thought that rations of onions, from Bermuda, are to be issued to the troops.

Your devoted;

Father.

Same Camp, June 7th.

Should the yankees come you must stand your ground, hid- ing all your supplies and valuables, or send them away, if you know where to send them. You might have your pieces of bacon hid away in various parts of the house. Peggy should pack some away in her mattress as the yankees will, I suppose, respect her race, or at least not suspect the hiding place. The household must exert its ingenuity to devise safe hiding places for your things. It will, perhaps, be better to lend your bacon and flour to the commissary department, returnable in kind, if you find the yankees about to occupy the place. It can fur- nish transportation very easily.

We are eating new beautiful onions from Nassau,—whether raised in Connecticut or not I cannot say,—they are imported at Wilmington. With our onions we have bacon cured in Ohio and shipped to Nassau to be sent us by blockade runners. It is said Beast Butler is engaged in this traffic. It is a good thing for us that he is. It is also said that when he commanded at New Orleans he promised to exchange bacon for cotton, but our departments, with great folly, refused to trade with him because of his violent orders. What difference did that make? They were, to some extent, blinds to enable him to carry on just such profitable schemes. Whether all this has any truth I cannot say. I tell the tale as it is told to me. Of course we believe anything of Butler.

June 9th, Night.

We have news,—authentic,—that Grant is crossing the James River below the mouth of the Appomatox and is pushing a heavy force towards Petersburg for the purpose of cutting our southern railroads. The wonder has always been with me that that effort has not been made before. This could have been done long ago and the failure to do so proves that any Federal successes will not be due to any military skill but natural depletion of our resources, both men and munitions.

June 10th.

To our delight this morning we learn the rumor is false, though fearful near the truth. Whoever permitted Petersburg to be thus defenseless is to blame. It was some of Bragg's work I think. Mark what I say: if the enemy occupies Petersburg the evacuation of Richmond must follow in three weeks. To leave such a strategic point to the protection of raw militia is great folly. Some of the fight took place in Poplar Grove, the pretty hospital on the upper end of Sycamore Street, just opposite Mr. George Bolling's. So you can see how close a shave it was.

I am constantly surprised that the Federal cavalry are not more efficient and more dangerous to us. The yankees are making a great fuss over General Sheridan in the Valley. If he had real merit he could have cut all our railroads supplying the army at Richmond on both sides of the James River, and, with our crippled resources, it would be very difficult for us to repair. He has a very large force, equipped with the finest and most improved repeating rifles and good horses, and with every possible supply known to the cavalry service. On our side our horses are worn down, and there is no source whence we can recruit. We have only pistols, sabres and old fashioned rifles, worn-out saddles, and none of the equipment in the way of portable furnaces, horse-shoes and transportation requisite for efficient cavalry work; and above all, we have not enough food to keep the horses up. Our cavalry is a very fine body of men, and we have some fine officers: Fitz Lee, Wickham, Rosser, Payne and others, but no horse can be kept efficient under the circumstances. The loss of a shoe from a horse where there is no convenient place to replace it, renders the cavalryman useless, and a horse unfed for several days is even more destructive. Sheridan vapors up and down the Valley, burning mills, scaring women and meeting, with doubtful effect, one-third his force in numbers and one-fifth his force when the matter of equipment is taken into consideration. Yet the whole yankee nation is showering glory upon Sheridan for the little he does, and is unmindful of the vast amount he might do if he displayed one-half the skill and courage of such men as Stuart, Forrest or Fitz Lee.

I was glad to see you say my report and General Lee's official report were exactly the same. They were written at about the same time. I pride myself upon giving about as accurate an account of army operations as is possible. This makes me so desirous that our letters shall be preserved. Some day they may be of use in settling disputed points. I never write anything down unless I am perfectly sure I am accurate, except when I give a rumor only as such.

How General Lee finds out Grant's intentions I cannot imagine, but, as soon as Grant commenced to move Lee commenced also, though, in some instances, as much as twenty miles apart; yet when Grant formed his new line, there was Lee in front of him as surely as if they had moved by concerted action. We have no news this evening of the yankee raiders under Sheridan. Two divisions of our cavalry have gone after them. Most people think they have gone to operate with Hunter. They say, however, they have gone towards Scottsville or Cartersville with the intention of crossing the James and cutting the Southside and Danville railroads, or even, perhaps, moving towards Lynchburg; a really bold and able man would attempt the latter plan and succeed, but Sheridan will not try it.

June 13th.

No one, so well as you, can imagine the deep solicitude the morning news gives me. The papers say the yankees are within eight miles of Lynchburg under Sheridan, and have destroyed all the bridges on the Orange and Alexandria Railroad. The very thing has happened that I thought would happen. It is needless for them to occupy Lynchburg long. They know that by going there they can destroy five or six important railroad bridges, and what is more, destroy the rolling stock of the Orange and Alexandria Railroad, for, by reason of change in gauge at that point, it cannot be taken off. The effect of which would be to put the railroad beyond our use for the rest of the war for we cannot supply any rolling stock. I am in agony of apprehension about you all. To think that my whole family, wife, child, mother, sister, are probably this very morning subjected to the insults and indignities of a band of freebooters makes my blood boil. From Lynchburg they will, of course, go down to Farmville and burn the High Bridge, and then cutting the line of the Danville Railroad, join Grant on the left flank near Petersburg. I do not know that Sheridan will do this, but a dashing and thoughtful man would do it. It is entirely possible and he ought to know it.

June 14th.

The glad news that Lynchburg is safe from Sheridan came yesterday for which I am thankful, but he should be ashamed. I am growing apprehensive of Hunter's movements now. He is moving up the Valley somewhere with quite a good army. He would be much to be dreaded if he were not conscience-stricken. No Virginian born and bred can lift a hand against her and not be afraid of his shadow. I wonder they should have picked him for such a command. No traitor to his blood and home can be trusted. No man upon whose head rests the scorn and contempt of all Virginians can stand up against it. He will be easily driven back. General Early has disappeared from our army in a most mysterious manner with his whole corps and we are very anxious to know where he has gone. He took fifteen days' rations with him. Some say he has gone to the Valley, some to Washington.

Grant has changed his front again. He will cross the James River and try to occupy Petersburg, which is the key to Richmond, as I have often said.

Camp on the Enroutey Town Road, June 16th.

The corps is moving now to Chafin's farm near Drewry's Bluff. I hear the enemy made a lodgement in our breastworks near Petersburg this morning. I hear heavy firing in that direction as I write, but all is quiet on our front. I am on the tiptoe of expectancy to hear the result, for it is very important we keep this line.

I do not regard Lincoln's renomination a very bad thing for us. Whether he is elected or not depends on Grant's success. He is supported by the whole army of office-holders and the power of the sword, and, unless some calamity befalls Grant's army, he is very sure to be elected. He seems to be a man of very good sense, rough, uncultivated, but I have no doubt is honest in his opinions. I am very anxious about our lines here. Lee has so few men with which to keep them up that it will be hard to maintain them. He has no mobile reserve to shift about whenever an attack is made. All are in the main line, and that is thin. If these lines are broken Richmond falls, and with the fall of Richmond the war and the Confederacy come to an end.

June 18th.

We have not moved yet, though most the men have crossed to the south side of the James,—I mean the men of our corps. I am very anxious about Lynchburg, and have no mail today. I hope a battle will be fought today. I have no doubt as to the result. What a glorious privilege Eugene has in fighting literally for "the green graves of his sires."*

* Major Eugene Blackford's line of sharpshooters ran directly through the Spring Hill Cemetery when Hunter was being repulsed. His position in the line at one time placed him beside his father's grave. General Early, who commanded the defense, is buried where he stood during the fight.
C.M.B.

Kean has received a letter from his sister in Caroline County. She says the enemy has been at his father's and have done them an infinite amount of harm. They took all the negroes, all the meat and chickens and broke open every lock in the house and stole everything they could carry away which would be of any use to them or their families. Everybody in Caroline and Spotsylvania Counties has suffered the same way; yet they keep their spirits up and are as undaunted as ever. They have nothing to eat but flour out of new wheat and such vegetables as the yankees have not stolen.

General Lee has endeared himself to the troops even more than before during this campaign. They idolize him now. Day before yesterday I was walking just in the rear of Hill's camp and came upon a poor sick man who was making his way slowly along in an effort to join his regiment. He said he had been in the trenches thirty-five days and was then quite sick, but he thought he would get well if a battle came on. He asked me what news from Petersburg. I told him that I did not know but Beauregard was over there. He replied, "General Beauregard is a pretty good general." I said: "General Lee has gone there also." He turned then to some sick and wounded men in an ambulance near by and called out: "You hear that, boys? It's all right now in Petersburg. General Lee's gone over there. I ain't goin' to make myself miserable about the thing any more."

If Grant is foiled during this campaign Lee becomes the most distinguished man now living.

As our troops passed Drury's Bluff on Friday the men made great fun of the garrison stationed there, shouting out, "You stay there, boys, and make onions for us. We'll do your fighting for you and won't let you get hurt!" One ragged fellow stepped out of the ranks, and with his musket in his hands, said to a particularly dapper and clean looking member of the garrison, at the same time holding out his musket as I would hold one to you to show you how it worked. "Look here, my friend, you take this thing . . ." pointing to the hammer, "and draw it back, then you can put a cap in this . . ." (showing him). "Now you pull the trigger and snap it. It won't hurt you, just try it. You've got to learn some day when they make a soldier out of you, and you'd better commence at once." All this in the most innocent and insinuating tone of voice, as if speaking to a timid child. It caused a great laugh. The men on the bluff have charge of the great guns there and have seen little service. They have built themselves nice houses and have little gardens around them.

I fear all these stories bore you, but they illustrate the spirit of the war, and of the camp. They are lost to history usually, and hence I take this mode of preserving them for my children.

CHAPTER XV

☆ ☆ ☆ ★ ☆ ☆ ☆

LYNCHBURG

☆ ☆ ☆ ☆ ☆ ☆

From Mrs. Blackford.
May 7th.

YESTERDAY was my regular time for writing you, but I really did not have the time to do so. The wounded soldiers commenced arriving on Saturday, and just as soon as I heard of it, which was before breakfast, I went to see Mrs. Spence to know what I could do for them. She said the ladies had been so shamefully treated by the surgeons that she was afraid to take any move in the matter. I told her I would go and see Dr. Randolph and ask him if we could not do something. I went down and did so at once and asked him what we could do. He said we might do anything we pleased in the way of attention to them; send or carry anything to them we wished and he would be glad of our help. As soon as I reported to Mrs. Spence what he said she started messengers in every direction to let it be known and I went to eleven places myself. We then determined to divide our provisions into two divisions: the bread, meat and coffee to be sent to the depot, the delicacies to the hospitals. The reception of wounded soldiers here has been most hospitable. You would not believe there were so many provisions in town as have been sent to them.

On Saturday evening I went up to Burton's factory, where most of the wounded were taken, and found the committee of ladies who had been selected, of whom I was one, just going in with the supper. I went in with them. We had bountiful supplies of soup, buttermilk, tea, coffee and loaf bread, biscuits, crackers and wafers. It did my heart good to see how the poor men enjoyed such things. I went around and talked to them all. One man had his arm taken off just below the elbow and he was also wounded through the body, and his drawers were saturated with blood. I fixed his pillow comfortably and stroked his poor swelled and burning arm. Another I found with his hand wounded and his nose bleeding. I poured water over his face and neck, and after the blood ceased to flow wiped his pale face and wounded hand which was black from blood and powder. They were very grateful and urged us to come and see them again.

On Sunday evening news came that six hundred more would arrive and Mrs. Spence sent me word to try and do something. The servants were away and I went into the kitchen and made four quarts of flour into biscuits and two gallons of coffee, and Mrs. Spence gave me as much more barley, so I made, by mixing them, a great deal of coffee. I am very tired.

May 12th.

My writing desk has been open all day, yet I have just found time to write you. Mrs. Spence came after me just as I was about to begin this morning and said she had just heard that the Taliaferro's factory* was full of soldiers in a deplorable condition. I went down there with a bucket of rice milk, a basin, towel, soap, etc. to see what I could do. I found the house filled with wounded men and not one thing provided for them. They were lying about the floor on a little straw. Some had been there since Tuesday and had not seen a surgeon. I washed and dressed the wounds of about fifty and poured water over the wounds of many more. The town is crowded with the poor creatures, and there is really no preparations for such a number. If it had not been for the ladies many of them would have starved to death. The poor creatures are very grateful, and it is a great pleasure to us to help them in any way. I have been hard at work ever since the wounded commenced coming. I went to the depot twice to see what I could do. I have had the cutting and distribution of twelve hundred yards of cotton cloth for bandages, and sent

---

* "Factory" as used here generally means a tobacco warehouse where tobacco is stored and aged. They generally are bare stone or brick buildings with no means of heating or other comforts.   C.M.B. III.

over three bushels of rolls of bandages, and as many more yesterday. I have never worked so hard in all my life and I would rather do that than anything else in the world. I hope no more wounded are sent here as I really do not think they could be sheltered. The doctors, of course, are doing much, and some are doing their full duty, but the majority are not. They have free access to the hospital stores and deem their own health demands that they drink up most the brandy and whiskey in stock, and, being fired up most the time, display a cruel and brutal indifference to the needs of the suffering which is a disgrace to their profession and to humanity.

Next morning.

It is now but a little after five o'clock, and as I go to the hospitals directly after breakfast I have arisen early to finish my letter. Almost all the men at Taliaferro's are Longstreet's men and express the greatest desire to see the General. When I told the men I had been in East Tennessee with them they seemed most pleased. Your mother is much interested in the soldiers. They seem to arouse her more than anything else. She does a great deal for them.

Evening.

I have been in the hospital nearly all day dressing wounds and nursing. I went to enquire about General Longstreet and saw Captain Gorse and was glad to hear that the general was better and that he rested well last night.

May 18th.

I have been constantly engaged with wounded soldiers. My work, however, is much reduced, as the men have been scattered about to the different hospitals and are better cared for. I shall not undertake so much again. I was nearly broken down by my efforts and could not perform any other duties. I went up yesterday evening to see Eliza Gordon, not expecting to see General Longstreet. I had been there but a short time when he sent for me and insisted I should come up and see him which, of course, I did. He is very feeble and nervous and suffers much from his wound. He sheds tears on the slightest provocation and apologizes for it. He says he does not see why a bullet going through a man's shoulder should make a baby of him.

I stopped just here on yesterday to go to church and thence in pursuit of little Spratt. Mary and I found him,—a most forlorn looking person with a wound in his face and most miserably clad. He was very gentlemanly, but the saddest person I ever saw. He did not have the ghost of a smile about his face while I was talking with him. I promised to send him down some soup and rice milk, for the hospital rations are very indifferent for the men, and most uninviting. From Miler's we went to the college, where all the patients have been put into tents. Some of my patients have been placed in the Langhorne Hospital, so I can see and attend them every day. There are three wounded yankees there, one of them a splendid looking man from Ohio. I have talked with him a good deal and found him very intelligent and very sick of the war. He says he has been kindly treated ever since he has been here, and does not intend to fight any more. The yankees are mixed up with our men and are treated exactly alike. They seem well contented. The hospital fare is very bad. I broke open a corn pone prepared for one of the sick and found it full of dry meal; no pains had been taken in making it up, though water was the only ingredient, enough was not supplied.

June 21st.

It is amusing to me, reading your letters of the 17th and 19th to see how little idea you had of the stirring times through which we were passing in Lynchburg. On Monday the 13th we began to fear that Hunter would make Lynchburg his point of attack, but it was not a definite fear until we heard of his being in Lexington and that he had turned this way. On Thursday the 16th we heard of his being at Liberty, marching this way, and then all the excitement and apprehension. General Breckenridge, with some troops, got here on Wednesday night, and as we saw them passing out West (now Fifth) street, it was a most reassuring sight, and never were a lot of bronzed and dirty looking veterans, many of them barefooted, more heartily welcomed. The streets were lined with women waving their handkerchiefs and cheering them as they moved out to a line on the hills west of the city. We were cheered also by the knowledge that General Early, with several brigades, was in Charlottesville en route to reinforce the small command of Breckenridge. He arrived with some of his troops on the evening of Friday the 17th, but could do little more than get what he had into position. On Saturday more of Early's men were here, and it was a delightful sound to hear their cheers during the night as they passed out to the lines. Eugene was amongst them, and seemed to delight in this chance of making a fight right at home. That was a day we will not soon forget. There was no general engagement, but a constant cannonade and heavy skirmishing went on all day. Our lines were out in and near Spring Hill Cemetery, the enemy's further out. Their skirmish line was in Mr. Johnson B. Lee's yard, where a number were killed by our cannon. I went out on College Hill and watched the fighting much of the time. It was very exciting to watch the cannon-fire from both sides and the explosion of shells on the opposite side. It was fascinating beyond all description. I could see our troops moving and taking new positions, and could see the yankee batteries doing the same thing, and then the fearful reality of the scene was forced upon me by the line of ambulances which was kept busy bringing the wounded men into town.

Col. Floyd King called at our house and told me, on Friday night, that we should put our most valuable things in the cellar for protection and should stay down there ourselves. Many things were carried into the basement including the pictures, china, silver, etc., but we did not go there to sleep, thinking it time enough when the shells commenced to fly. Our people, of course, were very much excited but on the whole behaved very well. I had so much to do I did not have time to get scared, though I was deeply anxious. The sight of the familiar faces of the veterans as they marched through our streets reassured me completely. Early got his men into line Saturday evening, but, for some reason, did not attack, and the next morning the coward Hunter was gone. Early at once started after him but has not yet overtaken him I hear. Eugene had his headquarters of his sharpshooters at one time in the cemetery close to his father's grave. He went on with his command. It was a great relief when we heard Hunter was gone.

Hunter's headquarters were at old Major Hutter's. He told them that he proposed to capture or burn Lynchburg. He was, of course, politely treated but after the general left it the officers and men robbed it,—robbing Miss Hutter's chamber of all its clothing and valuables. Many wounded men were left in Major Hutter's yard. Hunter's whole campaign seems to have been a farce. He was gallant where there was no enemy and a coward when they were in sight. He fled so hastily that he left even the slightly wounded, many small arms and some cannon behind. He burned the Military Institute which was not garrisoned, set fire to Governor Letcher's house which only women protected.

The soldiers who came up with Early give the most distressing accounts of the condition of affairs in Louisa County, where the yankee raids have done so much harm to the unprotected. They say that the desolation is so great that as they marched through women and children flocked to the road begging for something to eat, and would grasp eagerly the bit of cold corn-bread they could spare from their own haversacks. Is it not horrible to think of?

Mrs. Blackford's narrative.

My letters for some time are scattered, many having been lost from the files and others too faded to be copied due to the poor ink available at that time. I remember writing that the drought was terrible and that Mrs. Chalmers and I were planning to go out to Blacksburg to buy coal for the winter and have it shipped to Lynchburg.

Around the 25th of July I went to Charlottesville, to the University where I stayed with Professor John B. Minor's family. Mary Blackford, Mr. Blackford's sister, had gone to

Dewberry to nurse Churchill Cooke to whom she was engaged and who had been seriously wounded. The ever-growing list of those we knew who were being killed and wounded kept our hearts filled with dread that the next list would have the name of someone we most dearly loved. Already I had lost several cousins; one, Randolph T. Colston, who was particularly dear to me was buried in the University graveyard where I could visit it but others were scattered in unmarked graves throughout the South. Daily also came word of misery and suffering, the ever-arriving wounded who both drained our hearts and our small supply of food, clothing and comforts. Also were seen the destitute from beyond the yankee lines where the yankees, finding they could not destroy the spirit of Virginia, were starving it into impotence.

CHAPTER XVI

☆ ☆ ☆ ★ ☆ ☆ ☆

PETERSBURG

☆ ☆ ☆ ☆ ☆ ☆

From Capt. Blackford.
The First Corps headquarters, Petersburg, Va., July 11th, 1864.

W^E are camped just outside of town. Not enough change of any sort since my last, except possibly, the dust is thicker, the grass more parched and the sun hotter. The whole country around here is filled with refugees from Petersburg in any kind of shelter, many in tents. Mr. Watkins is about a mile from here in a barn. His party consists of his wife and himself, Mrs. Hall, Miss Carry and all the children. They sleep on the barn floor. I called to see them yesterday. Every yard for miles around here is filled with tents and little shelters made of pine boards, in which whole families are packed; many of these people of some means and all of great respectability. There must be much suffering. Thus far, while the shelling has done much harm to houses and property, only one *soldier* has been wounded and none killed. Some five or six women have been killed and as many wounded most of whom were negroes. And this is all they have done. Yesterday, about the time they thought the people were going to church, they commenced a tremendous cannonade, as if with the hope of killing women and children en route to church.

The sinking of the Alabama gives us great concern, and we are very anxious to hear from Early. I fear he has undertaken more than he can do with his small force, and he is likely to come to grief.

July 15th.
I am amused at the plan Mrs. Chalmers and yourself had for getting coal. If you succeed it will show an amount of

skill and energy with which I did not credit either of you. I hope you will succeed. I am much troubled to know what you are going to do for coal next winter.

July 17th.

No news, and no movement except the incessant shelling and the constant ring of the rifles of the sharpshooters on the lines. Last night, about eleven some five or six mighty siege guns were fired, which made the most terrific sound I ever heard. Early has withdrawn from near Washington.

I have taken cold and have a headache and fever. I believe the terrible dust has much to do with it and the hard fare. I can get little or nothing to eat, the best is blue-looking beef and the terrible bread cooked in camp. We have no coffee, tea or sugar. There is much unfavorable comment in the army about Johnston's constant retreats. Lee would have fought Sherman at Dalton. It is said Hood is to relieve him. Hood is not the man for such a place. Longstreet would be better. Johnston's army has been taught that falling back is the aim of a campaign and that fighting is an incident. Lee has taught us that an occasional retrograde movement is an incident and fighting is the aim. There have been more desertions of late than ever before. I hear that even some Virginians have deserted to the enemy. The hard lives they lead and a certain degree of hopelessness which is stealing over the conviction of the best and bravest will have some effect in inducing demoralization hitherto unknown.

The Richmond papers give me great anxiety. There is a shadow in them of a defeat of Early in the Valley. It is only a rumor, but I find bad rumors are always true while good ones are often false. My cold seems touching my vitals. I cannot see, hear or smell, and, but for you and Nannie, would as soon be dead as alive. Grant is making some move. He is taking troops to the north side of the James River, and as a consequence Kershaw's division moves today. There is a rumor Grant is dead. I do not believe it, but it would make little difference to us. He is a hard fighter but no match for Lee as a commander of an army.

July 27th.

I went to Richmond day before yesterday on business. Not satisfactory as almost all I wanted to see were out of town. I took breakfast with Col. Robert L. Owen, president of the Virginia and Tennessee Railroad. His bill was $141 for three but it was elegant. It was at Tom Griffin's. It was the best meal I have had for two years. I am glad that he, not me, had to pay the bill. News from Early is encouraging.

The schedule of prices fixed by the commission shocked me beyond measure and it is hard to believe they were such fools. I take that view because it is more charitable than calling them knaves. It is, as the Albemarle farmer would say, an official acknowledgment of bankruptcy, and is a deathblow to the currency. It carries starvation to the non-producers for the market price of everything to eat is far higher than those fixed by the commissioners. If they put wheat at $30 a bushel the farmers will at once charge the starving consumers $120. How are our people to live? The soldiers' wives and families? How are you and Nannie to live? It is a fearful question. The non-producer has nothing to sell, and one can make no money even if not in the army; and what can a soldier do at seventeen dollars a month in Confederate money? The producer has everything. He is exempted from military service if a large producer because he is. He exchanges his corn and wheat for coffee and sugar, prates about the hardships of war and the high prices, buys nothing and complacently asks the starving wife of his friend who is in the army $100 a bushel for wheat, $4 a quart for tomatoes, and if he does not get it he locks the wheat up for higher prices and feeds the tomatoes to the hogs. You and mother are suffering from this now. This does not apply to the farmers of Orange, Culpeper, Fauquier, Loudoun and the Valley whom the enemy have robbed so heavily. They are as liberal as they are brave and valiant.

Camp near Drewry's Bluff, July 31st.

I am down here on duty with Pickett's division. There is much activity but I do not know what it is. Reports reached us last night of quite a severe attack at Petersburg on yesterday morning. Grant's mining operations culminated there in blowing up one of our batteries, by which twenty-one men and three guns were disabled. An assault on the breach was at once made with negro troops who, report says, carried the fort in spite of Hayward's South Carolina brigade.* This is the story, whether true or not you will know long before this reaches you. We certainly hold our old line, and the enemy took nothing by his attack but a severe repulse. Grant had moved three corps to the north side and General Lee followed with three divisions. Yesterday morning they had all disappeared and the mine exploded at Petersburg, from which we infer that Grant had contemplated a general advance on our lines with his whole force massed at Petersburg. If this is correct he got badly worsted. His strategy was a complete fizzle. The news from Petersburg which has just come in says we captured nine hundred prisoners, thirteen stands of colors, killed about seven hundred and have the same line as before.

Same Camp, August 2d.
My Darling Nannie;

We are camped in a sweet grove by the side of a large brick house, and I often wish you and your mother were here to enjoy it. I would like you to see Drewry's Bluff and the big cannon down there,—big enough for you almost to crawl into. The breastworks there are very high and they have little rooms in them in which the powder and shells and shot are kept so they may not be injured either by rain or the shells of the enemy. The fortifications are all turfed which makes them look much nicer than any you have ever seen. The soldiers live in small cabins, all of which are whitewashed, and they have beautiful walkways between them and flowers and grass to make them look better. Would you like such soldiering as that? The fort is so situated that we could sink any yankee gunboats with our big guns if they try to pass up the James River, which is just at the foot of the bluff, to Richmond. We are camped at a place where there was a battle fought three

---

*This is the famous battle of The Crater.   C.M.B.

months ago, and there are some very curious signs now left. Very near us the yankees had their field hospital, and many of them are now buried all around us. In one hole they threw all the arms and legs they cut off, and as they threw only a little dirt over them many of them are sticking out now making a very horrid sight, but one we get used to. All the trees around us are marked with cannon and musket balls. A shell from one of our batteries struck a large oak tree and went to the heart of it before it exploded, then one piece of the shell went up the heart of the tree and the other down. It split the tree, of course, but stuck fast and stands there now like a great wedge. I hope the owner of the place will let it stand as it is as a memento of the war, which will be very striking when you are an old woman.

The most remarkable thing I have seen is a cabin a few hundred yards from here where a dead yankee is lying still unburied. He seems to have been wounded and carried into this cabin and laid on some straw on the floor. There he died, and had, as many bodies do, dried up, for the cabin was between the two lines and neither side could get to him to aid him or bury him. Right by his side lies the body of a great Newfoundland dog, which the negroes at the house in which we are camped say died of starvation rather than leave his dead master. Master and dog lie there together, strangers in a strange land, unburied and unwept, and perhaps, far away in the North, he has some little girl like you who is still hoping for her father's return and picturing the joy of having him back and romping with the faithful dog. War is a sad thing but if the poor man had stayed home and not come down here to desolate our homes and burn our houses he would have been with his little girl now. The negroes say they tried to get him to leave his master. They tempted him with food. Once he came out, ate something, but went back and afterwards they could not get him to leave his place or eat anything. So, there he died. Men are not so faithful as dogs.

Same Camp, August 1st.

The firing towards Petersburg was very severe yesterday but

no harm done. The enemy are digging another mine in the direction of our batteries, and General Lee found it out. He countermined and ran a gallery out under their working party and yesterday evening blew them up so effectively as to stop them. As soon as the explosion took place the enemy anticipated a charge from our lines, and at once commenced a furious cannonade upon them which lasted about an hour, but, though very expensive in the manner of ammunition, was not remunerative in that no harm whatever was done to us. This ends Grant's second great affair.

I went early this morning to General Field's headquarters to see him on business. I think we will move over to him tomorrow. He is on the other side of the river.

August 8th.

I was much pleased with General Field. He has greatly distinguished himself during the campaign and has won the esteem and confidence of the corps. He was shot through the hip at Second Manassas and tells me he still suffers from his wound, which is still running.

The Adjutant-General, at the request of the acting Judge-Advocate General, made a request that I be temporarily detailed to do some work in the Judge-Advocate's office, but General Lee declined to let me go, saying very kindly that he could get no one to fill my place or do my duties so well. This is very gratifying, of course, and I was perfectly satisfied. There are some reasons why I should enjoy a stay in Richmond for awhile, but I do not see how we could afford to be there together, and unless you and Nannie are to be there, I would greatly prefer being in the field.

A few moments ago there was a mighty explosion down the river in the direction of the Howlett House followed by a mighty volume of smoke, which rose straight to the clouds. We are all on tiptoe to know what it was.

Chafin's Farm, August 10th.

We are now camped on the north side of the river. Our gunboats all came up from their anchorage near the Howlett

House yesterday morning and are now lying just below the bluff on which we are camped. They do not inspire me with awe, because I can but regard them as machines destined to be blown up if the enemy gets very close. We have not the materials to build such boats. I begrudge the large number of able-bodied men in white pants who cover their decks.

I swam out yesterday to one of our gunboats, several hundred yards to the middle of the river, and crawled up its sides. I must be lacking in that native dignity which asserts itself unaided by outward insignia, for I was not saluted and, indeed, had no attention paid me by officers or men. So I showed my contempt for the rival branch of the service by diving off and swimming back to shore, making a total of nearly three-quarters of a mile. I find I have not lost my art as an expert swimmer.

Our living is now very poor: nothing but corn-bread and poor beef,—blue and tough,—no vegetables, no coffee, sugar, tea or even molasses. I merely eat to live, and live on as little as possible. You would laugh, or cry, when you see me eating my supper,—a pone of corn-bread and a tin cup of water. We have meat only once a day. It is hard to maintain one's patriotism on ashcake and water. The mighty explosion we heard was the blowing up of a powder ship at City Point. It is said to have been done by a Captain Z. McDaniel, of the secret service, with some kind of an infernal machine.

August 17th.

Yesterday was quite an active day along the front. The enemy made an attack on our whole line, and at one point broke through, making a gap in a brigade of Georgians, belonging to the Third Corps, commanded by Brigadier General Girardey, who was promoted a few days since from the position of Captain and assistant adjutant-general. He rushed to the front in an endeavor to rally the men and was shot through the head and was instantly killed. His adjutant was by his side, and, with his pistol fired five shots at the man who killed the general. One ball only took effect. The yankee ran at him, and they closed in a death-grapple and both fell over the breastworks. The adjutant finally succeeded in putting a ball through his adversary's head, but was at once captured. He soon, however, escaped with only a slight wound.

General Field brought up Anderson's brigade of Georgians and soon drove the enemy back and re-established our line, taking some three hundred prisoners. Captain Mason, of his staff, I am sorry to say, was badly wounded and is a prisoner. Most persons think he was killed. His horse returned with an empty and bloody saddle. The enemy's loss was heavier than ours. General Chambliss, of the cavalry, was wounded and left in the hands of the enemy. I like Field more than ever the better I get acquainted with him. He is affable and courteous and yet intelligent and, unlike some of our generals, especially some of those educated at West Point, does not think it detracts from their dignity to be a gentleman in his intercourse with his subordinates. We repulsed the enemy all along the whole line with a great loss to him and very little to us.

CHAPTER XVII

RICHMOND

By Susan Leigh Blackford.

O N THE 10th of September, Mr. Blackford, who had made a reputation in the Adjutant-General's office from the character of the papers which came from him, received the following order from that office, addressed to him:

"Captain James Taylor, having been appointed recorder of a court of inquiry at Abington, Virginia, by order of the Secretary of War, you are temporarily assigned to duty in this office, in charge of the Judge Advocate's duties until he returns.

S. Cooper
A&I General."

It was endorsed:

"Captain Blackford reported for duty in this bureau as directed in this order, on the 18th of September, 1864.

John W. Riely
A.A.G."

It was a surprise to him, but after his three and a half years in the field it was a pleasant change. By the invitation of his friend, R. G. H. Kean and his wife, I joined Mr. Blackford and secured two rooms on the second floor of a house inhabited by Dr. George, on Grace St. on the corner of Jefferson. We had also the use of a stable and a small room in the yard. Mr. Blackford kept one horse in the stable and John Scott slept in the small room, which was also used as a kitchen. We were fairly comfortable, and to Mr. Blackford it was a haven of rest.

It is a cause of great regret we kept no record of the events which passed during the terrible and feverish months we spent in that beleaguered and starving city. We were very much troubled to secure the necessities of life as Mr. Blackford's salary, as Captain of Cavalry, was of small use. I remember that our Christmas turkey absorbed nearly all he received for the month of December. Fortunately he had kept all he had made speculating in tobacco in that article, and as necessities required it, would order a box to be sold. And thus, making a box of tobacco as a standard of value, we lived very cheaply. But we lived very hardily, and counted many meals as sumptuous over which now the most patient would grumble. We had no butter, tea or sugar, molasses or many of the things which are accounted as essentials, or rather as foundations, of every meal, and are taken as given factors in any civilized system of domestic economy. We had flour and meal, and the flour made up into very fair biscuits. We had fat middling and sometimes a potato or cabbage. On extra occasions we would buy a quart of oysters and at Christmas had a turkey.

We were, however, very happy in the first taste of domestic life for nearly four years, and what, as we look back, were hardships didn't seem so then. Our only trouble was our anxiety in regard to the state of the country.

When in the field Mr. Blackford saw much to indicate the failure of our munitions and supplies, but active service and plenty of work enabled him to forget the deductions he drew from what he saw. But when he came to Richmond and was placed in a position which gave him a view behind the scenes, he soon determined that our cause was lost and that all our leaders knew it. He found out from the morning reports from General Lee's army, which he had an opportunity to inspect, that it was rapidly growing less and that the difficulty of keeping it supplied in rations, ammunition and arms was daily becoming greater. This preyed upon his spirits and upon mine, and it was harder to keep cheerful for, independent of our patriotic feelings, our personal fate and future were so beclouded that nothing but our long training in a life of uncertainty and danger enabled us to keep up—but keep up we did.

I remember, one day, late in February 1865, the despair with which Mr. Blackford told me General Lee did not have in his whole army as many as thirty thousand men fit for duty, and that he had but a few days' rations accumulated ahead. Of course all this was not generally known, not even in the Adjutant's office, but the statement was unfortunately true.

Even with these depressing influences there was, however, until the latter part of the winter, some gaiety and I went to several parties which I well remember. One was at Dr. William S. Morris', head of the telegraph service of the Confederate States. His ingenuity and energy made him invaluable to the government. At this entertainment, except for the dresses of the ladies, there was little to remind one of war. The viands were very abundant and consisted of oysters, turkey, game and everything usual for such occasions including champagne and other wines. The men were, as a rule, in uniform, but while the dressing of the ladies seemed to us at the time very nice, I have no doubt that it would have struck the eye of a lady of that time in New York or Paris as extremely old-fashioned, both as to materials and styles.

One night in February Mr. Blackford brought up to our room from the Adjutant-General's office a number of most beautiful captured flags—as many as a negro could carry. He borrowed them from the officer who had them in charge that I might see them. They remained in our room several days. I have often wished we had kept them, as they were destroyed when the Adjutant-General's office was burned six weeks later, at the time of the evacuation. There was a large room full of them.

The suffering of the people of Richmond at that time was terrible, and it, together with the general demoralization incident to the war, so largely increased the criminal classes that every night had its many stories of violence and robbery. But while that was true, the patience and heroism of the mass of people was beyond praise. The more so as hope had ceased to be the steadying and staying comforter. All anticipated the near approach of the end, all were calm and resigned, though defiant.

Sometime about the end of February Mr. Blackford became so well convinced that Richmond would soon be abandoned, that, to prevent me being left behind in the enemy's lines, he sent me to the University of Virginia. At first I stayed at Professor Minor's but soon rented a room at Professor Bledsoe's on the lawn, which I occupied with Nannie and my faithful girl, Mary. Almost as soon as I got there, to my horror, Sheridan's cavalry took possession.

CHAPTER XVIII

☆ ☆ ☆ ★ ☆ ☆ ☆

CHARLOTTESVILLE

☆ ☆ ☆ ☆ ☆ ☆

Capt. Blackford to Mrs. Blackford.
Richmond, March 5th, 1865.

YOU KNOW better than I can possibly describe how painful has been my anxiety during the past few days. I cannot suppose you have been in any actual personal danger, but you have been subject to possible insult and impertinence from the yankee soldiers around you, all of which you have had to bear without an avenging or protecting hand. I trust the University is not injured. We yet have no accounts of it having been burned though much apprehension is being felt on the subject. I do not apprehend such a breach of the law of nations and the decorum of war. I know you have blessed me for sending you away from here when you might, thus far, have remained in safety. I do not think you have, as Nannie would say, "got me down" on that point. Still I think, with my lights, I did the proper thing; for if the yankees burn all the bridges on the Central Railroad, as they say they propose doing, how would you have gotten away from here if General Lee withdraws his army?

You left me very few things for my comfort. Not a single spoon, or dish, and only one plate. Mrs. Robert Maury, Jr. and Dr. Tom Maury called to see you a few evenings ago and expressed their disappointment at not seeing you. They sat with me awhile.

We hear that owing to the negligent mode of destroying the bridge over the Rivanna the enemy crossed yesterday at four o'clock, and that another party is at North Garden, in Albemarle. The opinion here is that they will not try Lynchburg but will come down the Central Railroad destroying bridges, depots, etc. I fear the people of Albemarle will suffer much, though I cannot see what more they can lose, as they have been stripped of everything either voluntarily for our army or involuntarily by the enemy. I hope you will avail yourself of the first chance to send me a telegram announcing your safety. As I write I have no idea how this letter will reach you, but it is, nevertheless, a comfort to write, for I am very lonely.

Richmond, March 8th.

You can little imagine how anxious I am about you. I judge the enemy has left Charlottesville and I am hoping hourly to hear you and Nannie are safe and well.

Churchill Cooke is staying with me, and is very miserable because of the uncertainty of the times and the roads and the effect on his marriage. He is seriously contemplating a trip in his sulky. I went over from Lynchburg to Charlottesville in a buggy to get married, and in these times we ought to be able to use a sulky. It is raining again, very hard, much to my delight. Every drop that falls makes movement harder for the yankees and gives us more time to get our scattered men together. Things at the South are brighter. Johnston is collecting a good army, we hope. If we had even a second-class victory it will have a wonderful effect in inspiring our men. Old Virginia, as ever, is giving the keynote to the reaction which is going on. The response of the people to the call for supplies has been generous. They have given almost all they had and have divided the last dust of their flour and meal. If all the others would do as well we would be free yet. I think there is some comfort to be derived from the hope of war between France and the United States. Such a war would do us good. The relations between the two countries are much strained.

Richmond, March 10th.

This is Friday and the fast-day ordained by the President. Not a word from you. I am kept on the rack. To name one day as a fast day is most amusing since almost any given day is a fast-day for all, whether citizen or soldier. I see no chance for you to get through to Lynchburg as the bridges are burned, and the James River is too high to be forded. I wish you were out of their track. I would be a happier man.

This is the evening of the fast-day, and nothing has been done in the city, nor in our office. I never have seen such a day so devoutly kept by every class of the community.

From Mrs. Blackford.
University, March 6th, 1865.

My Dearest Husband;

Just what I told you when you insisted upon my leaving Richmond would happen has happened, and what I ran away from I ran into.

The rumor that the soldiers were coming down from Waynesboro reached us on Wednesday, but it was only a rumor. Many Ragged Mountain people came in with eggs and other things to sell and said they "hearn" that the yankees were this side of Staunton, but they are so ignorant and stupid we put little confidence in their statements. The next day came men and women flying with their cows and horses and little produce, hoping either to put them under the protection of our troops or conceal them. The alarm then became deadly, and everybody set to work to prepare for the raiders by hiding everything of value. I first stored away the hams I brought away from Richmond in a safe place in the cuddy of Mr. Minor's house, and then directed my attention to the silver I had with me and which I did not want to lose. The news flew from house to house of fresh accounts of the outrages the raiders were committing as they came down towards Rockfish Gap. Each act of depredation, doubtless, much exaggerated, but each served to increase the excitement. We were told, as it turned out to be true, the negroes were stealing their master's horses and were flocking to the ranks of the enemy. It had been raining for days and the roads were bottomless. They had been cut through by the long wagon trains crossing from the Valley to Charlottesville, and then when Sheridan's army came, with his trains and the cannon, they were in such a condition that every vehicle was up to its hub and the axles actually dragged in the mud. Many wagons had to be abandoned. All day Thursday the rain continued to pour until late in the afternoon, when the sun came out. We waited for the yankees all day most anxiously, indeed in a state of wild excitement.

I took my silver sugar-dish, cream pot, bowl, forks and spoons and put them into the legs of a pair of your drawers I had in my trunk, tying up each leg at the ankle and buckling the band around my waist. They hung under, and were concealed by, my hoops. It did well while I sat still, but as I walked and when I sat down the clanking destroyed all hope of concealment. Of course the ridiculous side of the situation struck me and I could not restrain my laughter, which sister said was very unseemly at such time. But I could not help it. It was partly nervous, but there were many amusing scenes, as you can well imagine, and what is amusing will amuse me, you know, whatever the surroundings.

Sister had a few gold coins, twenty dollar pieces, I was only allowed to peek at them, under the promise of secrecy, because she needed counsel as to how best to hide them. After gravely debating the matter as to whether they should be put into the chimney, sewed in the mattress or worn in a belt we determined the safest mode of carrying them would be to rip up some flannel strips, which decorated her homespun linsey balmoran skirt, which gave her some satisfaction, and so excited the envy of her friends, and sew the coins at intervals under it all around. This we did and she wore her fortune thus encircling her as long as there was a yankee in sight. All that night we wandered from Mr. Minor's to Mr. Maupin's and hence to Mrs. Taliaferro's, who occupied the next house, and even invaded the sacred precincts of Mrs. Scheles' home, exciting and being excited by fresh horrors as each imparted to the other all and more than she knew.

When I was out of sister's presence and with the Maupin's, Mary Minor and the other college girls, as they would collect in the other different professor's houses, I could not keep up the solemnity of the occasion, and could see nothing but the ludicrous features of the performance, and of a consequence, would go into uncontrollable laughter. People in their alarm did many foolish and ridiculous things, and said more, which, with the clanking of our precious silver around my own person was more than I could stand, and I found a great relief from the nervous intensity in this equally intense amusement. The dreadful night ended at last, and though there were frequent alarms that the yankees had passed the toll-gate, they did not come, and the sun rose upon the University untouched by a single yankee soldier.

We had breakfast and I lay aside my tinkling treasures believing the mode of concealment entirely too noisy to insure success. We waited the arrival of the dreaded vandals almost impatiently. At last our pickets came in at speed and reported the yankees in sight, coming down the hill from the toll-gate. The women all wanted to fight,—how I do not know, —and thought we should defy Sheridan and all his host. The professors were not so bold, and, in accordance to a plan they had already devised, met on the lawn and then marched, with Mr. Minor at the head of the procession, with a white handkerchief fastened to a walking-cane as an emblem of peace, to meet the general and ask for protection for the college and its inmates. The women were very indignant and scolded what they were pleased to call very dastardly conduct, though it was the wisest and the only thing which could have been done. The yankee general who met them, who was Custer, behaved very well and at once put the place under guard and maintained perfect order.

My brother, who you know is connected with the quartermaster department at Charlottesville, was forced to leave home to avoid being captured. Sister Gert and the girls were in great distress about him, as it was midnight when he left, and he had no idea where he was going. I think Mr. Charles Maury went with him.

At first the ladies were all determined they would not look at the yankees, but curiosity got the better of them, and they went back to the Rotunda to watch them come in. They seemed to be countless to us who had been for the past year or so little accustomed to seeing such large bodies of cavalry. They made camp on Carr's Hill, and in the shortest time their campfires were blazing and they were busy cooking their dinner, which I suppose they needed very much, as they had been marching in the mud all night. The whole face of the earth seemed alive with them, but the guards placed around the University protected us well and we were not molested in the least, rather to our disappointment, for we were ready to play the role of martyrs for the cause. As it is we had nothing personally of which we could complain or boast. We had planned all kinds of sarcastic speeches to be hurled at them and were almost sorry to miss the opportunity.

The places in the vicinity were not so fortunate. At Oakhurst, Mr. Gildersleeve's place, just outside the University grounds, the stragglers intruded themselves and ran all over the house, ransacking bureau drawers, trunks and wardrobes. Taking out the ladies' underclothes and dresses and finally dressing themselves up in them and wildly dancing about the yard, much to the terror of the ladies. Mr. Gildersleeve's sister, Mrs. Howard, had put all her silver and things in her baby's crib. The baby was asleep and the old nurse was sitting by rocking it, but the ruse did not answer, they turned the baby out on the floor, found and took the hidden treasure. They shook the old nurse to find out if she had anything concealed on her person much to the old negro's indignation.

They went to Mr. Jesse Maury's and ransacked the house, although General Custer made his headquarters there. Nannie Maury was so frightened that it brought on a sort of convulsion and she had to be put into a hot tub to restore her to consciousness. They burst open the door of the room where she was being bathed and it was with the greatest difficulty they could be gotten out again and that was only after they found out there was nothing to steal. They took all of Mr. Maury's meat and provisions, and left him without anything to eat for his large family. General Custer sat in the dining room while all this was going on. Lizzie Maury found a teaspoon on the floor which had fallen out of the pocket of one of the intruders. She picked it up, carried it to General Custer and asked him demurely if he dropped it. He was very indignant but she pretended to a great innocence of motive. Old Mr. Rubin Maury, the grandfather, was much outraged, and, venturing on his age and feebleness, remonstrated in very strong terms, when one of the men raised a whip to strike him, but Lizzie jumped in between and received the whip on her shoulders. It was a most terrible experience for them and their house was almost left a wreck, plundered of everything that could be carried off.

The night of the day of the yankee arrival was almost as exciting as the night of the day we were expecting them. The campfires blazed on all the hillsides around and made a most beautiful sight, and had they been our people we should have enjoyed the camp very much. A guard was placed at every home in the University limits where one was desired. One was sent to brother's and sister Gert put him in the parlor, leaving the door open between it and room in which the family sat. I had gone there to spend the night. We talked in a low half-tone, loud enough for him to hear if he wished to do so, yet low enough so as to induce him to think we did not wish him to hear. One of us would say: "I saw a man this evening who told me Colonel Mosby and his command were coming as fast as they could, and would be here tonight." And another would tell of a rumor that Hampton and Fitz Lee were at Gordonsville coming this way, and that Sheridan and his army would be captured. We went on this way awhile, then we heard a noise in the other room, and looking found our guard had taken flight, doubtless to report the advancing hosts. It was very foolish in us, but it was a great temptation. I confess I was glad he was gone. I was more afraid of the guard inside than the troops outside.

The next day came a notice that the houses were to be searched for arms. This, of course, was fresh excitement and a trying ordeal in anticipation. Really it amounted to very little. The search was conducted by Col. Sheridan, brother to the General, and one or two other officers, and was purely perfunctory. They were very gentlemanly and respectful. At Mr. Minor's they went into the parlor and thence into his study, where they had a conversation with him about books and the character of the college, winding up with a question as to whether he had any arms, and upon being told he had none they bid him good-by and left. Where they got the idea there were arms stored at the University, or anywhere else indeed, in the South, I cannot imagine. I felt like telling him that all we had were in the hands of the men, not under the guard of a lot of old men, cripples and children.

When they went to brother's there were no men there. Sister Gert received them. She had some sort of an idea they would run away with her three pretty daughters so she made them take their seats in the parlor, each with a book and enjoined them not to raise their eyes while the officers were in the room. I have no idea they obeyed. They are very pretty and very bright and clever and doubtless cast many glances at the fine-looking officers in their handsome uniforms, who, of course, kept their eyes on them.

I heard a very funny story about Cousin Eliza Maury. She has been very sick and confined to her bed, but when the search commenced she got up and dressed herself. Mrs. Charles Maury, upon going to her room, was much surprised to find her in that condition, and expostulated with her. The old lady, who has infinite humor, replied she had no idea of staying in bed; that she heard that the yankees said that in every house in which they found some damned old rebel woman sick she was in bed with the silver, and she did not intend to be dragged out of her bed by men looking for silver she did not have.

The yankees stayed only two days, in order that the men and horses might rest and that their wagon train might come up. They were days of much excitement and full of incident though, as far as we were concerned, without any tragedy. Many negroes from every direction flocked to meet and go with their friends, much to the disgust of their friends. All sorts and conditions came, men, women and children, old men bent with rheumatism, women with small children, carrying large bundles, and some young men upon horses they had stolen from farmers. What they expected I do not know. The great mass of negroes remained quietly at home; those who seemed to seek this haven were of no use at home and could not take care of themselves anywhere. One fat old woman on a lame and very poor Confederate horse came up the road from towards Charlottesville, which is knee-deep in mud. The horse, swaying from side to side under its burden, finally fell, pitching its portly rider into the mire along with a huge bundle, hopelessly ruining the flounced red calico in which she was dressed. After much labor she reached the sidewalk with her possessions, scraped the mud off her and started back on foot, leading her horse, remarking in no uncertain tone: "I'se gwine home, I is! I'se seen 'nuff of the yankees I is. Old missus is good Enuf fo' me!"

It is reported that the sufferings of the poor creatures on the road between here and Scottsville, whither the yankees moved, has been very great. They were not prepared for such a trip through the mud and cold, and the yankees were very impatient of their presence. It is rumored that they threw some of the babies into the river but that, of course, is not true. Yesterday morning, when they all went away, many ladies collected down at brother's house to see them pass as they went along the Range. A guard was placed in the yard to protect us from stragglers and we took the opportunity for guying him in a good-natured way, as he was very polite. He was very proud of his command and pointed out to us the officers he most admired as they passed, but whenever a particularly forlorn or disreputable looking man passed we would ask him, in a most innocent way, whether that was General Sheridan or General Custer, much to his disgust. They are all gone now, and we are in the most terrible state of uncertainty as to where they are going and whether they will come back here or not. All we know is that they started for Scottsville. This uncertainty as to their movements makes mine equally uncertain, for we cannot move in the same direction. The railroads both to Lynchburg and to Richmond are much injured, we hear, but how much we do not know. I shall have to wait for the development of affairs. I know you are terribly uneasy about Nannie and myself, and I hope this letter will reach you some time in the future, and I am on the lookout for someone going to Richmond and will get him to take it. I wish very much I had not left Richmond, for then I would at least have you to direct me. Nannie has behaved beautifully.

March 11th.

I was truly tnankful, as you well know, to get your letter by Mr. Corbin. You are right in thinking that I have blessed you out for sending me away. You know I told you there was no use in it, and that it was premature. This house is very much crowded. There are five persons in every room and we sleep three in a bed. I am trying to rent a room in one of the houses on the lawn so as to relieve sister of the pressure to some extent. They are all very kind, both here and at brother's. Brother occupies the house on the Western Range, just in the rear of Prof. Bledsoe's, and they have a very merry establishment, with the three pretty girls, all of whom, though so young, are great belles. Commodore Maury's family occupies the infirmary and Mr. Jesse Maury is moving his family, for protection, into one of the houses on Dawson's Row. They were very badly treated by the yankees out at their home; indeed they nearly ruined it. Their home was robbed and they were mistreated in every possible way, and that not altogether by stragglers, but by officers of high rank. Col. Thomas L. Preston was treated the same way. All his horses, meat, corn and everything to eat was taken and five of his negro men left him. He says by the strictest economy he can possibly make out to live three weeks on what was saved from the vandals. He has, in addition to his white family, thirty negroes dependent upon him, all women and children.

Henry Massie called on me just now, and he says Mr. Whitcomb says he can have all the bridges save the one over the Rivanna rebuilt in a few days. The cars will be running from Richmond to Shadwell soon. Mr. Massie says he will return Tuesday, but I am not sure I can get off then or not. I shall make every effort to do so; my heart leaps with pleasure at the idea. I see no reason why we cannot remain in Richmond, for General Lee shows no sign of giving up.

CHAPTER XIX

☆ ☆ ☆ ★ ☆ ☆ ☆

THE CONFEDERACY CRUMBLES

☆ ☆ ☆ ☆ ☆ ☆

Capt. Blackford to Mrs. Blackford.
Richmond, March 13th, 1865.

RICHMOND has no attractions for me now that you are gone, and I am trying to get a release from my detail to be sent back to the field. I see little chance of your return. The Central road has been cut, but even if you were here there would be so much difficulty in getting you away that we would live in a state of constant anxiety.

I went to see Mrs. Kean, and dined there yesterday. She has accounts from Edgehill. Col. Randolph lost all his provisions and the ladies were insulted and mistreated. Their jewelry was torn from their persons and they were kept in a constant state of alarm. You have, of course, heard all this.

The report this morning is that Sheridan occupied Ashland last night and burned all the bridges on the Central and Fredericksburg roads across the North and South Anna and Little Rivers. It seems to me General Longstreet, who commands in that district, should have sent two brigades of infantry to protect them. I received a telegram from Eugene yesterday asking what had become of Churchill. He left here on Sunday morning and has not been heard of since. I suppose he has been at Burkesville all the time. Launcelot joined him there, I presume, and possibly Lewis. I hope they will get there in time for the wedding. Churchill is quite a necessary party for such an occasion. None but soldiers are allowed to leave Richmond by the Danville road as it is occupied in carrying returned paroled soldiers. A vast number are arriving daily. Some say our forces have been driven back near Ashland. There is no such report at the War Department.

I spend most my time at the War Department where I take

the place of the officer of the day if he so desires. I have no-where else to go and prefer being at work to doing nothing in my room. I almost always have some pleasant company, and as we get the reports of the operations of the day we are well posted before twelve o'clock as to all that is going on. I always take Col. Palfrey's night as he lives far out and has to walk back very late. If nothing prevents, and I see no signs of active operations, I shall get a short leave of absence, go up to Lynchburg, hire a wagon and drive over and take you and Nannie home. I should feel much safer if you were in Lynchburg than at the University.

Beef is now ten dollars a pound, and I gave two hundred and fifty dollars for a single ham of bacon,—more than my month's pay.

Col. Funston is going to Charlottesville tomorrow and will take this with him. Your long and graphic letter of the 6th has only just reached me and right joyful did it make me. I enjoyed your description of the raid very much, it was very well written and very characteristic. I sent you yesterday thirty-nine and a half yards of cotton cloth and one bale of No. 8 cotton yarn. I hope you will get them. I will try to send you a calico dress and a pair of hooped skirts also.

The wedding took place Thursday night. Churchill got to Lynchburg in time for it to have taken place Wednesday, but it was postponed on account of the uncertainty of his arrival. Launcelot, who has returned and will take his place as adjutant of Dick Maury's twenty-fourth Virginia regiment, tells me the supper was abundant, though the guests were few. William and Lewis could not get there. Living is now harder than ever, owing to the cutting of the railroads. The people in the country will bring nothing for fear their horses will be pressed. I have been quite sick for three days and I wish you were here to nurse me, but this is no place for you,—the end is near at hand.

March 24th.

I write this to send by Major Noland, who will go in a day or two. In these terrible times, when the future of the country is so dark and our personal future is so uncertain, I miss you and your counsel very much. Now that father is dead, I have no one but you with whom I can confer and upon whose judgment I can safely rely.

Charles Minor and his wife and Col. Noland, of Hanover, took tea with me last night,—a pretty hard supper we had but it was all we had. Eugene has just been here. He, Mary and Churchill have just come from Lynchburg. Churchill and Mary are at the hotel, and will go up to Dewberry. Tomorrow Eugene will return to his regiment. I must hurry around and see them.

Our men are deserting quite freely. It looks very blue to them, and the fact that Sherman marched from Atlanta to Savannah without seeing an armed Confederate soldier is well calculated to make them despondent.

A note by Mrs. Blackford.

Shortly after this our letters stopped and I have to fall back on a narrative, written by Mr. Blackford much later, of the last days of Richmond:

Capt. Blackford's final narrative.

On Saturday, the 1st of April, there seemed to be a very intense but quiet anxiety in the War Department. I was one of the officers on duty in the Adjutant-General's office, and it was our duty to go in about twelve o'clock and see if the Secretary of War wished to send any messages. About twelve I went in as usual to report. The Secretary was not in his office, but the Assistant Secretary, Judge John A. Campbell, was stretched out on a hard bench with a book under his head and his arms folded over his chest. His face, which was the most intellectual I have ever seen, was so pale and thin that you could almost think you could see the brain working. I supposed he was asleep and stood quietly waiting until, without apparently opening his eyes, he said, "Captain, what do you think of the situation?" I replied, "Judge, it is not up to me to think."

"But what *do* you think?" he asked with some earnestness.

"That we cannot hold out a week longer," I answered.

He gave a deep groan, and, after a pause, said, "No orders tonight, I thank you, Captain." I never saw him again.

I was early at the department the morning of Sunday, April 2d, but all seemed quiet. I went back to my frugal breakfast, after which I went to St. Paul's Church, meeting many people on like errands. I had not been long in church when I saw a messenger come in and whisper something to President Davis. The President, without any show of excitement, got up and walked out. I soon followed him as did many others, feeling there was some important news. I went at once to the Adjutant General's office, where I learned that General Lee's attenuated lines were broken, and that he had ordered Richmond evacuated.

I went to work, and with the other officers, soon packed up all the papers which were deemed essential to remove, and they were, in a few hours, sent to the Danville depot and packed in the cars. It is a great pity more were not saved, for all left in the house were burned the next day in the great fire, and thus much material for history was lost. After my work was done I was given an official order to report to Longstreet wherever he could be found.* I went back to my room and packed up my round valise which strapped to the back of my saddle, had some rations cooked, and just before sundown I mounted my horse and rode down to the canal and took up

---

*Captain Blackford was also given a 30-day leave of absence. Why he didn't mention it here cannot now be explained, but the story, as I heard it from my father, is about as follows: After everything was done and orders given all the officers, Capt. Blackford lingered, somewhat at a loss as to what to do with himself. His former superior officer noticed him and said:

"Can I do anything for you, Captain Blackford?"

"Well," said my grandfather, "I would like to get back to see my family if I could."

The other officer made out the pass and handed it to him with the following comment:

"When that pass expires, Captain Blackford, there will be no more Confederacy."

I was brought up under the impression that this paper was the last official act of the Confederacy in Richmond, and it has been treasured by the family as such.   C.M.B. III.

the tow-path thinking I thus could get ahead of our army, and by crossing through Buckingham, join it about High Bridge, where I thought possibly a stand could be made.

The streets were full of scared people, ladies and gentlemen, all in great distress, but all powerless to accomplish anything. I went down by Grumble's Hill.

My slave, Gabe, who was hired out under Dr. Morris to the telegraph department, as soon as he heard the news, came to my room to know what he must do. I told him he was free to do what he pleased, and that as he was, I should try to get work with the yankees, I advised, as soon as they came. He and John Scott did all they could to make me comfortable. I left John in charge of our little furniture, and told him to come through the lines as soon as he could and join me at Longstreet's headquarters. Both went with me to the canal bank. Gabe shed tears and kissed my hand when I told him goodbye and sent his love to his mistress and Nannie. He took my word for it and got employment but soon sickened and died without my hearing of it or being able to help him. A more honest and faithful man never lived. John Scott said he would get through the lines very soon and so he did, but not before the surrender. He was never again in my service but I aided him as long as he lived and buried him with some pomp when he died.

All the cars of the Richmond and Danville Railroad were pressed into service for the government officials and stores, and many trains left full of people during the evening and night of the 2d. The road and the canal were the only avenues of escape by public conveyance. The canal was filled with boats extemporized into packets and loaded with people,—gentlemen, ladies, children and servants — all seeking, very foolishly, some safe place, and seeking it in a direction in which safety was not to be found.

I had not traveled more than a mile when I overtook a flat-bottomed open boat full of people for Albemarle and among them I found Mrs. Kean and a number of other acquaintances. I kept with them near all night but we parted about daylight. As I reached the canal I came upon a small shop which was open, Sunday as it was. On the counter I spied some hooped skirts, and, as I had some Confederate money left I asked the price in that currency and purchased them for three hundred dollars, which was about the amount of my store. It was a good financial deal on my part. I rolled them into a ball and tied them to my saddle, and they remained there until I got to where my wife could use them.

I had to move very slowly, as I could get no food for my horse but grass and none for myself but what I had brought with me, and I had no money with which to buy anything. At night I slept either on the ground or in some old barn or shed. I found the bridges all burned and that I could not ford the river. I pushed on, however, determining to go to Lynchburg as I could not hear where our army or the yankees were. When opposite Appomatox County I learned that Lee's army was at or near the courthouse, and that yankee cavalry were filling the country between that point and the river. The next day I met a cavalryman, one of my regiment, who told me of the surrender, and I turned at once with him and took up the march for Charlottesville and the University. He was a better forager than I was and made me much more comfortable. We got to Charlottesville about midday the 11th, bringing almost the first definite information of the surrender.

My wife, Nannie and myself stayed at the University living in one room, and with only three dollars and fifty cents in current money for two months. We made the money go very far. I purchased flour on credit, we had some bacon, and with the money we bought some sugar and coffee which we hoarded. Strange as it may appear the time passed pleasantly, for all were trying to make the best of everything. There were a great many charming people there at the time and a great many pretty girls. There were quite a number of crippled soldiers who had entered college for awhile also. Vegetables and milk were given us by Mr. Colston and others and we got along very well. I had managed through Mr. John M. Miller, of Lynchburg, to get some money in gold for my mother's use in Lynchburg; and though I had none myself I was quite happy, except as to how I was to secure bread and meat in the future. But my long experience as a soldier had taught me to let the future take care of itself in a very philosophical degree.

This state of things could not last, and I determined to go back to Lynchburg on a prospecting tour. On the morning of the 10th of June I started out to walk. My horse had been making his own living grazing on the University grounds but he had cast a shoe and I did not have the money to replace it. At that time there was a gravel train which ran out from Lynchburg to Tye River where they were repairing the bridge. It started back at four o'clock. There was also a sort of hand car which left Covesville at ten o'clock and connected with it. My intention was to reach Covesville in time to use it, though I did not have any money. I told my wife good-bye at five o'clock and struck out in a swinging gait, without stopping a moment, until I reached Covesville where I found the car started at nine o'clock and had been gone some twenty minutes. I did not hesitate but pushed on determined to make the whole forty-two miles to Tye River before four o'clock. I did, stopping only at Peggy Rives' where I spent ten cents, all I had, in eggs for myself and a negro man whom I overtook and promised a ride in the cars if he would carry my coat, vest and watch, which he faithfully did to my relief. I reached Tye River at half past three, having made the forty-two miles, including a stop to boil eggs, in ten and one half hours on a hot summer day. I induced the conductor to permit my colored friend and myself to go over on the flats deadhead, yet strange to say I never have paid anything for travelling on it since.*

I got in town by sundown, and on the route up to my

*My father told me that, when my grandfather reached Lynchburg and was going up to his mother's home, he met a friend and a stranger and stopped to talk to them. When they found that he was just in from Charlottesville the stranger asked him many questions about the condition of the railroad which my grandfather was able to answer. When he was finished the stranger explained he was sent to reorganize the railroad and offered him a directorship although, for the time, without pay. My grandfather, having nothing to lose, accepted and remained with the road and the Southern System when it was organized until his death.

C.M.B. III.

mother's met William T. Booker, to whom I told my condition as to finances and asked him for a loan, meaning only to borrow five dollars. He drew out five twenty-dollar pieces and offered them to me. Seeing no chance of paying him back, I took only twenty dollars, telling him that I feared he would never see it again. While talking to him I saw Mr. Abell, a bank officer in Charlottesville, passing down the street on horseback. I hailed him and found he was going over to a friend's in Amherst to spend the night and the next day to Charlottesville. I gave him the twenty dollars to give my wife which he did.

I found mother well, Launcelot was with her. I at once went to work, getting ready for any employment that might come. I got back into my office and had my books unpacked, and some furniture I had at mother's and a carpet put down, making quite a respectable appearance. I was the only lawyer in town who kept his office open, for there were no courts and no business. People on Main Street sat out on the sidewalks gossiping and smoking, and some with tables playing chess, backgammon and cards. As the sun moved they moved from one side of the street to the other to get the shade. Some men were settling up their books and old matters, and occasionally a controversy would arise about "Confederate contracts" as they were called, and my services would be invoked to settle them. I was very rusty in the law, of course, and stuck close to my office trying hard by study to catch up.

I shall never forget my first case. Two gentlemen, who afterwards became very prominent business men in the city and good clients of mine, walked into my office and startled me by saying they wanted me to decide a question in regard to a contract payable in Confederate money. I looked wise, heard them both and gave my decision. They then asked me my fee. I told them I charged nothing as the matter was small. They said they must pay something and each laid down a half-dollar and walked out. I was amazed at my wealth, seized it, closed the office and went home to show the spoils to my wife, who had come home via Scottsville and the canal. With part of it we bought our first herring and a slice of cheese. No one can tell how good a herring and a piece of cheese is until they have had none for four years. Other small work of the same character came in, and in July I made good laborer's wages by giving opinions and sitting as an arbitrator.

I was very earnest and very needy, and attended faithfully to small matters; very soon the courts were opened, larger matters became plentiful and I got my full share.

When I got home the yankees were in full possession and the town under military law, but they did nothing to annoy us, and we got on with them very smoothly, for which we are very thankful to General Gregg, who was in command, and who acted with wisdom and consideration.

By Mrs. Blackford.

This ends the story I proposed at the outset to preserve. I cannot but feel that what I have transcribed is not without value as a contribution to the history of the times of which it speaks,—a value derived principally from the scarcity of such contemporaneous records of domestic life during the long night of the war.

I close this work without comment or reflections on the result of the transactions of which it speaks, or their effect upon the destinies of our people. My proposed task has been accomplished when I place in print facts and incidents which would otherwise be lost, and which, though of little public interest, disclose, with the accuracy of contemporaneous records, the daily life of the people of that time.

THE END

APPENDIX

APPENDIX

Muster of Wise Troop, Company B
2nd Virginia Cavalry *

1st Captain	John S. Langhorne
2nd "	Chas. M. Blackford
3rd "	Geo. B. Horner
4th "	William Steptee
1st Lieutenant	C. M. Blackford
2nd "	Van R. Otey
" "	Wm. H. Stratton
" "	A. D. Warwick
" "	John Alexander
" "	John O. Thornhill
" "	J. P. Robertson
" "	R. B. Isbell
1st Sergeant	William Langhorne
" "	Robert B. Lacey
2nd "	E. G. Scott
" "	John S. Massie
3rd "	A. S. Watson
4th "	W. B. Cross
" "	M. B. Langhorne
" "	C. Christian
" "	James Chalmers
" "	John B. Luckett
Corporal	S. M. Alexander
"	C. V. Donahue
"	F. M. Stone

*From the "Campaign and Battle of Lynchburg, Va.," by Chas. M. Blackford.

Privates

Abbott, J. P.
Akers, E. A.
Alexander, E. A.
Allen, T. W.
Barnes, A. J.
Bays, John R.
Barnes, E. F.
Berkley, Joseph
Bibb, John R.
Bolling, W. R.
Bowman, N. B.
Boyd, Andrew
Boyd, James
Bradley, Wm.
Brook, St. George
Browning, C. P.
Browning, John
Callahan, J. E.
Carnefix, E. M.
Caruthers, John
Clay, D. C.
Coles, John
Cox, John C.
Cox, P. S.
Cox, Samuel
Cox, Thad.
Crumpton, Robert
Dameron, C. D.
Dobyns, Joe
Dunnington, V. G.
Earley, S. H.
Edwards, J. E.
Edwards, J. T.
Edwards, W. P. M.
Eubank, W. E. J.
Everett, H. B.
Fariss, J.
Flemming, F. W.

Flood, T. W.
Floyd, C. A.
Godsey, F. M.
Green, Charles
Green, John L.
Hammerling, C. D.
Holley, W. E.
Hunt, H. C.
Ingram, J. R.
Irvine, W. A.
Jones, J. W.
Kasey, J. R.
Kefauver, Wm.
Kemper, Hugh
Kinnear, Geo. A.
Kinnear, John A.
Kinnear, William
Langhorne, J. Kent
Lawson, Joe
Lawson, S. M.
Leake, F. M.
Leman, A. H.
Lewis, John C.
Lock, Daniel
Love, A. D.
Love, S. A.
Love, T. H.
Lucado, Wm. F.
Luck, Henry
Mays, C. J.
Mays, C. R.
Mays, H. H.
McCorkle, S. M.
Meriweather, C. J.
Mitchell, J. E.
Moore, Sampson
Morgan, J. H.
Norvell, Chas.

Offterdinger, H.
Palmer, C. F.
Percival, George
Perrigo, George
Perriman, Wm. P.
Pettyjohn, S. W.
Phelps, J. C. W.
Purvis, W. C.
Read, John A.
Roberts, H. T.
Rucker, James G.
Sale, J. E.
Seabury, E. C.
Seabury, R. M.
Seabury, W. J.
Sherrar, John C.
Smith, John Thomas
Smith, Wm. N.
Sneed, S. Emmit
Spencer, W. R.
Stone, Frank
Sullivan, Dennis
Sumpter, S. R.
Taylor, John O.
Taylor, O. P.
Taylor, Thomas P.
Thurman, Alex.
Thurman, P.
Toler, W. D.
Tucker, Willis
Tyree, Richard
Wall, Thomas
Watson, W. H.
Whitlow, W. H.
Witt, J. C.
Woodruff, A. M.
Wright, J. I.

INDEX

Alabama, the, sinking of, 266
Albemarle County, Virginia, 96, 180, 212, 278, 279
Aldie, Virginia, 50, 75
Alexander, General (E. Porter), C.S.A., 213, 214
Alexander, Capt. Jack, 18, 43, 82, 158, 170
Alexandria, Virginia, 18
Alsop, Mrs., 156–159
Ambler, Dr. Cary, 177
Amherst County and Courthouse, Virginia, 9
Andrews, Col. Snowden, 106
Appomatox Courthouse, 293
Armistead, General, 189
Army of Northern Virginia, 114, 164, 224
Arnold, Capt., U.S.A., 36
"Articles of War," new edition prepared by Capt. Blackford, 223
Ashland, Virginia, 90, 167, 288
Atlanta, Georgia, 210
Augusta, Georgia, 209

Baily, Miss, 47
Baker, General E. D., U.S.A., 52
Ball, Mr. and Mrs. Thomas A., 228, 229
Ball's Bluff, battle of, 51, 52
Baltimore and Ohio Railroad Company, houses and depot burned, 130
Banks, General Nathaniel P., U.S.A., 100
Barbour, Mr. James, 116

Barker's Crossroads, 135
Barksdale, Colonel, C.S.A., 52, 187
Barton, Mrs., 177
Barton, David, 151
Bartow, General, 27
Bayard, General, U.S.A., 111
Baylor, Col., W. S. H., 104
Bealton, Virginia, 78
Beauregard, General P. G. T., C.S.A., 41, 43, 45, 48, 49, 53, 257; at Manassas, 24, 26, 29
Beaver Dam Depot, 94, 95
Bee, General, C.S.A., 27
Belleview, Bedford County, 236
Belmont, Virginia, 67
"Belvedere," 205
Benning, General, C.S.A., 243
Berlin, Maryland, 63
Bernard, Arthur, 205
Bernard farm, 145
Berryville, Virginia, 179–181
Blackburn's Ford, 24, 30
Blackford, Dr. Ben, 12
Blackford, Capt. Charles M., C.S.A., 1, 2, 4, 54, 152; farewell to family, 5, 8; ill health of, 24–26, 80, 81, 83, 97, 112, 114, 116, 117, 126, 127, 220, 225, 227, 229; promotion to captain, 40; visit at home, 80; under General Jackson, 82 ff.; under General Lee, 114 ff.; appointment to Judge Advocate: possibility, 133, 139, fact, 142, 150, 151, 154; narrow escapes, 100, 134, 135, 142, 234; complaint to Post-

master General and reply, 159, 164; at Longstreet's headquarters, 175, 213, 231, 243; his impression of Yankees, 184–186; at Hood's headquarters, 200; in the Army of Tennessee, 209; receives commission from State of Virginia, 222; at Richmond, 274 ff., 288 ff.; his handbook for military court, 223; despair for victory, 275, 276; last days in the War Department, 289–291; back in law work, 295, 296

Blackford, Mrs. Charles M., 36, 59–61, 76, 77, 161; visits to her husband, 39, 40, 71 ff., 170–174, 207, 208, 239–241; letter written on death of her baby, 162, 163, 171; breaking up housekeeping, 211, 212, 217, 218; help with the wounded, 259–262; hiding of valuables, 252, 263, 280, 281; with Capt. Blackford in Richmond, 274 ff.; at Charlottesville, 278–280

Blackford, Capt. Eugene, C.S.A., 23, 46, 47, 53, 54, 128, 142, 146, 152, 160, 176, 192, 193, 246, 263, 290; anxiety about, 35, 108, 177, 187; at Spring Hill Cemetery, 256, 264

Blackford Home in Fredericksburg, damaged by battle, 149, 150

Blackford, Landon Carter, 152

Blackford, Launcelot, 46, 56, 98, 100, 104, 106, 112, 146, 162, 181, 193, 201, 227, 241, 289, 295

Blackford, Lieut. Lewis, C.S.A., 14

Blackford, Lucy, 79

Blackford, Miss Mary, 173, 264

Blackford, Nancy (Nannie), 5, 37, 39, 71, 79, 80, 151, 161, 170–172, 236, 240; letters from father, 111, 165

Blackford, Susan Colston, 40

Blackford, Dr. Thomas, 37

Blackford, Lieut. Col. W. W., C.S.A., 35, 46, 55, 58, 78, 108, 112, 118, 119, 128, 132, 138, 142, 146, 156–160, 165, 176, 189, 197, 248

Blackford, Mrs. W. W., 158–160, 165, 217

Blackford, William M., Sr., 91, and wife, 36, 37; diary quoted, 40, 53, 58, 70, 152, 160, 162, 229, 230; death of, 241

Blackford, William (Willy), 5, 59, 71; death of, 76, 77

Booker, William T., 295

Bowling Green, Virginia, 92

Boyden, Mary, 98

Bradfute, Mrs., 123

Bragg, Major General Braxton, C.S.A., 211, 213, 219–224

Brandy Station, Virginia, 108, 116, 175, 178

Breckenridge, General, C.S.A., 252, 262, 263

Breckenbridge, Gilmer, 249

Bridgeport, Alabama, 211, 220, 221

Brigades, Branch's, 105; Cocke's, 24–26; Georgian, 272, 273; Hayward's South Carolina, 269; Hood's, 234; Jackson's, 31; Jones', 178; Kershaw's, 224; Law's Alabama, 207; Lawton's, 126; Lee's, Fitzhugh, 143, 157; Longstreet's, 38; McLaw's, 240; Pender's 105; Robinson's Texas, 234; Texas, 244; Taylor's, 82; Trimble's, 82

Bristol, Tennessee, 240
Bristow, Virginia, 24
Broad Run, Virginia, 68
Brockenborough, Major John
 B., C.S.A., 119
Brooke, Judge, 205
Brown, Thompson, 243
Brownlow, 226
Bull Run, 14, 23, 24, 27, 30, 31,
 32; *see also* Manassas
Bull's Mill, 50,
Bunker Hill, W. Va., 127, 128,
 193, 197
Burnside, Major General Am-
 brose E., U.S.A., 140, 146, 161,
 221; army of, 242
Burt, Colonel, C.S.A., 52
Butler, "Beast," 252, 253

Cabell, Stuart, 151
"Camden," 207
Cameron, Secretary of War, 58
Camp Blackford, 23, 38
Camp Mason, Virginia, 20–22
Campbell, Judge John A., 290
Caroline County, Virginia, 257
Carr, Lieut. Frank, C.S.A., 57
Carroll, Mrs. Grey, 158, 177
Carr's Hill, Charlottesville, Va.,
 282
Carter, Charles, 206
Carter, Rev. George W., 182
"Carter Hall," 179
Carter, Landon, 206
Carter, Lucy Landon, 206, 207
Carter's farm, Mrs. George, 50
Cedar Fork, 174
Centreville, Va., 23, 24, 30, 32,
 33, 49; letters from, 15–20
Chalmers, James, 17, 44, 45
Chambersburg, Pennsylvania,
 128, 181, 184–186
Chambliss, General, C.S.A., 273
Chancellorsville, Virginia, 200,
 204

Charleston, W. Va., 179
Charlottesville, Va., 11, 53, 61,
 71, 75, 78, 81, 83, 96, 127, 238;
 Yankee raid on, 282 ff.
Chattanooga, Tennessee, 210,
 219, 222
Chickamauga River, 210
Chickamauga, Tennessee, 209;
 battle of, 221, 224
Chilton, General, C.S.A., 157
Chisholm, Col., C.S.A., 221
Christian, Jack, 18
City Point, blowing up of pow-
 der ship at, 272
Clagett, Dr., 62
Clark, General, C.S.A., 53
Clark, Major, C.S.A., 222
Clarke County, 179, 180
Clark's Mountain, 112, 113
"Cleve," 206, 207
Cobb, General Thos. R. R.,
 C.S.A., 148
Cochran, Col., C.S.A., 201, 205
Cochran, Captain John L.,
 C.S.A., 166
Cocke, General Philip St. George,
 C.S.A., 12, 17, 24, 29, 47, 53
Cockerille, Mr., 18
Coleman, Lewis Minor, 151
Colston, Anne, 161, 170, 171
Colston, Betty, 36
Colston, Col. Raleigh E., C.S.A.,
 47
Colston, Randolph T., C.S.A.,
 265
Colston, Capt. William B.,
 C.S.A., 47, 151
Columbia, S. C., 228
Company A, 4, 20
Company B, 2nd Va. Cavalry,
 1, 4, 7, 8, 23, 36, 42, 128, 129,
 158, 248, 249; men of, 17, 18,
 23; election of officers, 81, 82;
 difficulty securing horses for,
 137, 139

Confederate Army, inadequate supply of arms and horses, 32, 33, 80; hospitality shown soldiers of, 10, 11, 13, 19, 169; hardship and lack of food, 78, 140; election of officers a weakness of, 81; losses, 101, 245; improved conditions of, 159, 181; snow "battles," 165, 166; morale, 168; supplies, 233; confronting Grant, 247

Conrad, Holmes, 19, 130, 181

Cooke, Churchill, 141, 173, 265, 279, 288, 289

Cooke, Mrs. Edmonia, 173

Cooke, Gen. Philip St. George, U.S.A., 57, 58

Corbin, Nannie, 138

Corbin, Richard, 205, 206

Corbin, Welford, 206

Corse, Col., C.S.A., 38

Covesville, Virginia, 294

Crater, the, battle of, 269

Crawford, General S. W., U.S.A., 111

Crittendon, Mrs., 103; house of, 106, 110

Crooked Run, 101

Cross, Sgt., W. B., C.S.A., 17

Crutchfield, Oscar, 141, 155

Culpeper, Va., 204; County, 100, 110, 174, 268; Courthouse, 11, 12, 99, 114, 197; Road, 103

Cumberland Valley, Md., 185

Cunningham farm, 118

Custer, Gen., U.S.A., 282, 283

Dandridge, Stephen, his home "The Bower," 132

Danville Railroad, 255

Darksville, W. Va., 181

Davis, Dr., 76, 79

Davis, Eugene, 199

Davis, President Jefferson, 45, 46, 85, 86, 216. 221, 222, 291

Davis, Lucy, 76

Davis, R. J., 217

Deep Creek, 145

Deep Run, 204

Dewberry, 173, 248, 265

Dickenson, Mr., 91

Douglas, Henry Kyd, 94

Dranesville, Virginia, 15, 67, 68

Drewry's Bluff, 257, 268, 269

Dunnington, Laura, 74, 75

Dunnington, Virginius, 17, 134

Early, Everett B., 31

Early, General J. A., C.S.A., 103, 129, 238, 255, 256, 266, 267; cut off at the Rappahannock, 124–126; at Lynchburg, 263, 264

Early, Mr., 136

Early, Captain Samuel Henry, C.S.A., 129, 189

East Tennessee and Georgia Railroad, 227

"Edgehill," 288

"Edgemont" (Mrs. Blackford's old home), 133, 180

Edgewood, Va., 174

Edward's Ferry, Va., 73

"Enquirer" of Richmond, Va., 197

Evans, General George Nathan ("Shanks"), C.S.A., 35, 39, 49–51, 61, 62

Evans, Mrs., 57

Ewell, Lieut. Gen. R. S., C.S.A., 21, 82, 103, 175–177, 179, 181, 184, 187, 192, 243, 250

Fairfax, Randolph, 151

Fairfax, Va., 19, 20, 21, 23; County, 143

Fairfax Courthouse, Va., 20, 23, 24, 40, 46, 49, 57

Falling Waters, Virginia, 190, 191

Falmouth, Virginia, 145, 204

Falls Church, Va., 43, 46, 55; letter from, 42

Fauquier County, Virginia, 98, 110, 135, 177, 268

Fauquier White Sulphur Springs, 13, 122, 127

Featherstone, Colonel, C.S.A., 52

Federal Army, 32, 130, 249; in Virginia under Grant, 242; losses, 245, 246, 250, 251; cavalry, 253

Field, Major-Gen. W. C., C.S.A., 245, 246, 271, 273

Finley, Mrs., 182

Fisher, Eddie, 201

Fisher, Robert, 189

Fitzhugh, Major Norman, C.S.A., 159, 176

Flood, Captain, C.S.A., 82

Flournoy's Regiment, Col., 82, 83

Floweree, Colonel, C.S.A., 169

Fontaine, Edmund, 32

Fontaine, Lucy, 173

Fortress Monroe, 80

Fourneybough farm, 145

France, prospect of war with the United States, 279

Fredericksburg, Va., 84, 91–95, 112, 138, 140, 141, 157, 159, 201, 204, 245; evacuation of, 137; battle of, 142–148; damage to, 149, 150

Fryingpan Church, 20

Gabe (Blackford slave), 162, 292

Gaines Crossroads, 177

Garland, Col., C.S.A., 38

Garland, John, 57

Garland, Jr., Mr. and Mrs. Samuel, 3, 40

Garnett, Mr., 201

"Gaymont," 206

Germanna Ford, 243

Gettysburg, Pa., 187, 188, 189, 190

Girardey, Brigadier Gen., C.S.A., 272

Glass, Senator Carter, 70

Goodwin, Mrs. Arthur, 164

Goose Creek, 68

Gordon, Mrs. Wellington, 98

Gordonsville, Virginia, 80, 82, 83, 85, 89, 91, 95, 90–101; retreat to, 111

Grant, Gen. Ulysses S., U.S.A., 242, 246, 256, 267; near Richmond, 249; push towards Petersburg, 253, 254, 269, 271

Grattan, Peachy R., 84

"Great Battle of Vienna, The," 15

Green, Charles, 17

Green, John, 65, 66

Green Springs, Virginia, 97, 98

Greencastle, Pa., 183

Greenville, Tenn, 239

Gregg, General Maxcy, C.S.A., 15, 296

Griffith, General, C.S.A., 61, 69

Guest, Mrs., 165; Mr., 166

Guilliard, Col., C.S.A., 243

Hackett, Mr., 172

Hagerstown, Md., 183

Hale, Captain, C.S.A., 82

Halsey, Doc, 82

Hamilton's Crossing, 145, 156, 162, 164, 201

Hamilton's farm, 143

Hampton, Col. Wade, C.S.A., 29

"Hampton's Legion," 29

Hanover, Virginia, 167; county, 172; junction, 247

"Happy Creek," 135

Harmon, Major John, C.S.A., 101, 102
Harper's Ferry, W. Va., 26, 63, 130, 153
Harris, Captain, C.S.A., 82
Harris, Val, 188, 189
Harrison, Major Carter, C.S.A., 25
Hart, Mr., 156, 201, 208
Haskell, Major John C., C.S.A., 169
"Hayfield," 205
Hazel River, 118, 119
"Hazelwood," 206
Heiskell, Mr. & Mrs. Jesse L., 10, 11
Henry, Mrs., 27; house of, 14
Herndon, Dr. Brodie, 94, 137
"Hill and Dale," 127
Hill, Betty, home of, 89
Hill, Colonel, C.S.A., 163, 205
Hill, General A. P., C.S.A., 97, 99, 103, 105, 125, 175, 181
Hill, General D. H., C.S.A., 61, 62, 66–69, 163, 197, 243
Hoffman, Mr., 69
Holcombe, Prof., 11
Holt, John D., 218
Home Guard, the, 23, 25, 188
Hood, Lieut. Gen. J. B., C.S.A., 168, 178, 267; wounded, 187
"Hood's Brigade, an appeal for," article by Capt. Blackford, 234
Hooker, Major Gen. J., U.S.A., 175, 178
Horner, Ned, 18
Howard, Mrs., 283
Howlett House, the, 271, 272
Hudgins, Mr., 13
Hunt, Private Henry C., 18
Hunter, General, U.S.A., 255, 262, 264
Hunton, Colonel Eppa, C.S.A., 52

Hutter, Major, house used as Hunter's headquarters, 264

Isbell, Bob, 105, 117

Jack (Blackford slave), 60, 225
Jackson, Major General Thomas J. ("Stonewall"), C.S.A., 53, 82, 84, 89–91, 93, 95–97, 100, 101, 106, 108, 119, 121, 128, 129, 138, 161; at Manassas, 27, 31; description of, 86, 105; stories of his popularity and heroism, 87, 88, 90, 104, 105, 109, 110, 131; other anecdotes, 102, 103, 113, 114, 117, 118, 120, 125–127; origin of nickname, 111; compared with Lee, 115, 116; comment by Capt. Blackford on, 231
James River, 253, 256, 267, 269
Jenifer, Colonel, C.S.A., 56, 67
Jenkins, General, C.S.A., 49–52, 165, 166, 180, 244
Johnson, General (Edward), C.S.A., 245
Johnston, General J. E., C.S.A., 26, 29, 45, 48, 53, 77, 78, 239, 267, 279; Capt. Blackford's impression of, 180
Jones, General, C.S.A., 53, 243
Jones, Mrs., 57

Kean, Mr., 92, 93, 142, 150, 257, 274
Kemper, General, C.S.A., 15, 185
Kershaw, General J. B., C.S.A., 240, 243, 245, 246, 250, 251, 267; story of young boy in his regiment, 167, 168
Kinckle, Mr., 193, 199
King, Col. Floyd, C.S.A., 263
King sisters, Mamie and Lilly, 3
Kirkpatrick, Captain Thomas J., C.S.A., 193

Knox, Miss, 228
Knoxville, Tennessee, 227

Lacy, Major, 155
Langhorne, Capt. John S.,
  C.S.A., 2, 4, 8, 21, 60, 151;
  story of his servant, 46
Langhorne, Sgt. Marion B.,
  C.S.A., 18
Langhorne, Mrs., 38
Langhorne, William, 152
Latrobe, Major, C.S.A., 243, 244,
  246
Law, General, 165
Lawley, Hon. Charles, M.P.,
  132
Lee, Major General Fitzhugh,
  C.S.A., 137, 157, 158, 254
Lee, General Robert E., C.S.A.,
  85, 111, 157, 161, 175, 178,
  183, 193, 197, 244, 252, 267,
  287; Capt. Blackford's im-
  pressions of, 86, 114–116, 184,
  231; at the Rappahannock,
  121, 129, 136, 137, 148; orders
  no pillaging, 181, 186, 188;
  crossing the Potomac, 182; at
  Gettysburg, 187, 188; address
  after Vicksburg, 190; confidence in, 211, 219, 223, 224,
  251, 257; at Spotsylvania and
  Mechanicsville, 247–249; opposing Grant, 254, 271; surrender, 293
Lee, Gen. William H. F. ("Rooney"), C.S.A., 145
Leesburg, Va., 20, 49–52, 56, 59,
  62, 67, 68, 178; Mrs. Blackford's visit to, 71 ff.
Letcher, Governor, 52, 53, 85
Lewis, Henry Byrd, 207
Lewis, John C., 56
Liberty Mills, 101
Lincoln, Abraham, 58, 80, 256
Linden Station, 134

Little River, 288
Little River turnpike, 50
"London Times," the, 132
"London Illustrated News," the,
  132
Longstreet, Lieut. General
  James, C.S.A., 53, 54, 86, 157,
  161, 169, 197, 219, 241, 245,
  246, 267; promotion to Major-
  General, 48, 127; Blackford's
  association with, 46, 49, 55,
  132, 133, 154, 155, 174, 180,
  193, 198, 223, 233; joined by
  Jackson, 139; at the Rappahannock, 108, 117, 121, 129;
  near Fredericksburg, 138; in
  Culpeper County, 175; at Gettysburg, 187; his opinion of
  General Bragg, 221, 222;
  credit for Chickamauga, 224;
  incidents connected with, 225,
  236; Blackford's evaluation
  of, 231, 288; condition of men
  in his corps, 238; in East Tennessee, 239, 240; at Mechanicsville, 243; wounded, 244,
  250, 261
Lookout Mountain, 210
Loudoun County, 19, 63, 268
Loudoun, Tennessee, 227
Louisa Courthouse, 95; County,
  264
"Louisiana Tigers," 23
Lovingstone, Va., 9
Lucado, Capt., I. F., C.S.A., 172
Lynchburg, Va., 1, 2, 3, 4, 5, 70,
  77, 80, 99, 154, 167, 170, 180,
  214, 222, 228, 237–239, 279,
  286, 293, 294; Battle of Manassas heard in, 36; Court
  Street Church, 182; threatened by Sheridan, 255; the
  war in, 262–264
"Lynchburg Republican," 234
Lyons, James J., 123

McClellan, Maj. Gen. George B., U.S.A., 45, 62, 67, 78, 128
McDaniel, Capt. Z., 272
McGuire, Dr. Hunter, 110
Macon, Lieut., C.S.A., 54
Madison Courthouse, Va., 101, 127
Major's Gate, 100, 103, 106; *see also* Slaughter's Mountain
Manassas Gap Railroad, 14, 24, 71, 74, 75
Manassas, Virginia, 4, 20, 39, 53, 70, 71, 75, 101, 242; junction, 13, 14; First Battle of, 2, 23–36, 47, 55
"Mansfield," 205
Markham, Virginia, 135, 178
Marshall, Agnes, 122
Marshall, Colonel Charles, C.S.A., 121
Marshall, James, 188
Marshall, Thomas G., 136
Marshall, Ed. C., 135
Martinsburg, W. Va., 19, 179, 193
Martinsville, 129, 181
Marye, John M., 92, 93, 160, 204
Marye's Hill, 146, 147, 149
Maryland, 153, 179; march to, 180
"Mason's and Dixon's Line," 183
Mason, Capt., C.S.A., 273
Mason, Mrs., 69
Mason and Slidell affair, 57
Mason's Hill, 45
Massaponax Creek, 145
Massie, Sgt. John S., C.S.A., 17, 23
Mattapony River, 247, 248
Maury, Commodore, 287
Maury, Dick, 155
Maury, Eliza, 285
Maury, Jesse, 283, 287
Maury, Mrs. Matthew F., 151

Maury, Nannie, 283
Maynard, 226
Mayo, Colonel, C.S.A., 169
Meachen, Mr., 24, 38, 39
Meade, General Geo. G., U.S.A., 193
Mechanicsville, Virginia, 242, 243, 248
Mechanicsville Pike, 84
Mercer, Hon. Charles Fenton, 75
Middleburg, Va., 19, 178
Milford Depot, 247
Miller, John M., 293
Millwood, Va., 179
Milroy, General Robert H., U.S.A., 176, 179
Minor, Berkley, 189
Minor, Dr., 58, 161
Minor, James, 89, 92
Minor, General John, 146
Minor, Mrs. John B., 163
Minor, Prof. John B., 11, 76, 77, 264, 284, 285
Minor, Launcelot, 59
Minor, Robert, 236
Mississippi regiments, 13th, 17th and 18th, 52
Mitchell, Major Sam, C.S.A., 155
Mitchell, Robert C., 155
Mitchell's Ford, 24, 25, 30
Mitchell's Station, 109
Moore, Maurice, 136
Morrison, Mr., 129, 130
Moses, Major, C.S.A., 232
"Moss Neck," 205, 206
Munford, Col. T. T., C.S.A., 18, 28, 31, 38, 62, 63, 67, 81, 133, 142
Munson's Hill, 45
Murell, Dr., 3

Nance, Col. C.S.A., 243
Nancy, Mr., 136

Nashville and Tennessee Railroad, 211, 220, 221
Nassau, onions from, 252
Nelson County, Va., 9
Nelson, Dr., 76, 79
Nelson, Mrs. Judith, 173
Nelson, Thomas, 173
New Market, Tenn., 239
New River Bridge, 204
"New York Herald," 111
Noland, Mr. and Mrs., 19
North, the, attitude toward the war, 58
North Anna River, 247, 288
North Carolina, 215
North Carolina, 83, 159

"Oakhurst," Charlottesville, Va., 283
"Oaklands," 173
Officers, their treatment of privates, 41
Old Fork Church, 90, 172
Opaquan, the, 193
Orange County, Virginia, 174, 268
Orange Courthouse, 101, 108, 238
Orange and Alexandria, 78, 109, 255
Osborne, Logan, 134
Otey, Colonel, C.S.A., 169
Otey, Kirk, 188
Otey, Van, 17, 55, 63
Otey, Mrs. John M., 22
Owen, Col. Robert L., 268
Owen, Dr., 22

Paris, Fauquier County, Va., 178
Parker, Dr., 75
Patterson, General, U.S.A., 26
Pelham, Major, C.S.A., 159
Pender, General W. D., C.S.A., 97

Pendleton, Col. A. S., C.S.A., 85, 95, 99, 106, 108, 112, 113, 127
Pendleton, Dr., 155
Pendleton, Rev. General, 176, 178
Peninsular campaign, the, 153
Penn, Davison, 123
Penn, Imogene, 123
Pennsylvania, march to, 180 ff.; division of sentiment in, 183
Petersburg, Virginia, 170, 171, 253, 255, 256, 266 ff.
Pettigrew, General, C.S.A., 193
Pettus, John C., 140
Pickett's Division, 173, 174, 178, 180, 181, 187, 188, 190; officers of, 169; at Drewry's Bluff, 268
Piedmont, the, 153, 177, 178
Pinkerton, Alan, 67
Plains, the, Virginia, 75
Pleasanton's raid, 222
Poague, Capt., 106
Polk, Maj. Gen., C.S.A., 239
Pope, Major General John, U.S.A., 100, 110, 111, 126, 127
Port Royal, 159, 205–207
Porterfield, Miss., 63
Potomac, the, 24, 26, 33, 49, 179, 181, 182
Powell, Mrs. Humphrey, 72
Pratt farm, 145
Pratt, Mr., 205
Pratt, Mrs., 207
Preston, Capt. and Mrs. Samuel D., 60
Preston, Col. Thomas L., C.S.A., 287
Prices, increase in, 59, 81, 85, 170, 171, 199, 237, 250, 268
Prince, General, U.S.A., 100
Prince William County, 143
"Prospect Hill," 205

Raccoon Ford, 108, 112

Radford, Col. R. C. W., C.S.A., 2, 4, 18, 20, 31, 32, 43, 46, 63, 81

Radford, Capt. Winston, C.S.A., 32

Radford, Mrs. Winston, 36

Randolph, Dr., 259

Randolph, Col., C.S.A., 288

Rapidan River, Virginia, 100, 108, 112, 176

Rappahannock River, the, 114, 117, 124, 125, 144, 145, 148, 176

Rehobeth, Va., 174

Regiments, Garland's Eleventh infantry, 25; Rodes', 23, 182; *see also* South Carolina, Virginia, etc.

Richmond, Va., 90, 137, 164, 197, 238, 287; "Dispatch," 58; concentration of armies near, 78, 82–84, 111, 159; Forest Hill, 160; passage of Hood's division through, 168, 169; "Enquirer," 197; fighting near, 248, 249; suffering in, 250, 276; fears for the fall of, 256, 277; papers, 267

Richmond and Danville Railroad, 292

Ricketts, Captain, U.S.A., 35

"Ridgewood," 248

Robinson River, 101

Rockfish River, 10

Rockbridge Artillery, 56, 105, 164

Rodes, Col., C.S.A., 47; his regiment, 23, 182

Rogers, General, C.S.A., 19

Rose, Dr., 207

Rosecrans, General Wm. S., U.S.A., 211, 213, 219, 221

Rosser, Colonel, C.S.A., 119, 243, 254

"Roughugees," 155, 156

Russelville, Tenn., 239

Ryan, Tommy, 46

"St. Julien's," 205

"Santee," 205

Saunders, Mrs. Robert C., 36, 37

Saunders, Texanna, 60

Scott, E. G., 68

Scott, John, 8, 18, 25–28, 47, 64, 74, 99, 112, 126, 143, 144, 156, 158, 170, 189, 205, 231, 274, 292

Scott, Taylor, 176

Scottsville, Virginia, 286

Seabury, Private R. M., C.S.A., 18

Shenandoah Valley, 83, 153, 253, 268

Shepherdstown, W. Va., 180, 181

Sheridan, Col., U.S.A., 284

Sheridan, Lieut. Gen. Philip H., U.S.A., 253–255, 288; raid on Charlottesville, 280 ff.

Skinner, Major, C.S.A., 47

Skinner, Miss, 47

Slaughter's Mountain, battle of, 100–107; *see also* Major's Gate

Smith, James T., 67

Smith, Dr. John A., 104

Smith, Private John Thomas, 17–19, 41, 42, 81, 170, 199

Smith, Jno. Holmes, 188

Smith, Mrs. Jno. T., 74, 75

Smith, General Kirby, C.S.A., 53

"Smithfield," 205

Snead, Emmet, 65

Snicker's Gap, 133, 178

"Snowdown," 178

Sorrell, Major, C.S.A., 155, 243, 244

South Anna River, 288

South Carolina, 215

South Carolina regiments, infantry, 15; Eighteenth, 49

Southern Railway System, 78; Mr. Blackford's association with, 294 n.

"Speaks," 50

Spence, Mrs., 259, 260

Spies, 13, 92, 93, 95, 122

Spottswood Hotel, Richmond, Va., 168

Spotsylvania, Va., 245; country around, 139; courthouse, 138, 247; county, 257

Spratt, Colonel L. W., C.S.A., 163

Spring Hill Cemetery, 256, 263

Stafford, General, C.S.A., 243

Staunton, Va., 238, 280

Stoneman, Maj. Gen. Geo., U.S.A., 178

Stone Bridge Ford, 24

Strasburg, Virginia, 71

Stratton, Mr., 55

Stratton, Lieut. Wm. H., C.S.A., 67

Stribbing, Mrs. Robert, 158, 159

Stribling, Mrs., 178

Stuart, Maj. Gen. J. E. B., C.S.A., 42, 46, 53, 57, 58, 110, 111, 116, 119, 129, 157, 187, 222; raid in Pennsylvania, 128; headquarters of, 132; at Brandy Station, 175; criticism of, 195, 196

Stuart, Mrs. J. E. B., 43, 57, 156, 158

Stuart, Rev. Kelsey, 97

Styles, Captain Robert, C.S.A., 73, 74

Sudley farm, 28, 30

Sullivan, Dennis, 56

Suter, Rev. Mr., 133

Swann, Mr. Thomas, 69

Sweeney, Sam, 140

Taliaferro, Col., A. G., C.S.A., 122

Taliaferro, General William B., C.S.A., 121, 127

Tarleton (Capt. Cochran's body-servant), 166, 172, 180, 208, 240

Taylor farm, 145

Taylor, Capt. James, C.S.A., 274

Taylor, Mrs., 205

Taylor, General, 223

Taylor, W. P., 205

Taylorsville, Virginia, 172, 174, 248

Tebbs, Captain, 158

Tennessee, 209, 231 ff.; attitude toward war, 226; East, 227; Mrs. Blackford's visit to, 239–241

Tennessee River, 210, 211, 220, 226, 227

Terry, Captain, C.S.A., 4, 8, 14, 15, 20

Thom, The Misses, 150

Thom, Ruben, 150

Tilden, John F., 167

Toombs, General, C.S.A., 53

"Traveler" (Lee's horse), 115

Tucker, John Randolph, 250

Tucker, Mr., 149

Tye River, 294

Union Mills, Va., 49

University, the, *see* Charlottesville

Upton's Hill, 45

Valuables, hiding of, 252, 263, 280, 281

Van Dorn, General (Earl), 48, 53

Venable, Colonel C. S., C.S.A., 121

Vicksburg, Mississippi, 179, 189, 190
Vienna, Va., 15, 18, 22
Virginia, attitude toward the war, 2, 226
Virginia and Tennessee Railroad, 203
Virginian hospitality, 173, 174
Vizetelly, Mr., 132
Von Borcke, Major Heros, C.S.A., 119, 159

Wade, Dick, 145
Warrenton, Va., 13, 14
Warwick, Lieut. Abram D., C.S.A., 17, 39
Warwick, Major Daniel, C.S.A., 39
"Washington Artillery," 29, 49
Washington, D. C., 78
Watauga, River, 233
Watkins, Mary G., 85
Watts, Lieut. Col., C.S.A., 82, 133, 138, 139, 175
Whaling, Capt., 239
Wheat, Colonel (R. C.), C.S.A., 23
Wheeler, General, C.S.A., 220, 221
Whitehead, Capt. Thomas, C.S.A., 175, 177
White's Crossing, 179
Wickham, Col. Williams C., C.S.A., 143, 144, 254

"Wilderness, The," 139, 243, 247
Willcox, Col. O. B., U.S.A., 35, 39
William (Blackford Negro), 152
Williams, Colonel, C.S.A., 169 and n.
Williams, Rev. Walter, 51, 57, 69, 72, 73
Williamsport, Md., 179, 180, 181, 188, 190, 192
Willis' Hill, 147
Wilmington, North Carolina, 215
Winchester, Virginia, 71, 127, 176, 238
Winder, General (Charles S.), C.S.A., 97, 106
Wise, Henry A., 1
"Wise Troop, The," 1
Women, southern, devotion to the cause, 94
Wood, Col., C.S.A., 201, 205, 243
Woodroof, Private A. M., 18
Wounded, the, 30; care of, 259–262

Yankees, strategy of, 160, 161; admiration for General Jackson, 105; destruction caused by, 179, 180, 207, 257, 288; plane of living, 184
Yowell's Tavern, 175